A HERALD OF THE
EVANGELICAL REVIVAL

A HERALD OF THE EVANGELICAL REVIVAL

A CRITICAL INQUIRY INTO THE RELATION OF
WILLIAM LAW TO JOHN WESLEY
AND THE BEGINNINGS
OF METHODISM

BY

ERIC W. BAKER
M.A. (Cantab), Ph.D. (Edin.)

THE NEW-WORLD LIBRARY

WIPF & STOCK · Eugene, Oregon

Wipf and Stock Publishers
199 W 8th Ave, Suite 3
Eugene, OR 97401

A Herald of the Evangelical Revival
A Critical Inquiry into the Relation of William
Law to John Wesley and the Beginnings of Methodism
By Baker, Eric
Copyright©1948 Methodist Publishing - Epworth Press
ISBN 13: 978-1-5326-0031-9
Publication date 6/24/2016
Previously published by Epworth Press, 1948

Every effort has been made to trace the current copyright owner of this publication but without success. If you have any information or interest in the copyright, please contact the publishers.

TO

MY WIFE

Contents

INTRODUCTION	. . . . . .	vii

Part One
Historical Survey

1.	BEFORE 1738	3
2.	1738	17
3.	1738 TO 1756	30
4.	1756 AND AFTER	47

Part Two
Wesley's Indebtness to Law

5.	THE ETHICAL IDEAL	65
6.	PRACTICAL OUTWORKINGS	86

Part Three
Wesley's Disagreement with Law

7.	WESLEY'S OBJECTION TO MYSTICISM . . .	103
8.	THE FUNDAMENTAL DOCTRINAL ISSUE . . .	117
9.	THE 1756 LETTER	140

Part Four
Law and the Beginnings of Methodism

10.	THE TESTIMONY OF CHRISTOPHER WALTON . .	161
11.	THE INFLUENCE OF LAW ON METHODIST BELIEF AND PRACTICE	174
	SUMMARY AND CONCLUSION	187
	BIBLIOGRAPHY	190
	INDEX	195

Introduction

NO ONE COULD tell the story of John Wesley and the beginnings of Methodism without referring to the influence exerted by the writings of William Law at one particular period of Wesley's life. When it comes, however, to assessing the permanence and importance of that influence we find a considerable disparity. Scores of volumes have been devoted to expositions of Wesley's life and work, and in many of these the references to Law are of a cursory nature and confined to one of the early chapters. Such treatment would suggest that the relationship of the two men was an episode, important enough indeed, at the time of its occurrence, but of temporary interest, which can safely be forgotten when the reader passes on to Wesley's later adventures. These writers would agree with the judgement of Dr. Henry Bett in a recent work: 'A great deal has been made (and a great deal too much by some writers) of the influence of Law'.[1] In startling contrast to this, we find other judgements, some emanating from the eighteenth century itself and others from modern writers, suggesting that Law's influence was paramount; Charles Wesley himself, we are told by one of his early biographers,[2] used, even in old age, to refer to Law as 'Our John the Baptist'. Two of John Wesley's earliest biographers writing in the year after his death were equally emphatic: 'This considerable writer was the great forerunner of the revival which followed, and did more to promote it than any other individual whatsoever; yea, more perhaps than the rest of the nation collectively taken.'[3] Dr. Trapp, the eminent contemporary of Law and Wesley, and an opponent of both, described Law as the parent of the Methodists, and John Wesley himself agreed that there was some truth in this description.[4] In later days Dr. G. A. Wauer has called Law 'the father of the English revival of the eighteenth century, and the grandfather of

---

[1] *The Spirit of Methodism*, p. 57.
[2] *Life of Charles Wesley*, Moore, Vol. I, p. 107.
[3] *Life of Wesley*, Coke and Moore, p. 6 (1838 edition).
[4] *Wesley's Works*, Vol. VII, p. 203.

Methodism'.[5] Similarly, Miss Evelyn Underhill writes: 'Law has a certain right to be called the spiritual father of Methodism.'[6] Other instances could be cited, but the above suffice to indicate the scope and interest of the present inquiry, which is a careful examination of the relationship of Law and Wesley with an attempt to assess the genuine and permanent contribution of Law to Wesley's religious experience and outlook. As it is impossible to discuss Wesley apart from the movement he founded, a brief section has been added to indicate to what extent Law's influence on Wesley was reflected in the beginnings of Methodism.

The whole is a fresh treatment of the life and work of Law and Wesley from the definite viewpoint of their mutual relationship, which not only sheds light on the development of religious life in England in the eighteenth century, but also on certain central religious issues of perennial interest, especially the subjective and objective approaches to the doctrine of the Atonement.

In certain parts of the thesis, especially in Chapters 3 and 8, it has been found necessary to include fairly lengthy extracts from Law's writings. In this connexion it is interesting to note F. D. Maurice's judgement: 'The remark of a friend, that Law is the most *continuous* writer in our language, each of his sentences and paragraphs leading on naturally, and as it were, necessarily to that which follows, makes me doubt whether the experiment of reducing one of his books into aphorisms, could be successful in any hands'.[7] Commenting on this, Law's biographer, J. H. Overton, remarks: 'The perfect truth of this description I have felt most painfully while endeavouring to select specimens which might give the reader the best insight into Law's tenets.'[8] Alexander Whyte experienced a similar difficulty,[9] and Dr. Newton Flew quotes Maurice's words in explanation of the lengthy quotations he makes from Law.[10]

---

[5] *Die Anfänge der Bruderkirche in England*, quoted by Dr. Henry Bett, op. cit., p. 57.
[6] *Worship*, p. 304.
[7] *Remarks on the Fable of the Bees*, by William Law, with an Introduction by F. D. Maurice, p. v.
[8] *Life and Opinions of the Rev. William Law*, pp. 267-8.
[9] *Characters and Characteristics of William Law*, pp. v, vi.
[10] *The Idea o Perfection in Christian Theology*, p. 293.

The method adopted has been first to sketch the events of the whole period concerned, in so far as they are relevant to the subject, after which sections are devoted to specific aspects of theological and practical importance, and a brief summary states the conclusions arrived at.

The general reader is likely to find the concluding sections the most interesting in the first instance and is advised to spend on Part I only sufficient time to enable him to understand the background of the later sections.

A good index is an indispensable adjunct to a book of this kind. My especial thanks are accorded to my friend, Rev. Eric Harrop, for so generously devoting time to compiling the index and correcting the proofs.

Wartime difficulties have delayed the publication of this work, which was completed in 1941. In the meantime my friend, the Rev. J. Brazier Green, has published his admirable study, *John Wesley and William Law*, which was the theme of his Fernley-Hartley Lecture in 1945.

While, of necessity, much of the same ground is covered here, the present work ranges over a wider field. Mr. Green's work was mainly confined to the theological aspect of the Wesley-Law controversy, whereas I have dealt more fully with the historical background and have also included a section on 'Law and the beginnings of Methodism'. This section includes material which, as far as I am aware, is set forth here for the first time.

Important as the subject is, Mr. Green's book was the first serious discussion of it to be published for two hundred years. It is my hope that Mr. Green's book will have aroused interest in the subject and that the present volume will prove in some sense complementary to his.

ERIC W. BAKER

LONDON
February 1948

Notes

1. Whenever the name Wesley occurs with no Christian name prefixed, it is John Wesley who is referred to.
2. The spelling 'Boehme' has been adopted throughout instead of the Anglicized 'Behmen', even in quotations where 'Behmen' is in the original. The adjectival form 'Behmenish' has, however, been retained.
3. References to Law in the ensuing pages are to the complete edition in nine volumes, printed in London for J. Richardson (1762); privately reprinted for G. Moreton, Setley, Brockenhurst, New Forest, Hampshire (1892): Abbreviated in footnotes: *Law's Works*.
4. References to Wesley are, where possible, to the Standard Editions of the *Journal*, *Letters*, and *Sermons*; and otherwise to the *Collected Works*, Third Edition, Jackson (1829): Abbreviated in footnotes: *Wesley's Works*.

The Standard Editions are as follow:

Journal, 8 Volumes, edited by Curnock (1904-16);
Standard Sermons, 2 Volumes, edited by Sugden (1921).
Letters, 8 Volumes, edited by Telford (1931).

PART ONE
Historical Survey

CHAPTER ONE

Before 1738

STRICTLY speaking the relation of William Law to John Wesley does not begin until 1727, when Wesley first read Law's *Christian Perfection*, but it is desirable for a clear understanding of events in that and subsequent years that we should have in our minds a brief sketch of the earlier history of the two men.

William Law was born in 1686 at Kingscliffe in Northamptonshire, where he was also to spend his later years. He came of a good middle-class family. After a serious and devout upbringing he entered Emmanuel College, Cambridge, as a sizar in 1705,[1] graduating as a B.A. in 1708. He was elected to a Fellowship in 1711, in which year he also took Holy Orders. He became an M.A. in 1712 and appeared to be launched on a brilliant and successful career when, by refusing to take the oath of allegiance to King George the First, he forfeited his fellowship in 1716 and with it all prospect of advancement in the Church. This action on his part, which was in marked contrast to the aptitude for compromise at the expense of principle displayed by many of his contemporaries, affords ample evidence alike of his intellectual honesty and his sensitive conscience. A further anticipation of what was to come was furnished by the 'Rules for my Future Conduct' drawn up on his entering the university and found among his papers.[2] This document, comprising some eighteen principles of practical piety, taken in conjunction with certain prayers of his which have also survived from this period,[3] shows that the seeds were already present of what was to come to full flower in the *Christian Perfection* and the *Serious Call* and should cause us to modify Mr. Stephen Hobhouse's judgement of the extent of the conversion which the publication of these latter works revealed.[4]

[1] *Notes and Materials for an Adequate Biography of William Law*, Christopher Walton, p. 344.
[2] ibid., p. 345.   [3] Walton, op. cit., pp. 346 et. sqq.
[4] *William Law and Eighteenth-century Quakerism*, p. 260.

Little is known of Law's whereabouts during the next few years, but it is probable that he lived quietly in London. In 1717 he published the *Three Letters to the Bishop of Bangor*.[5] These letters, addressed to the latitudinarian Dr. Hoadly, contain the essence of the High Church position[6] and constitute what Mr. Hobhouse describes as the 'first phase'[7] of Law's churchmanship. In them he insists on the absolute necessity of a strict apostolic succession in order to constitute a Christian priest and complains to the bishop: 'You have left us neither Priests, nor Sacraments, nor Church.'[8] The importance of these letters for our purpose is that Law's position at this time is so different from that adopted by him later when one of Wesley's main strictures on him arose from his alleged depreciation of the outward ordinances of the Church. So far was the pendulum to swing. Law's only other published work during the period under review in this chapter was his *Remarks upon 'The Fable of the Bees'*,[9] published in 1721.[10] This was a reply to Dr. Bernard Mandeville and concerned the origin of the moral sense. We need only make passing mention of it as it does not concern our subject, though Mr. Hobhouse sees significance in the fact that Law chose an ethical theme, albeit a remote one, for his second field of controversy.[11] His next writings were to be those which exercised so profound an influence on Wesley.

John Wesley was some seventeen years younger than William Law, having been born in 1703 at Epworth in Lincolnshire where his father, the Rev. Samuel Wesley, was rector. Our direct knowledge of his earliest years is slight. The dominant influence in Wesley's early upbringing was his remarkable mother, Susanna Wesley; at first she was almost entirely responsible for his secular and religious training, but for long after he left home, during his years at school and the university, and even when launched on his evangelical campaign, she remained his main counsellor and guide.

At the age of ten he entered Charterhouse, the nominee

---

[5] *Law's Works*, Vol. I.
[6] *Dictionary of National Biography*, Vol. XI, p. 677.
[7] *William Law and Eighteenth-century Quakerism*, p. 255.
[8] *Law's Works*, Vol. I, p. 9.
[9] *Law's Work.*, Vol. II, pp. 1-54.
[10] Walton, op. cit., p. 355.
[11] *William Law and Eighteenth-century Quakerism*, p. 261.

of the Duke of Buckingham, and in due course proceeded to Christchurch, Oxford, where he continued until after his ordination in 1725. His religious development up to this time is perhaps best traced in the sketch which he himself prefixed to his account of the occurrences of 24th May 1738.[12] Until he was ten, he tells us, he had not sinned away that 'washing of the Holy Ghost' he had received at baptism. He had been taught that he could only be saved 'by universal obedience, by keeping all the commandments of God'. With these instructions he outwardly complied, without understanding or remembering what was said of inward obedience or holiness. So that, to quote his own words: 'I was indeed as ignorant of the true meaning of the law as I was of the Gospel of Christ.' At school, freed from outward restraints, he became negligent even of outward duties, though he still read the Scriptures and said his prayers. He now hoped to be saved by:

(1) not being so bad as other people; (2) having still a kindness for religion; and (3) reading the Bible, going to church, and saying my prayers.[13]

At Oxford he continued in prayer and Scripture reading but declared he had not

'so much as a notion of inward holiness' and could not say what he hoped to be saved by now unless by transient fits of repentance which he experienced 'especially before and after the Holy Communion'.

Then in 1725, when his father pressed him to take holy orders he first met with à Kempis's *Christian Pattern*. This proved the beginning of those stirrings which were to move him so profoundly when in the following year, during which he was elected a Fellow of Lincoln College, he made his first acquaintance with the writings of William Law.

It was probably about the year 1723 that Law accepted the post of tutor to the son of Mr. Gibbon, of Putney.[14] In 1726 he published *A Practical Treatise upon Christian Perfection*,[15] the first of the two works which were so profoundly to influence

---

[12] *Journal*, Vol. I, pp. 465 et sqq.   [13] ibid., p. 466.
[14] *Selected Mystical Writings of William Law*, Stephen Hobhouse, p. 389.
[15] *Law's Works*, Vol. III.

Wesley. In this work he included almost without alteration a tract on the stage published earlier in the same year, entitled *The Absolute Unlawfulness of the Stage-Entertainment Fully Demonstrated*.[16] Three years later, in 1729, there appeared *A Serious Call to a Devout and Holy Life, Adapted to the State and Condition of all Orders of Christians*.[17]

These two works reveal, as Mr. Hobhouse observes,[18] a remarkable change of emphasis on Law's part. Instead of the ecclesiastical purist of the Bangorian letters, we discover a man dominated by a consuming passion for the ethical implications of his religion. As the title of the first suggests, they are great practical treatises on the Christian way of life. Their whole plea is that the essence of Christianity consists not in the formal execution of outward ordinances but in the consecration of the whole life to God. So great a transformation does this appear when placed side by side with the Bangorian letters that it is impossible to demur when Mr. Hobhouse describes it as being necessarily caused by 'something in the nature of a conversion',[19] though we have already noticed earlier traits in Law's character, which suggest that even then there was present in him the spark of that moral passion which now bursts forth with consuming fire.[20]

'Few books have had such a marvellous effect upon a nation as these two volumes.'[21] This is Mr. Hobhouse's verdict, but we can only agree in so far as we hasten to add that the effect on the nation was due to the effect produced first on Wesley. Other notable men such as Dr. Johnson and Edward Gibbon paid their tributes to the works in the highest possible terms but 'effect upon a nation' is a very different matter, and it is extremely improbable that Mr. Hobhouse would have passed such a judgement apart from the effects of the works on Wesley and what happened in consequence. These were not the only, indeed they were not even the first, books responsible for Wesley's ethical awakening at this period. Let him tell the story himself. Writing in May 1765 to John Newton, Wesley says:

[16] *Law's Works*, Vol. II.　　[17] ibid., Vol. IV.
[18] *William Law and Eighteenth-century Quakerism*, p. 260.
[19] ibid., p. 260.　　[20] vide *supra*, p. 2.
[21] *William Law and Eighteenth-century Quakerism*, p. 261.

In 1725 I met with Bishop Taylor's *Rules of Holy Living and Dying*. I was struck particularly with the chapter upon Intention and felt a fixed intention to *give myself up to God*. In this I was much confirmed soon after by the *Christian Pattern* and longed to *give God all my heart*. This is just what I mean by Perfection now: I sought after it from that hour. In 1727 I read Mr. Law's *Christian Perfection* and *Serious Call*, and more explicitly resolved to be *all devoted to God* in body, soul, and spirit.[22]

This account may be supplemented by his autobiographical review in the *Journal* for 24th May 1738:

But meeting now with Mr. Law's *Christian Perfection* and *Serious Call*, although I was much offended at many parts of both, yet they convinced me more than ever of the exceeding height and breadth and depth of the law of God. The light flowed in so mightily upon my soul, that everything appeared in a new view. I cried to God for help, and resolved not to prolong the time of obeying Him as I had never done before. And by my continued endeavour to keep His whole law, inward and outward, to the utmost of my power, I was persuaded that I should be accepted of Him, and that I was even then in a state of salvation.[23]

Thus Jeremy Taylor, Thomas à Kempis, and William Law formed a triumvirate jointly responsible for what happened to Wesley in 1725 and the years immediately following. But though Law's writings were the last of the three to attract his notice, it may be fairly claimed that from the time when Wesley first read them they occupied the chief place in his esteem. As evidence of this we may cite the great number of references made to them by Wesley in later years, and there is a natural explanation in the fact that, unlike Jeremy Taylor and Thomas à Kempis, William Law was still living and could be visited and consulted. Not only his writings but the man himself could become a source of enlightenment and inspiration. This is what actually occurred and in the succeeding years Law became 'a kind of oracle' to Wesley. This is Law's own phrase in a letter of February 1756,[24] and Wesley acknowledges its truth in his letter to the *London Chronicle* in September 1760.[25] There is abundant evidence that this description is no exaggeration.

In the Introduction to the Standard Edition of the *Journal*

[22] *Letters*, Vol. IV, pp. 298-9.
[24] *Law's Works*, Vol. IX, p. 168.
[23] *Journal*, Vol. I, p. 467.
[25] *Journal* Vol. IV, p. 410.

there are set forth the reasons for believing that Wesley's introduction to the works of all three devotional writers concerned was due to his association with a group of friends who formed a correspondence and reading circle, the headquarters of which was at the rectory at Stanton. It was after a visit there that Wesley 'began an almost furious study of William Law'.[26] In August 1727 he removed to Lincolnshire where he acted as his father's curate for over two years, paying a visit to Oxford to be ordained priest in July 1728. During Wesley's absence from Oxford his brother Charles with a few like-minded companions had formed the 'Holy Club', and on John's return in November 1729[27] to resume his tutorial duties at Lincoln College, he joined them and was from that time their acknowledged leader. This company distinguished themselves alike by personal religious devotion and good works, and their regularity of behaviour earned for them the nickname 'Methodists'.

Here we must turn aside to take note of an incident which may or may not concern Law. In *Fog's Journal* for December 1732 a letter appeared attacking the Oxford Methodists. To this a reply was made in an anonymous pamphlet entitled: *The Oxford Methodists: being an Account of some Young Gentlemen in that City, in Derision so called; setting forth their Rise and Designs, with Some Occasional Remarks on a Letter inserted in 'Fog's Journal' of December 9th, 1732, relating to them*.[28] Wesley himself refers to this reply in the Preface to the *Journal*:

I have prefixt hereto a letter wrote several years since, containing a plain account of the rise of that little society in Oxford, which has been so variously represented. Part of this was published in 1733; but without my consent or knowledge.[29]

Two further editions were published in 1737 and 1738, to the former of which was prefixed an explanatory letter in cordial terms to Whitefield, Wesley then being out of the country in Georgia. This reply is printed in full in the *Wesleyan Methodist Magazine* for 1848.[30] The author made a

[26] *Journal*, Vol. I, p. 15.   [27] ibid., p. 89.
[28] See Townsend, Workman, and Eayrs, *A New History of Methodism*, Vol. I, plate vi, facing p. 144.
[29] *Journal*, Vol. I, p. 84.
[30] pp. 754-63, 874-80.

personal investigation at Oxford, as a result of which he completely vindicated the Oxford Methodists. His comprehensive description of their aims and behaviour concludes:

> Let all the serious part of mankind, who alone are appealed to in this case, be judges between them and this letter writer, who has so ludicrously and, in some cases, so wilfully misrepresented them. To live by rule, especially a good rule, was ever esteemed a sure sign of wisdom: to live by none, much more to be against all rule and method, must be a flagrant mark of folly. And I will venture to add, that if these young gentlemen persevere to the end in this good method, they shall receive a crown of glory.[31]

Our special interest in this work derives from the ascription in many quarters of its authorship to Law. This was done by Thomas Marriott in a footnote in the same magazine,[32] and by the late Dr. Simon, who writes:

> The attack, however, had one good result. John Wesley, in July, had made his way to the house of William Law, in Putney, and had been welcomed by the famous Nonjuror and mystic, to whom he owed so much. A copy of *Fog's Journal* being sent to Law by a friend, who in a letter asked for some information concerning the 'Methodists', he determined to go to Oxford and make investigation on the spot. . . . He gathered up the facts he had ascertained by observation and conversation, and stated them in a pamphlet he published anonymously.[33]

On the strength of this, the British Museum catalogue also ascribes the pamphlet to Law. In recent years, however, the question has been reopened by Rev. F. F. Bretherton in his article, 'The First Apology for Methodism', in the *Proceedings of the Wesley Historical Society*.[34] In the second part Mr. Bretherton quotes Canon C. H. Lambert, who gives cogent reasons for doubting Law's authorship. It must be remembered, however, that though we are not aware of its nature, those who originally claimed Law as the author must presumably have had good authority for doing so. Judgement must be suspended, but if the pamphlet was indeed a product of Law's pen, it affords most interesting evidence of the

---

[31] ibid., p. 880.   [32] ibid., p. 754.
[33] *John Wesley and the Religious Societies*, by J. S. Simon, p. 97.
[34] Vol. XIX (December 1934,) pp. 181-3; Vol. XX (June 1935) pp. 30-2 (privately published).

warmth of his approval of Wesley and Methodism at this early stage.

Wesley remained at Oxford until 1735 and during all this period strove after that ideal of Christian Perfection set forth in Law's writings. '*John Wesley avait appris de ses maîtres, notamment de W. Law, que la religion n'est point chose extérieure, affaire de pratiques, de gestes et de formules.*'[35] In July 1732 he visited Law at Putney and began that friendship which lasted until 1738. No doubt personal intercourse, as Sugden says, 'deepened the strong impression which Law's works had already produced upon him', and from this time, on Law's advice, he began to study the *Theologia Germanica* and other writings of the mystics.[36]

It seems probable that Wesley's decision to undertake the Mission to Georgia in 1735 was largely due to the new scale of values inculcated by Law's works. It is true that Law is reported to have described the project as that of a 'crack-brained enthusiast',[37] but for all that it sprang from an idealism and devotion the Wesleys had largely learned from Law.

Our end in leaving our native country [writes Wesley], was not to avoid want, God having given us plenty of temporal blessings, nor to gain riches or honour, . . . but singly this—to save our souls, to live wholly to the glory of God.[38]

Other writers do not hesitate to attribute the decision directly to Law's influence. So for example Thomas Jackson:

By reading the writings of Mr. Law, and others of a similar kind, they were deeply impressed with the necessity of holiness. According to their apprehensions, true holiness is attained principally by means of sufferings, mental and bodily; and hence they adopted this mode of life, resolved to do and suffer whatever it should please God to lay upon them. . . . Holiness of heart and life was the object of their eager pursuit; and this they sought, not by faith, but by works, and personal austerity, according to the misleading doctrine of Mr. Law.[39]

Similarly M. Leger, in his brilliant study, *La Jeunesse de Wesley*,[40] writes of this choice:

[35] *La Jeunesse de Wesley*, Augustin Leger, p. 175.
[36] *Sermons*, Vol. I, p. 264.
[37] *Journal*, Vol. I, p. 418, n. 1.
[38] ibid., p. 109.
[39] *Memoirs of the Rev. Charles Wesley*, p. 28.
[40] p. 228.

... *de deux chemins, quand on est convaincu que l'un plaît moins à Dieu et conduit moins à la perfection de l'âme, l'Evangile du Christ ne nous permet pas de nous flatter qu'en préférant celui-là nous puissions plaire du tout à Dieu ni recevoir de lui la grâce qui seule est capable de nous élever au moindre degré de perfection chrétienne. C'etait toujours le principe de Law.*

So the brothers Wesley turned their backs on academic and ecclesiastical careers and set sail for Georgia in 1735.

On board the *Simmonds* and afterwards in Georgia, Wesley made constant use of Law's *Christian Perfection* and *Serious Call*, as frequent references in the *Journal*[41] for this period testify. One occasion may be singled out as showing the central position Law's teaching occupied in Wesley's religious outlook at this time. Referring to a certain Mrs. Lawley, Wesley tells us: 'I thought it concerned her to be first instructed in the nature of Christianity and accordingly fixed an hour a day to read with her in Mr. Law's treatise of *Christian Perfection.*'[42]

This is the period at which Law's influence on Wesley was at its height, and it might be well to attempt to assess its significance and extent before tracing the events which led to the breach in 1738. Our judgement on this matter will obviously largely determine our final conclusion as to the importance of Law in relation to Wesley and Methodism.

It is the traditional, and among Methodists the unanimous, view to single out 24th May 1738 as the all-important date in Wesley's life. This interpretation of events has been recently challenged in the remarkable work of Father Maximin Piette who terms it a 'Wesleyan legend',[43] and asserts that the famous experience of that day 'enjoyed but a very modest role' in Wesley's life, the effect of which time was quickly to dull and which would possibly have been entirely forgotten by Wesley, if it had not been entered in the first extract of the *Journal*. Father Piette suggests that Wesley's true conversion should be dated, as M. Leger dates it, fourteen years earlier. This is, however, to stretch M. Leger's meaning. He calls the experience of 1725 *'la première conversion'*,[44] and that of 24th May 1738 'Le coup de grâce',[45] and after first stating

[41] Vol. I, pp. 115-285.   [42] ibid., p. 122.
[43] *John Wesley in the Evolution of Protestantism*, p. 306.
[44] *La Jeunesse de Wesley*, p. 77.   [45] ibid., p. 322.

that he is thinking of the moment when the soul begins to turn to God says: 'En ce sens, *la conversion de Wesley date de 1725, non du 24 mai 1738.*'[46] With this judgement we may well agree, as many Methodist scholars do. Sugden, for example, says of 1725:

> It is not too much to speak of this as his (i.e. Wesley's) first conversion: though it was not till 24th May 1738 that he received the consciousness that his sins were forgiven and the witness of the Spirit that he was a child of God.[47]

And Dr. Rattenbury, referring to Father Piette's criticism of the Methodist authorities, says:

> He was justified if conversion be regarded as the decisive turning of a man of the world to God. When in 1725 Wesley . . . decided upon a completely religious life, that he would not be a half Christian but a real one, he made a decision from which he never deviated and which determined the whole course of his career.[48]

To admit, however, the positive importance of 1725 does not necessarily involve any belittling of 1738, and Dr. Rattenbury, whose frank recognition of the former experience we have just quoted, proceeds to examine and reject Father Piette's position.[49]

After a cordial reference to Dr. Piette's deep appreciation of Wesley and the sympathetic and charitable spirit of his writing, and a recognition of the element of truth in Dr. Piette's assertion that Wesley, though a Protestant, adopted many positions which are those of the Catholic tradition, Dr. Rattenbury finds it quite impossible to accept Dr. Piette's view of the superficiality of the experience of 24th May 1738. It is true that the doctrine of conversion is the corner stone of Methodist theology, but this, claims Dr. Rattenbury, is because Wesley himself and not his followers made it to be so.

Dr. Piette had formulated a theory that Tyerman had represented Wesley before conversion as a very great sinner with the object of magnifying the conversion experience, on the principle, 'the greater the conversion, the greater the sinner', but Dr. Rattenbury shows how this is an entirely

---

[46] *La Jeunesse de Wesley*, p. 366. (The italics are mine. E.W.B.)   [47] *Sermons*, Vol. I, p. 263.
[48] *The Conversion of the Wesleys*, p. 42.   [49] ibid., pp. 103-18.

distorted interpretation of Tyerman's position, which would never have been adopted by anyone familiar with Methodist phraseology of the nineteenth century, when all unconverted men, in the Methodist sense, were deemed great sinners. All Tyerman was intent upon, in those passages which Dr. Piette made the foundation of this theory, was to show how exaggerated were the conceptions of Wesley, then gaining currency among Methodists, according to which he was portrayed as a stained-glass-window saint. Far from Dr. Piette's theory being in accordance with the facts, the excessive piety of Wesley after he took Orders, rather than his sinfulness, was usually stressed by Methodists, including even Tyerman who actually called the date 1725 the turning point in Wesley's history.

The truth appears to be, continues Dr. Rattenbury, that Dr. Piette fails to understand the Methodist doctrine of 'Evangelical Conversion', which is not only concerned with a prodigal's return to God, but is as much concerned with moral people. All men, good and bad, need the converting grace of God. Thus Wesley, though 'converted' in the Catholic sense in 1725, after which for thirteen years he had striven, by every means in his power, to be good, still needed conversion in 1738. In support of this Dr. Rattenbury quotes the verses by Charles Wesley, inscribed on his mother Susanna Wesley's tombstone, containing the line, 'A legal night of seventy years', demonstrating that the Methodists believed that even a woman as good as she lacked something which she received at her evangelical conversion. The same fact is illustrated by the conversion hymn of the Wesleys themselves: 'He died for *crimes* like yours—and *mine*.' A good man like Wesley was helpless and hopeless, except for the saving grace that bad men needed. But on 24th May 1738 Wesley, who had the form of godliness, received the power. Any objective reading of the *Journal*, *Letters*, and *Sermons* abundantly proves that. Dr. Rattenbury agrees with Dr. Croft Cell[50] that if we had no knowledge of 24th May we should be compelled to invent some such day to account for the changed tone in Wesley and the sudden success of his mission.

Dr. Rattenbury then notes Dr. Piette's own striking

[50] *The Rediscovery of John Wesley*, p. 62.

admission that on 24th May Wesley, 'after fourteen years of struggle . . . found calm, equilibrium, peace of the soul, in love', though denying that it was Wesley's first experience of the love of God. In the concluding section of his argument Dr. Rattenbury suggests that it was impossible for Dr. Piette, a Roman Catholic priest, to ignore the controversial aspects of the doctrines of 'Justification by Faith' and 'Instantaneous Conversion', otherwise he could scarcely have failed to see the importance of what happened on 24th May 1738. Such, briefly summarized, is Dr. Rattenbury's argument, and our own consideration of the relations between Law and the Wesleys in the years up to 1738, to which we now proceed, reinforces Dr. Rattenbury's contention that, important as was the experience of 1725, something vital was still lacking which was only supplied by the experience of 1738.

First of all we observe in Wesley a certain impatience with the scanty results of his preaching during this period.

> I preached much, but saw no fruit of my labour. Indeed, it could not be that I should: for I neither laid the foundation of repentance nor of believing the gospel.[51]

Writing to Ann Bolton nearly sixty years later, Wesley recalls how Law said to him:

> Sir, you are troubled, because you do not understand how God is dealing with you. Perhaps if you did, it would not so well answer His design. He is teaching you to trust Him further than you can see Him.[52]

Wesley's impatient desire to win men for Christ called forth from Law the remark that he must wait God's own time.[53] Then later, while in Georgia, Wesley made his first protest against the teaching of the mystics, whose works he had begun to read on Law's advice. In a letter to his brother Samuel in November 1736 he writes:

> I think the rock on which I had the nearest made shipwreck of the faith was the writings of the Mystics; under which term I comprehend all, and only those, who slight any of the means of grace.[54]

This is the first sign of that opposition to Mysticism which,

[51] *Letters*, Vol. II, p. 264.   [52] ibid., Vol. VIII, p. 110.
[53] *Journal*, Vol. I, p. 418.   [54] *Letters*, Vol. I, p. 207.

as we shall see, was to play such a large part in the estrangement between the two men.

Meanwhile things were not going well with Charles Wesley who, leaving John at Savannah, had proceeded to Frederica. Jackson unhesitatingly attributes this lack of success in preaching to the defectiveness of his theological views which were

precisely those of Mr. Law ... as in the eloquent volumes of Law, we look in vain for correct views of the atonement and intercession of Christ, and of the offices of the Holy Spirit. No satisfactory answer is given to the question 'What must I do to be saved?'[55]

Charles Wesley returned to England in 1736, some eighteen months before his brother, and in his *Journal* for that period we find several references to Law.[56] At first they reveal Charles's continued adherence to Law's principles, but the later references reveal a growing dissatisfaction, particularly in connexion with two visits paid by Charles to Law on 31st August and 9th September 1737.[57] Further evidence of the growing unrest in Charles's mind is to be found in the Journal of John Byrom, Law's devoted friend and admirer, who also knew the Wesleys. In an entry dated July 1737 (considerably earlier, be it observed, than the interviews described above) Byrom tells of a visit paid to him by Charles in which the latter 'mentioned several objections against Law's teaching, especially against his mysticism', defining the mystics, in terms rather similar to John's, as 'those who neglected the use of reason and means of grace'.[58] Byrom's comment on the incident was that Charles had met with somebody who 'does not like Mr. Law', and concluded:

I believe that Mr. Law had given his brother or him or both very good and strong advice which they had strained to a meaning different to his.[59]

These references are important as showing that the divergence between Law and the brothers was already developing in the minds of both John and Charles before it issued in the

[55] *Memoirs of the Rev. Charles Wesley*, p. 34.
[56] *Journal of the Rev. Charles Wesley*, Vol. I, pp. 47, 70, 72, 75.
[57] ibid., Vol. I, p. 74.
[58] *Remains of John Byrom*, Vol. II, Part I, p. 181.
[59] ibid., p. 182.

dramatic events of 1738. They also confirm Dr. Rattenbury's position against that of Father Piette as to the inadequacy of the 1725 experience by itself either to solve the Wesley's own personal religious problem, or to explain the widespread revival largely initiated and carried on by them, which swept England in the years following 1738.

CHAPTER TWO

1738

John Wesley landed at Deal on 1st February 1738[1] after an absence from England of two years and nearly four months. His spiritual state at this time was one of deep discontent as his *Journal* shows:

> What have I learned myself in the meantime? Why, what I the least of all suspected, that I, who went to America to convert others, was never myself converted to God.[2]

He does not hesitate to describe his condition at the time in terms of Paul's classical dilemma set forth in Romans 7.

> I was now properly 'under the law'; I knew that 'the law' of God was 'spiritual; I consented to it that it was good'. Yea, 'I delighted in it, after the inner man'. Yet was I 'carnal, sold under sin'. . . . 'To will is' indeed 'present with me: but how to perform that which is good, I find not. For the good which I would, I do not; but the evil which I would not, that I do. I find a law, that when I would do good, evil is present with me': even 'the law in my members, warring against the law of my mind', and still 'bringing me into captivity to the law of sin'.[3]

It is evident that the 1725 experience was not enough. Something more was needed. Wesley was as a man who has seen the goal, but lacks the means of attaining it.

> For thirteen years [says Dr. Rattenbury], he had striven to do all a man could, by every means in his power, to be good. No one ever denied that; nor that he had accomplished as much as any man was likely to accomplish in his own strength. The point is that, even then, he needed conversion.[4]

On 7th February, described by him as 'a day much to be remembered',[5] Wesley met the Moravian, Peter Böhler, with whom he conversed as often as possible during the succeeding weeks and months. Böhler spoke to Wesley of true faith in Christ in a manner that at first aroused the latter's amazement.[6]

[1] *Journal*, Vol. I, p. 421. [2] ibid., p. 422. [3] ibid., p. 470.
[4] *The Conversion of the Wesleys*, p. 110 [5] *Journal*, Vol. I, p. 436. [6] ibid., p. 447.

When Peter Böhler, whom God prepared for me as soon as I came to London, affirmed of true faith in Christ (which is but one) that it had those two fruits inseparably attending it, 'dominion over sin and constant peace from a sense of forgiveness', I was quite amazed, and looked upon it as a new gospel. If this was so, it was clear I had not faith.[7]

Wesley at first resisted this doctrine, but with his customary fairness agreed to submit the issue to the test of Scripture. He had to confess that Böhler's teaching was in accordance with Scripture, but further insisted that living witnesses should be produced who would testify to the truth from their own experience.[8] This was done and Wesley was thoroughly convinced.

This took place on 23rd April, and for the next month Wesley carried out his resolve to seek this faith, which he believed to be the free gift of God, by renouncing all dependence on his own works, and continuing unceasingly in prayers. So finally on 24th May 1738, three days after the conversion of his brother Charles,[9] there came to him the decisive experience of conversion.

In the evening I went very unwillingly to a society in Aldersgate Street, where one was reading Luther's preface to the *Epistle to the Romans*. About a quarter before nine, while he was describing the change which God works in the heart through faith in Christ, I felt my heart strangely warmed. I felt I did trust in Christ, Christ alone for salvation; and an assurance was given me that He had taken away *my* sins, even *mine*, and saved *me* from the law of sin and death.[10]

The correspondence with Law occurred in the days of waiting which preceded the experience of 24th May, the initial letter from Wesley being dated 14th May.[11] This was the first open breach between Law and Wesley. In spite of the signs of Wesley's growing dissatisfaction with his spiritual state and his definite rejection of mysticism while still in Georgia,[12] the relations between the two men appear to have remained cordial at any rate up to the time of Wesley's return to England and his subsequent meeting with Böhler. The evidence for this, though to a certain extent negative, is

---

[7] *Journal*, Vol. I, p. 471.
[8] ibid., pp. 455, 472.
[9] *Journal of Charles Wesley*, Vol. I, pp. 90-2.
[10] *Journal*, Vol. I, pp. 475-6.
[11] ibid., Vol. VIII, p. 319.
[12] vide *supra*, p. 14.

by no means entirely so. In September 1736 James Hutton, in a letter to Wesley in Georgia, refers to visits paid by Law to Wesley's mother first at Gainsborough and again in London.[13] M. Leger does not hesitate to describe Wesley in 1737 as '*toujours disciple de Law*'.[14] More emphatic evidence is contained in Wesley's first letter in the correspondence of 1738 with Law when he states: 'For two years (more especially) I have been preaching after the model of your two practical treatises.'[15] The two years concerned were plainly those immediately preceding the writing of the letter. Wesley's self-confessed amazement at the novelty, to him, of Böhler's teaching[16] affords further proof that up to that time his inward discontent had not found expression in any conscious rejection on his part of Law's religious position as inadequate. In the vital weeks between Wesley's return to England and his evangelical conversion he does not appear to have consulted Law as one would have expected. How are we to account for the fact that even in the critical month of May Wesley did not visit Law in person? The *Journal* shows that he was in and around London throughout that time, and Law was still at Putney. In 1732 a journey on foot from Oxford to Putney was cheerfully undertaken, but in 1738 he makes no attempt upon the few miles to Putney from London.

The explanation must surely be that he did not want to meet Law. It is evident from the general impression created by reading Wesley's own story of that period, that from the time of the first meeting with Böhler, six days after Wesley's landing at Deal,[17] there was set up in Wesley's mind a disturbance which culminated in the experience of 24th May. Böhler's teaching was novel, and although at first unable to understand it, Wesley also found himself quite incapable of ignoring it. To have consulted Law at that time would very probably, as Wesley would consciously or unconsciously realize, only have brought on himself once more a rebuke for his impatience and an injunction to bide God's time.[18] The events in Georgia had convinced Wesley that Law had nothing to offer. He had preached a Christianity drawn from

[13] *Methodist Magazine*, 1848, p. 1,102.
[15] *Journal*, Vol. VIII, p. 319.
[17] *Journal*, Vol. I, p. 436.
[14] *La Jeunesse de Wesley*, p. 318.
[16] vide *supra*, p. 17.
[18] vide *supra*, p. 14.

à Kempis, the *Theologia Germanica*, Law's *Christian Perfection*, and *Serious Call*, and had failed. He knew the failure was in himself and that the serene detachment of the Putney tutor had no solution to offer to his problem. It is significant also in this connexion that although Wesley, as we have noticed, made regular use of Law's two practical treatises on board the *Simmonds*, and in the early days in Georgia, the last reference is in October 1736,[19] after which we hear nothing of them, save the solitary reference in the autobiographical passage in the *Journal* introducing the events of 24th May, which we have already quoted. Hence the only contact between them during these critical days which preceded the correspondence seems to have been an indirect one through Böhler himself who had an apparently accidental interview with Law, on which he reported unfortunately to Wesley, as a result of which it became a subject of contention in the ensuing correspondence.[20] Such indirect contact, through a third party, himself a protagonist with definite and uncompromising views, could but tend toward estrangement rather than mutual understanding; it would also keep prominent in Wesley's mind the difference between Böhler's presentation of the faith and Law's, which had dominated his outlook for more than ten years past, so that it is not altogether surprising, though none the less regrettable, that as he became more and more convinced of the truth of Böhler's contention, his change of view should be accompanied by a reaction against his former teacher.

If this is correct, it may be asked why he should have bothered to write to Law when he did. For the answer to that, Wesley's first letter must be taken at its face value. He was genuinely suspicious that Law himself had not learned the secret, and anxious that Law too should share in the quest.

The correspondence of 1738 consisted of two letters each way, all of which were written within the space of a few days. The first three letters, that is Wesley's two letters to Law and Law's reply to the first of them, have been freely commented on by many writers, and are printed together as an Appendix to the Standard Edition of the *Journal*.[21] The fourth letter,

[19] *Journal*, Vol. I, p. 285.
[20] ibid., Vol. VIII, pp. 320-2; *Letters*, Vol. I, p. 242
[21] *Journal*, Vol. VIII, pp. 319-24.

that is Law's second letter which concluded the correspondence, has had a curious history. Christopher Walton,[22] criticizing Wesley's omission of those letters from his Diary, tells us that they were found by his executors among his papers after his death. The latter published them in their periodical in 1795[23] but omitted Law's second letter, which only came to light because a rough outline of it was found among Law's papers. Walton then in his book printed this hitherto unpublished letter in full, the only one of the four he does, and some of the earlier writers, such as Tyerman[24] and Overton[25] refer to it, though somewhat cursorily. Later on, however, its presence seems to have been overlooked and it was not included among the letters in the Appendix to the *Journal*. Later still, however, it is inserted in the appropriate place in the Standard Edition of the *Letters*,[26] prefixed by an explanation that it is copied from the original now in Dr. Williams's Library, to the existence of which Mr. Stephen Hobhouse had called attention; the suggestion is further made, quite erroneously, that it was now being printed for the first time in that form. Though by the inclusion of the letter in the Standard Edition of Wesley's *Letters* the previous omission has been corrected, Law's first reply to Wesley which had been previously printed in the Appendix to the *Journal* was naturally not repeated, so that for the complete correspondence recourse must be had to the Standard Editions of both the *Journal* and the *Letters* of John Wesley.[27]

Now to summarize the four letters themselves.

LETTER I. WESLEY TO LAW[28]

This first letter was written by Wesley on 14th May 1738. We have seen how he had become convinced, both by reference to Scripture and as a result of personal testimony, of the rightness of Böhler's views concerning the nature of saving faith. This seemed to Wesley to reveal a glaring omission

[22] *Notes and Materials for an Adequate Biography of William Law*, p. 94.
[23] Walton gives the date as 1795, but the correct reference is to the *Arminian Magazine*, 1797, pp. 147-53.
[24] *The Life and Times of John Wesley*, Vol. I, p. 187.
[25] *The Life and Opinions of the Rev. William Law*, p. 87.
[26] Vol. I, p. 242.
[27] *Journal*, Vol. VIII, pp. 319-24; *Letters*, Vol. I, pp. 238-44.
[28] *Journal*, Vol. VIII, pp. 319-20; *Letters*, Vol. I, pp. 239-40.

in Law's teaching as set forth in the *Christian Perfection* and the *Serious Call*. It is to draw attention to this omission that Wesley felt constrained to write to Law. After referring to this Wesley reviews the period immediately preceding his meeting with Böhler, of which period he says: 'I have been preaching after the model of your two practical treatises.' While all agreed, however, in their admiration for the law thus expounded, all discovered too that it was a standard too high to be achieved in spite of exhortations and earnest prayer. 'Both they and I were more and more convinced that this is a law by which a man cannot live.' To Wesley in his despair came Peter Böhler (described in this letter as 'an holy man'), with his message:

Believe, and thou shalt be saved. Believe in the Lord Jesus Christ with all thy heart, and nothing shall be impossible to thee. This faith, indeed, as well as the salvation it brings, is the free gift of God. But seek, and thou shalt find. Strip thyself naked of thy own works and thy own righteousness, and fly to Him. For whosoever cometh unto Him, He will in no wise cast out.

Why, asks Wesley, had Law never given this advice, when he must have discerned that Wesley lacked this faith? He beseeches Law to ask himself whether the true reason was that Law had it not himself. In support of this, Wesley recounts the story told him by Böhler of the latter's interview with Law, in which he alleged that Law was silent on the subject of faith in Christ, but twice diverted the conversation on to mystical matters. In a final paragraph Wesley further suggests that Law's lack of faith would account for his rough and sour behaviour.

LETTER II. LAW TO WESLEY[29]

Law's reply is dated 19th May and is the longest of the four letters. The opening paragraph is couched in a vein of delicate irony to the effect that, as Wesley claimed his letter was written in obedience to the divine call and at the instigation of one whom he knew to have the spirit of God, Law neither desires nor dares to defend himself. He then proceeds to state what would have been his reply had Wesley only acted 'by that ordinary light which is common to good and sober minds' and deals point by point with Wesley's letter.

While declining to comment on Wesley's ineffectual preaching on the basis of the two practical discourses, Law counters Wesley's professed ignorance of the doctrine of saving grace by reminding him of Thomas à Kempis's work, a new translation of which had been published by Wesley more than two years before. Surely he could not pretend ignorance of 'the most plain, open, and repeated doctrine' contained in it, and surely, too, he must remember Law's strong recommendation of it.

Furthermore, Law claims it as likely that in the many conversations they had had

> you never was with me for half an hour without my being large upon that very doctrine of which you make me totally silent and ignorant.

As proof of this, Law cites his putting into Wesley's hands the 'little book of the German Theology' which 'plainly leads to Jesus Christ', and reminds Wesley of his own (i.e. Law's) work written against the *Plain Account of the Sacrament*. A fair reading of this should help him to a right judgement of Law, who had been governed in all he had

> written and done by those two common, fundamental, unchangeable maxims of our Lord, 'Without Me ye can do nothing: If any man will come after Me or be My disciple, let him take up his cross and follow Me'.

In this connexion Law pleads that the doctrine of the Cross is inseparable from faith in Christ and following Him.

In the next section of the letter Law drives home the points already made, without introducing fresh arguments, and claims again that any blame must not be laid exclusively at his door but should be shared between à Kempis and himself.

Law proceeds to quote Wesley's description of the interview with Böhler and gives an entirely different account of it. The interview, he says, was accidental and when Böhler brought up the subject of faith in Christ, Law's silence was one of approbation. As for his own alleged introduction of mystical matters, Law flatly denies having done so. He then returns to an ironical vein, suggesting that as neither Wesley nor Böhler could have any part in the falsity involved in these contradictory versions, he is content it should be ascribed to him. As for Wesley's accusation of sour and rough behaviour, 'whatever you can say of me of that kind, without hurting yourself, will be always well received by me'.

LETTER III. WESLEY TO LAW[30]

Law's prompt reply to Wesley's first letter evoked an even more prompt rejoinder from Wesley who returned to the charge in a letter dated the very next day, 20th May.

Ignoring his opponent's irony, Wesley is brief and to the point. He sweeps aside as of little importance questions raised by Law concerning his translation of à Kempis and also the interview between Law and Böhler (though saying on this latter point that two besides himself were present), on which matters, says Wesley, 'the main question does not turn', and concentrates on one point:

whether you ever advised me, or directed me to books that did advise, to seek first a living faith in the blood of Christ?

Wesley restates Law's three contentions on this point: (1) that he put the *Theologia Germanica* into Wesley's hands, (2) that he published an answer to *The Plain Account of the Sacrament*, (3) that Law was governed through all he had writ and done by these two fundamental maxims of our Lord—'Without Me ye can do nothing' and 'If any man will come after Me, let him take up his cross and follow Me'. Wesley allows the fact but not the consequences. The *Theologia Germanica*, though speaking of Christ our Pattern says 'nothing express of Christ our Atonement'. The answer to *The Plain Account*, though in Wesley's opinion an excellent work, does not affect the question. The two maxims may imply but do not express that third—'He is our propitiation, through faith in His blood'. He then indicts Law on five counts.

'But how are you chargeable with my not having had this faith?' If, as you intimate, you discerned my spirit, thus: (1) You did not tell me plainly I had it not. (2) You never once advised me to seek or pray for it.

[30] *Journal*, Vol. III, pp. 323-4; *Letters*, Vol. I, pp. 241-2.

(3) You gave me advices proper only for one who had it already; and
(4) advices which led me farther from it, the closer I adhered to them.
(5) You recommended books to me which had no tendency to plant this faith, but a direct one to destroy good works.

As for Law's claim that he and à Kempis should share the blame, Wesley bluntly retorts that if Law saw that he was understanding à Kempis wrong, it was his business to explain and set him right.
The letter ends, as it had begun, with an expression of courteous respect.

LETTER IV. LAW TO WESLEY[31]

Law's concluding letter is simply headed May 1738 in the Standard Edition of Wesley's *Letters*, but Christopher Walton gives the date as 30th May.[32] He deals seriatim with the points already raised in the course of the correspondence.

He refers twice to the interview with Böhler, first to correct what he appears to think Wesley said in his second letter. This, he says, is his sole reason for writing again. Wesley had alleged that there were two others present at the interview, but Law maintains that the persons concerned though present were not witnesses, as the interview was conducted in Latin which they did not understand. At a later point in the letter, Law returns to this subject and severely criticizes Böhler's whole behaviour in the matter, in that after parting from Law on apparently friendly terms he then, describing the interview to Wesley, 'invents and tells things as false as if he had charged me with picking his pocket'.

Law reiterates his statement that, in translating à Kempis, Wesley's attention must have been deeply engaged to those very truths to which he complained of being a stranger through Law's conversation. The *Theologia Germanica* Law stoutly defends especially as a book suitable to be read by 'a clergyman that had made profession of divinity'. 'What that book has not taught you I am content that you should not have learnt from me.' On the subject of the two maxims of Scripture Law objects to being confined to them alone. The answer

[31] *Letters*, Vol. I, pp. 242-4.
[32] *Notes and Materials for an Adequate Biography of William Law*, p. 94.

to the *Plain Account* had been mentioned by him not in connexion with the question Wesley now makes central, namely, Law's manner of conversation with him, but rather as proof of his own faith in the Atonement, which Wesley had challenged. He then accuses Wesley of shifting his ground. Things which in his second letter he sweeps aside as irrelevant, had only been discussed by Law, in reply to Wesley's first letter. What Wesley now calls the main question had not been the main question of the first letter, and if it had been, that letter would never have been written. Law then roundly asserts that Wesley's real motive was to give vent to the dislike he had conceived for him by telling him he had been shown by a man of God the real poverty and misery of Law's state.

Then follows the attack on Böhler referred to above, after which Law in a concluding paragraph brusquely disowns any peculiar responsibility for Wesley's defects.

Who made me your teacher? or can make me answerable for any defects in your knowledge? You sought my acquaintance, you came to me as you pleased, and on what occasion you pleased, and to say to me what you pleased. If it was my business to put this question to you, if you have a right to charge me with guilt for the neglect of it, may you not much more reasonably accuse them who are authoritatively charged with you? Did the Church in which you are educated put this question to you? did the Bishop that ordained you either deacon or priest do this for you? did the Bishop that sent you into Georgia require this of you? Pray, sir, be at peace with me.'

Such is the correspondence between Law and Wesley in 1738. Law's conclusion to his second letter ruled out any further reply on Wesley's part. How this rankled with Wesley may be judged from the fact that after nearly twenty years Wesley, writing to William Dodd, expressed the hope that his correspondent would never receive from him such treatment as he (Wesley) had received from Mr. Law on this occasion.[33]

Many writers in commenting upon this Law–Wesley correspondence endeavoured to apportion the blame between the two men. In this there are many differences of opinion and it is interesting to note that whereas Wesley's biographer Tyerman is more critical of Wesley,[34] Law's biographer

[33] *Letters* Vol. III, p. 157.   [34] *The Life and Times of John Wesley*, Vol. I, p. 188.

Overton finds the greater fault in Law.[35] For our purpose in this historical survey it is more important that we should see how the controversy arose, wherein it consisted, and what effect it produced. We have already traced the events which gave rise to it. Wesley being the forthright man he was, it is difficult to see how the religious transition he underwent could fail to be accompanied by some sort of clash with his former spiritual director, although it might well have been that, if personal contact had taken the place of correspondence, all bitterness might have been avoided. Disputes of this kind at a distance always tend to greater acrimony, and the effect of the written word is harder to efface than that of the spoken. If Wesley had consulted Law personally at this period, it is likely that at any rate they would have understood one another better. The impression derived from the letters is that neither properly appreciated where the other stood. The situation was complicated by Böhler's intervention as a sort of go-between. The interview between him and Law seems to have loomed unnecessarily large in Law's mind, in connexion with the dispute, and a careful reading of the letters reveals a definite misunderstanding which, as far as I am aware, has hitherto escaped notice.

The fact is that Law was talking of one interview and Wesley of another. Wesley in his second letter says: 'whether Peter Böhler spoke truth in what he said when two others were present *besides me*. . . .'[36] This clearly refers to the occasion when Böhler gave an account to Wesley of his interview with Law, and Wesley is anxious to make it plain that two witnesses were present who could testify that Wesley was faithfully recording Böhler's words. Law, however, in his reply, in which moreover he gives the incident the most important place, says,

I had not sent you an answer to it [i.e. Wesley's second letter] had it not been for the part of it where you say there were two persons present with Mr. Böhler *and myself*,[37]

thereby taking Wesley's remark about the witnesses to refer to an entirely different occasion, namely Law's actual interview

---

[35] *The Life and Opinions of the Rev. William Law*, p. 82.
[36] *Journal*, Vol. VIII, p. 323. (The italics are mine. E.W.B.)
[37] *Letters*, Vol. I, p. 242. (The italics are mine. E.W.B.)

with Böhler, instead of to Böhler's subsequent account of the interview given to Wesley. The responsibility for the misunderstanding must rest with Law, as Wesley's original statement is perfectly clear. But a much deeper misunderstanding must also be attributed to Law, who could never have advanced his own reliance on the two maxims of our Lord, 'Without Me ye can do nothing' and 'If any man will come after Me, let him take up his cross and follow Me', as a defence against Wesley's accusations unless he had failed to appreciate the latter's position and the intensity with which he held it. Law's whole defence in this respect is weak. In so far as the *Theologia Germanica* and his own answer to the *Plain Account of the Sacrament* support his contention, they do so by implication rather than explicitly, but his third point, his citation of these two maxims as the basis of all he said and did, entirely begs the question at issue. Wesley's whole complaint had been his inability to fulfil the ethical demands of the Christian faith as Law taught them. For Law to quote these maxims, the first of which is altogether too general and vague, and the second of which is an ethical demand, as proof that he has faithfully pointed Wesley to a saving faith in Christ, reveals a complete misunderstanding of Wesley's viewpoint. Neither of the maxims has anything to do with the blood of Christ or with saving faith. With all respect, they must be dismissed as irrelevances introduced by Law when he was clearly out of his depth. Thus Wesley's main charge, at any rate in the narrower form in which he stated it in his second letter, remained unanswered.

On the other side it should be remarked that, considered purely as a debate, the contest resembled that between a rapier and a bludgeon. Wesley was no match in this respect for the older man, whose first letter, as Overton says,

Shows on a small scale what almost all Law's controversial pieces show—the handiwork of a consummate master of the art of controversy.[38]

On the broad issue, too, it cannot be denied that Law was fully justified when, at the conclusion of the correspondence, he objected to being thus singled out as solely to blame for any deficiencies in Wesley's faith. Wesley's genuine Christian

[38] *The Life and Opinions of William Law*, p. 86.

motive in initiating the correspondence cannot be doubted, and his frankness and sincerity go far to counterbalance that lack of judgement, tact, and even reasonableness which his attack on Law reveals, and the impression of which is accentuated by Law's own dignified restraint and skill in controversy. Wesley was no match for Law as a controversialist, but he was desperate, and desperate men are not greatly concerned for the niceties of controversial tactics. The awful gloom resting on his soul penetrated into his whole way of life, even into the tone of his letters, and it is doubtful if Law when he wrote his replies had the faintest grasp of the struggle then going on in the soul of Wesley.

Of the content of the correspondence more need not be said at this point, though we shall, of course, return to the whole subject of Justification by Faith in the doctrinal section of our inquiry. Before leaving the subject, we might note that Wesley's singling out of Law for attack in this way and his earnest vehemence furnish a revealing commentary on the degree of his previous dependence on Law and the dominant place Law had held in Wesley's regard.

The effect of the quarrel in 1738 was to make a clear and final breach between Law and Wesley, the significance of which is tersely summed up by Telford who, discussing the correspondence, says: 'Another pilot was dropped by the outspoken letters to William Law.'[39]

[39] *Letters*, Vol. I, p. 232.

CHAPTER III

1738 to 1756

THE BREACH between Law and Wesley was never healed; on the contrary, the gulf which separated them steadily widened, though it was not until 1756 that Wesley publicly attacked Law in the famous open letter.[1] After 1738 there was no further private correspondence and, as far as we are aware, the two men never met. Wesley being who he was, some record of such a meeting would almost certainly have come down to us, had it taken place. In Mr. Hobhouse's view the fact that they did not meet must have been due to a deliberate avoidance of it on Wesley's part.[2] There is, however, no real evidence of this and Mr. Hobhouse modifies his view in a footnote which shows clearly that Wesley would have had to make a special detour in order to pass through Kingscliffe, where Law lived from 1740 until his death. None of Wesley's usual lines of travel went through that district and in the thirty years between Law's death and his own Wesley never visited the neighbourhood.[3] Although Wesley made no effort to bring the issues between Law and himself to a definite head until 1756 there were, naturally enough, a good many indirect contacts between him and Law, and incidental references on the part of each to the other. Before examining these, it would be well for us to summarize the activities of the two men in turn during the intervening years, observing as we do so along what divergent paths their stories developed, rendering any possible reconciliation out of the question.

Of Law we may say with greater truth than of most writers that we see the man *in* his writings. Walton remarks that 'his works were severally and collectively the transcripts of his own experience'.[4] This was Overton's reason for devoting such a large section of his biography of Law to an account of the writings.[5] And if we are to understand the development of

[1] *Letters*, Vol. III, pp. 332-70.
[2] *William Law and Eighteenth-century Quakerism*, p. 313.　　[3] ibid., p. 314.
[4] *Notes and Materials for an Adequate Biography of William Law*, p. 532.
[5] *The Life and Opinions of the Rev. William Law*, p. 333.

Law's life and thought during these important years, it is to his written works that we must turn.

In Chapter One we described the first two phases of Law's outlook as expressed first of all in the Bangorian Letters and then later in the great practical treatises, the *Christian Perfection* and the *Serious Call*. In this chapter we are concerned with the last two phases each represented by a group of writings, the two groups being separated by an interval of nine years.[6]

The first group of writings with which we are concerned falls within the years 1737–40. These are the titles and dates:

1737: *A Demonstration of the Gross and Fundamental Errors of a late Book called 'A Plain Account of the Nature and End of the Sacrament of the Lord's Supper, etc.'*

1739: *The Grounds and Reasons of Christian Regeneration.*

1740: *An Earnest and Serious Answer to Dr. Trapp's Discourse of the Folly, Sin, and Danger of being Righteous Overmuch.*

1740: *An Appeal to all that Doubt, or Disbelieve the Truths of the Gospel, etc.*

1740: *Some Animadversions upon Dr. Trapp's late Reply.*

This group of writings represents an intermediate stage in Law's thought. It appears that he was no more content than Wesley with the purely ethical Christianity of the *Christian Perfection* and the *Serious Call*. When we remember how Wesley broke with Law because of his (Wesley's) dissatisfaction with a system which set before him an ideal, but no means of attaining it, there is a danger that we may overlook the fact that Law himself found the religion of the practical treatises equally inadequate. Indeed we may go farther and say that with him the process of development, though unaccompanied by any dramatic element such as characterized Wesley's

---

[6] For the sake of completeness it should perhaps be mentioned in passing that in the years that elapsed after the publication of the *Serious Call* and before 1737 Law had written in 1731 the *Case of Reason*, and also in 1731-2 the *Letters to a Lady inclined to enter into the Communion of the Church of Rome*, which were not published, however, until 1779. Besides these there were the letters written to Fanny Henshaw, 1736, mentioned by Walton (*Notes and Materials*, etc., pp. 52, 364), but not published until Mr. Hobhouse in his recent work makes them the starting point of his inquiry into William Law and Eighteenth-century Quakerism. None of these works, however, need detain us as they are irrelevant to our subject, except perhaps in so far as the letters to Fanny Henshaw, though containing the first signs of Boehme's influence, nevertheless reveal that as late as 1736 Law still showed no sympathy whatever with the religious outlook of the Quakers, with which he had so much in common in the last phase of his thought.

evangelical conversion, had actually begun earlier. Law, as he himself tells us,[7] had for long been a diligent reader of the mystic writers, and we have already seen how he endeavoured to communicate his enthusiasm for them to Wesley, by recommending to him that summary of mystical theology, the *Theologia Germanica*.[8] Then about 1736 he became acquainted with the writings of Jacob Boehme, the shoemaker-mystic of Silesia.[9] This proved a turning point in Law's life and from that time forward he became a 'lifelong student and disciple of Boehme'.[10] The important point to recognize is that though by an entirely different route, so that neither he nor Wesley realized it, Law by this means made the transition from νόμος to χάρις, which Wesley experienced on 24th May 1738. Though in this chapter our historical survey covers the years 1738–56, it should be noted that the first of the works in this group was written as early as 1737. Beginning in that year, as Law himself gradually absorbed the profound and often obscure teachings of Boehme, so he increasingly re-interpreted those teachings in his own writings, and it is in the group of writings of the years 1737–40 that we first discern Boehme's influence. In these works Law reverts to the Sacraments of Baptism and the Lord's Supper, which had receded into the background in the *Serious Call* period, as of primary importance without, however, adopting again the strict High Church position of the Bangorian Letters. As Mr. Hobhouse says:

There it was the 'validity' of the Sacraments, the question as to what body of men should administer them, and the like topics that he was discussing: here, he leaves all that on one side, assumes a valid administration, and sets out to interpret the deep significance of these divine mysteries.[11]

The *Demonstration*, for example, was written as a reply to a 'nameless author',[12] supposedly Bishop Hoadly, who in a recent work had sought to

---

[7] *Law's Works*, Vol. VI, pp. 203-4.
[8] vide *supra*, p. 24.
[9] Mr. Hobhouse, in *William Law and Eighteenth-century Quakerism*, p. 268, gives reasons for placing Law's first acquaintance with Boehme's writings in or about this year.
[10] ibid., p. 268.
[11] ibid., p. 266.
[12] *Law's Works*, Vol. V, p. 3.

confine us to the bare words of the institution for right and full understanding of all that is to be understood of the nature, end, and effects of the holy Sacrament.[13]

According to this teaching, the Sacrament of the Lord's Supper became little more than a memorial act. Law refutes this, urging the need for knowledge of 'who and what kind of Person this ME is, who is here to be remembered', also 'in what respects and on how many accounts He is our Saviour'.[14] Further:

It was the want of this knowledge, that made the Institution of the Sacrament useless to the Apostles when they first heard it; but when they had got this knowledge, and knew all the characters of their Saviour, and in how many respects He stood as the Mediator and Redeemer betwixt God and Man, then the Institution became highly intelligible to them, and every part of it plainly declared the mystery that in a certain sense was both concealed and expressed by it.[15]

Law then proceeds to expound the truths of Scripture that Christ as our Saviour is the Atonement for Sin and a Principle of Life to all that lay hold on Him. The acknowledgement of these two truths, he maintains, are the two essential parts of the Sacrament, which constitute its whole nature.

The first is in these words, 'This is My Body which is given for you, this is My Blood which is shed for the Remission of Sins'.

What is here said by our Lord Christ, we are to acknowledge to be true; therefore we are to own and acknowledge this great truth, that this bread and wine are made symbols and memorials of, viz., that His body is given for us, and His blood shed for the Remission of Sins; and consequently all that the Scripture teaches concerning the truth, reality and manner in which He is the Sacrifice, Atonement and Satisfaction for our sins, is in this Sacrament to be of all necessity acknowledged and confessed by us. . . . Therefore the acknowledgement of Christ's being the Atonement and Satisfaction for our Sins, is an essential and important part of the Sacrament. . . .

Secondly, the other essential, and no less important part of the Sacrament is, the eating the body, and drinking the blood of Christ. This is plainly another essential part of the Sacrament, entirely distinct from the other. The one respects Christ, as he is the Atonement and Satisfaction for our Sins; the other shows that he is to be owned and received as a Principle of Life to us.'[16]

[13] ibid., p. 8.   [14] ibid., p. 13.   [15] ibid., pp. 13-14.   [16] ibid., pp. 38-9.

The nature and end of the Sacrament is to exercise our Faith in this twofold manner,

For when our Saviour says, Do this, it is the same thing as if he had said, Do these two things appointed in the Sacrament, as your Act of Faith, that I am both the Atonement for your sins, and a Principle of Life to you. Don't say bare and empty outward words, when you say, 'This is My Body which is given for you, and this My Blood which is shed for the Remission of Sins'; but let Faith say them, and acknowledge the truth of them: When you eat My Body, and drink My Blood, don't let your mouth only eat, or perform the outward action; but let Faith, which is the true mouth of the inward man, believe that it really partakes of Me, and that I enter in by Faith; and when you thus by Faith perform these two essential parts of the Sacrament, then, and then only may what you do be said to be done in Remembrance of Me, and of what I am to you. For nothing remembers Me but Faith, nothing acknowledges Me but Faith, nothing finds Me, nothing knows Me but Faith.[17]

This faith is absolutely essential if the Sacrament is to be valid.

If we stand before this Atonement, without such dispositions as correspond to it, we are as absent from the Sacrament of Christ, as they are that refuse to come to it; if we eat that which is before us in the Sacrament, without such faith and purity as qualify us to receive the flesh and blood of Christ, we are only eating that, which might have been the bread of life to our souls.[18]

With this recaptured, though shifted, emphasis on the Sacraments is blended an ever-increasing infusion of mystical thought, derived from Boehme. This gradual spreading of Boehme's influence is, of course, one of the main themes of Mr. Hobhouse's study, and he is our best guide to its development. Over the pages of the earliest of these works, the *Demonstration* (1737), 'there is spread', says Mr. Hobhouse,

a kind of infusion of Behmenism that, quite apart from questions of Church and Sacrament, has not yet absorbed some of Law's more legalistic methods of explaining the ways of God with men.[19]

In the later works of this group the process has considerably developed, but even here

[17] *Law's Works*, Vol. V, p. 41. [18] ibid., p. 67.
[19] *William Law and Eighteenth-century Quakerism*, pp. 268-9.

the *Christian Regeneration* and the *Appeal*, while they are in themselves comprehensive statements of Law's newly thought-out mystical system, yet contain impressive descriptions of the supreme virtues to be found in baptism and the supper respectively.[20]

Law's teaching on the Sacrament of Baptism at this time is well expressed in this passage from the *Christian Regeneration*:

Our baptism is to signify our seeking and obtaining a new birth. And our being baptized in, or into the Name of the Father, Son, and Holy Ghost, tells us in the plainest manner, what birth it is that we seek, namely, such a new birth as may make us again what we were at first, a living real image or offspring of the Father, Son, and Holy Ghost. It is owned on all hands, that we are baptized into a renovation of some Divine Birth that we had lost, and that we may not be at a loss to know what that Divine Birth is, the form in Baptism openly declares to us, that it is to regain that first birth of Father, Son, and Holy Ghost in our souls, which at the first made us to be truly and really images of the nature of the Holy Trinity in unity. The form in Baptism is but very imperfectly apprehended, till it is understood to have this great meaning in it.[21]

This conception of a new birth being owned and sought by baptism into the name of Father, Son, and the Holy Ghost is expounded in similar terms by Law elsewhere in the *Regeneration* and the *Appeal*.[22]

The latter work also contains in its concluding passage what Mr. Hobhouse describes as 'the high-water mark'[23] of Law's devotion to the Eucharist. Certainly his thought has developed beyond the stage of the *Demonstration* and now it is the 'Flesh and Blood of Eternal Life which is offered to us in the Holy Sacrament that we may eat and live for ever'.[24] Considerations of space prevent the whole of the passage being quoted or even summarized, but Law concludes:

And thus is this great Sacrament, which is a continual part of our Christian Worship, a continual communication to us of all the benefits of our second Adam; for in and by the body and blood of Christ, to which the divine nature is united, we receive all that life, immortality, and redemption, which Christ, as living, suffering, dying, rising from the Dead, and ascending into Heaven, brought to human nature; so that this

[20] ibid., p. 266.   [21] *Law's Works*, Vol. V, p. 148.
[22] ibid., pp. 164, 170, and Vol. VI, p. 83.
[23] *William Law: Selected Mystical Writings*, p. 341.
[24] *Law's Works*, Vol. VI, p. 153.

great mystery is that, in which all the blessings of our redemption and new life in Christ are centred. And they that hold a Sacrament short of this reality of the true body and blood of Jesus Christ, cannot be said to hold that Sacrament of eternal life, which was instituted by our blessed Lord and Saviour.[25]

These quotations from his writings illustrate Law's position at this stage. It is interesting to note that Christopher Walton writing, of course, long before Mr. Hobhouse demonstrated the significance of the steady trend of Law's thought from the extreme High Church position to one approximating (in thought, if not in practising Churchmanship) to that of the Quakers, also describes this group of writings as representing an intermediate stage between that of the *Serious Call* period and Law's ultimate position. He writes:

Up to the year 1732 he had preached the gospel of the law, or the duties and obligations of wisdom and devotion: but now it had become his high privilege and duty after the intervening growth of his mind (as exhibited by his *Sacrament Book*, *Regeneration Tract* and his replies to Trap[26]) to preach the Gospel of the Spirit, in all its nakedness and fulness. He does indeed speak of the New Birth and influences of the Holy Spirit in exalted terms in the above works; and in the express treatise of *Regeneration*... clearly exhibits the orthodox mode of our becoming the subjects of the New Birth, or means we are to employ in order to pass through that gate of entrance into the spiritual life; yet he must be said therein to have more particularly reflected upon the truth of the doctrine of the old and new man and of that sublime holiness which the gospel sets before us, than upon the means and power, by which alone the practice of this latter could be freely and universally fulfilled. Which contemplation indeed necessarily precedes the high *Johannic* experience of the *Spirit of love*—the especial subject of these his last writings.[27]

So we pass to the other group of Law's writings which falls within the period we are discussing. They are five in number and the titles with dates are as follows:

1749. *The Spirit of Prayer*. Part the First.
1750. *The Spirit of Prayer*. Part the Second.
1752. *The Way to Divine Knowledge*.
1752. *The Spirit of Love*. Part the First.
1752. *The Spirit of Love*. Part the Second.

[25] *Law's Works*, Vol. VI, p. 155. [26] Walton's own mis-spelling.
[27] *Notes and Materials, etc.*, p. 532.

It will be seen that, like the earlier group, these were all written within a few years of each other but that the earliest of them is separated by an interval of no less than nine years from the latest work of the earlier group we have been considering. The importance of this interval was noticed by Walton but afterwards overlooked until attention was again drawn to it by Mr. Hobhouse.[28] Walton writes:

We have shown how Mr. Law's understanding became matured for his later works. Outwardly, by his masterly apprehension of Boehme, aided by the demonstrations of Freher and collateral elucidations of Lee, and based upon his previous acquaintance with the highest French, Spanish, and Italian masters of experimental mystical science. And, inwardly, by his own cultivation of the divine life, and demersions of his spirit in the internal abyss of the divine power and life.[29]

It was a period of meditation and study at the end of which Law's theological and ecclesiastical position, now finally settled, was expounded by him in the five above-mentioned works. Mr. Hobhouse describes these as Law's five most important books.[30] Doubtless that is true if we are taking as our standard Law's own maturity of outlook, but if we adopt a broader view and take as our criterion of importance the influence exerted on his contemporaries and on future generations, the *Christian Perfection* and the *Serious Call* must take pride of place. This is due mainly to the effect they produced on Wesley, but even today, in so far as William Law is not entirely forgotten by the ordinary man, as distinct from students of mysticism, it is as the author of the *Serious Call* that he is best known. However that may be, Mr. Hobhouse is right in saying that in the five books of this group, to which must be added the *Collection* of edited letters, all of which belong to this same period, we have

one harmonious system of thought—Law's final and considered views on creeds and sacraments, on the Incarnation and the Atonement, on the universe and God.[31]

Law's later writings after 1756 reveal no fresh development of thought and indeed show a certain deterioration in style and treatment.

[28] *William Law and Eighteenth-century Quakerism*, p. 282.
[29] *Notes and Materials, etc.*, p. 524.
[30] *William Law and Eighteenth-century Quakerism*, p. 283.   [31] ibid., p. 283.

The first of the two extracts from Walton quoted above has already hinted at the nature of these writings. He described them as containing 'the Gospel of the Spirit, in all its nakedness and fulness',[32] and spoke of 'the high *Johannic* experience of the *Spirit of Love*—the especial subject of these his last writings'.[33] In the period of the two practical discourses Law's main emphasis had been on the common duties of man. 'Here . . . while these duties are assumed, it is the inward states of the soul and the manner of God's revelations to the soul, which are all-important.'[34] The Sacraments which, as we saw, had regained prominence in the earlier groups of writings of this 1738-56 period, as having supreme mystical significance, recede once more into the background. The outward ceremony has only a value in so far as it can stir up within us the spirit of prayer and love.

The whole emphasis is on the need of 'continual immediate inspiration' of the Holy Spirit, and on the possibility of possessing this gift in field or shop, as much as at a service in church.[35]

Examples of this change of emphasis could be taken from almost every page of the group of writings, for Law is very repetitive, but we may cite the following as typical. In the First Part of the *Spirit of Prayer* Law writes:

All that is grace, redemption, salvation, sanctification, spiritual life, and the new birth, is nothing else but so much of the life, and operation of God found again in the soul.[36]

Then, on the inward nature of the Fall of Man and the New Birth:

The Kingdom of Self is the Fall of Man, or the great Apostasy from the life of God in the Soul; and everyone wherever he be, that lives unto Self, is still under the Fall and great Apostasy from God. The Kingdom of Christ is the Spirit and Power of God dwelling and manifesting itself in the Birth of a new inward Man; and no one is a member of this Kingdom, but so far as a true Birth of the Spirit is brought forth in him.[37]

A more than usually succinct statement of his position follows a little later: 'There is but one Salvation for all Mankind, and

---

[32] *Notes and Materials, etc.*, p. 532.
[33] ibid.
[34] *William Law and Eighteenth-century Quaker sm*, p. 284.
[35] ibid.
[36] *Law's Works*, Vol. VII, p. 38.
[37] ibid., p. 39.

that is the Life of God in the Soul.'[38] Similarly in the Second Part of the same work:

You should, once for all, mark and observe, where and what the true Nature of Religion is; for here it is plainly shown you, that its Place is within; its Work and Effect is within; its Glory, its Life, its Perfection, is all within; it is merely and solely the raising a new life, new Love, and a new Birth, in the inward Spirit of our Hearts.[39]

And with a contrast explicitly drawn between outward ordinances and the regenerating work of the Spirit within,

all religion is but a dead work, unless it be the work of the Spirit of God; and that sacraments, prayers, singing, preaching, hearing, are only so many ways of being fervent in the Spirit, and of giving up ourselves more and more to the inward working, enlightening, quickening, sanctifying Spirit of God within us; and all for this end, that the curse of the Fall may be taken from us, that death may be swallowed up in victory, and a true, real, Christ-like nature formed in us, by the same Spirit, by which it was formed in the Holy Virgin Mary.[40]

Such was the religious transition through which Law passed in the years 1738-56, and all that we know of his life and character during that time is in harmony with what such writings would lead us to expect. In 1737 his old friend Mr. Gibbon died.[41] Law, however, appears to have remained in town until 1740 when he took up residence at Kingscliffe. For a few years he lived alone, but in 1744 was joined by his two friends, Miss Hester Gibbon and Mrs. Hutcheson,[42] to whom also he acted as spiritual adviser.

What was the particular economy of the household does not now appear, ... but if we bear in mind ... that the directing head of the whole establishment was the piety and wisdom that indited the *Serious Call to a Devout and Holy Life*, we may justly infer that all was conducted according to the principles and with the regularity of a religious house.[43]

Walton then gives a detailed reconstruction of how a normal day is spent[44] and described Law's personal appearance and habits as far as they could be gathered from what testimony

---

[38] ibid., Vol. VII, p. 45.   [39] ibid., p. 110.   [40] ibid., p. 113.
[41] The date is given as 1736 by Walton (*Notes and Materials, etc.*, p. 364), and by Overton (*Life and Opinions of the Rev. William Law*, p. 77) as 1737. The latter appears correct.
[42] *Notes and Materials, etc.*, p. 428.
[43] ibid.   [44] ibid., pp. 497 et sqq.

remained on record. The impression we get from this is of a somewhat shy and retiring man—it is significant that there is no authentic portrait of Law in existence[45]—living in fact, if not in intention, almost the life of a recluse, seeing very few people outside the narrow circle of Kingscliffe society, attending with exemplary regularity the public ordinances of the Church, maintaining withal a strict devotional discipline in private, studying and reinterpreting the mystical writers, and together with his two friends exercising that piety and charity which his own practical discourses enjoined.

Meanwhile what was happening to Wesley? It has been necessary to examine Law's works in some detail in order to arrive at an adequate conception of his developing life and character during the years under review, and even so that conception is to a certain degree inferential. How different is it with Wesley, who almost from the moment of his 1738 experience was engaged on a crusade which was to transform the life of Britain and exert a world-wide influence. The story is too well known to need detailed description. After a brief visit to Germany Wesley returned to England to preach awakening sermons, the power and effect of which he discovered to be as great, as all too often they had seemed feeble in the pre-conversion days. When Whitefield had to interrupt his open-air preaching at Bristol, Wesley responded to the call to succeed him. That was the beginning of an itinerant preaching ministry throughout the length and breadth of the land, as Wesley travelled on horseback from place to place. From the preaching of that evangel there sprang up the Methodist Societies everywhere to meet the need for regular Christian fellowship. Those societies were scattered ever farther afield in fresh places and linked with one another. So Wesley became not only the inspired evangelist, awakening men to newness of life, but the incomparable organizer, appointing leaders and later ministers (known as helpers) responsible only to himself. He was the driving force of the whole movement, every part of which he kept under his own direct control.

Could a greater contrast be imagined than that between Law and Wesley? Wesley, like Law, spent hours in meditation,

[45] *Notes and Materials, etc.*, p. 502. Also *Serious Call* (1816 edition), p. vii (footnote).

but it was as he rode his horse from one town to the next in the prosecution of his campaign. Wesley, too, like Law, was a prolific writer, but his writing was incidental to his preaching and designed to meet the needs of that ever-increasing company of men and women who looked to him for the nourishment of their minds and their souls, as they already owed to him their spiritual re-birth. Temperamentally, there was a corresponding contrast. 'Was I so talked of as Mr. Whitefield is,' said Law to Charles Wesley on 10th August 1739, 'I should run away, and hide myself entirely.'[46] If Law was what the modern psychologist would term an introvert, Wesley, in spite of his introspective period prior to his conversion, ultimately found happiness, as Mr. Bonamy Dobrée has well observed,[47] when he lost himself in his work. Here then are the two men, the one a recluse at Kingscliffe, modest, retiring, too diffident even to have his portrait painted, the other directing, organizing, launching societies, touching contemporary life at a thousand points, knowing men and known of them, perhaps the most frequently portrayed figure of the century. Experience and temperament combined to make it almost impossible that these two should think in 1756 as they had thought in 1732. Those two divergent processes of growth must be given due weight as the dominant cause, rather than the effect, of their consequent theological disagreements.

With this general sketch in our minds of the ever-widening gulf between Law and Wesley, we conclude this chapter by filling into the picture such details as are available to us of Law's relation to the Wesleys and the Methodists during these years, while leaving the discussion of the doctrinal issues involved to a later chapter. The earliest record of any direct link between Law and the Wesleys after the quarrel of 1738 is a pleasing one, as it reveals on Law's part a certain tolerance and a greater measure of appreciation of the Wesleys position than at any other time. The occasion was the interview between Law and Charles Wesley, from which we quoted in the last paragraph above.

Charles Wesley apparently still had enough confidence in Law to take to him on 10th August 1739 a certain J. Bray

[46] *Journal of Charles Wesley*, Vol. I, p. 159.   [47] *John Wesley*, p. 83.

to consult him about his feelings and experiences. Law seems to have explained these away and then to have attacked Whitefield and his methods. He had hoped that the Methodists would have been dispersed into livings where they would have acted as leaven. Charles Wesley recounted his experience to Law, whereupon the latter said: 'Then am I far below you, (if you are right,) not worthy to bear your shoes.' Law then agreed with the notion of faith put forward by Charles, but held that all men had it. He then expressed his disapproval of laymen expounding as 'the very worst thing, both for themselves and others'. Charles said that Law had been his school master to bring him to Christ. Only Charles's desire to be sanctified before he was justified had prevented his coming to Him sooner. Then followed Law's profession of diffidence recorded above and the interview closed with Law disclaiming the role of adviser 'seeing we had the Spirit of God' and at the end, says Charles, Law 'came almost right over'.[48]

The impression we gain from this interview is that the door might still have been open for some reconciliation, but we must bear in mind that it was not John Wesley who was concerned but his brother Charles, who, as we shall see later, always had more in common with Law's mystical outlook than had John.

Any such prospect was rudely dispelled later in the same year when Law's *Christian Regeneration* was published. We are not concerned at the moment with the doctrinal issues between Law and the Wesleys which this work raised, but only with its effects upon the latter. In his *Journal* for 19th October 1739 Charles Wesley writes: 'I read part of Mr. Law on Regeneration to our Society. How promising the beginning! How lame the conclusion!'[49] After some detailed criticism of the contents he described the author as one who 'too plainly demonstrates . . . that his knowledge of the New Birth is mostly in theory'.[50] Four days later, on 23rd October, this is John Wesley's verdict:

In riding to Bradford, I read over Mr. Law's book on the New Birth: philosophical, speculative, precarious; Behmenish, void, and vain! 'Oh what a fall is there!'[51]

[48] *Journal of Charles Wesley*, Vol. I, p. 159.
[49] ibid., p. 191.
[50] ibid.
[51] *Journal*, Vol. II, p. 297.

This was not, however, the universal reaction to the book among the Methodists. Roger Shackleton, writing to his friend Law in the following month mentions that Benjamin Ingham, at that time one of Wesley's intimate fellow-workers, borrowed, read, and liked the *Christian Regeneration*. In 1742 Ingham separated himself from the Wesleys, and Mr. Hobhouse, who quotes the above-mentioned letter, surmises that Ingham's reading of Law's books may have been partly responsible.[52]

Ten years later, when after Law's long silence the *Spirit of Prayer* appeared, Wesley commented:

I read Mr. Law *On the Spirit of Prayer*. There are many masterly strokes therein, and the whole is lively and entertaining; but it is another gospel.[53]

After attacking Law's denial of the wrath of God which Wesley said struck at the root of the Christian doctrine of reconciliation, he continued: 'An excellent method of converting Deists by giving up the very essence of Christianity!'[54] Law seems to have made no direct reference by name to the Wesleys in his writings during this period, but Walton makes a most interesting suggestion that in the Second Part of the *Spirit of Love* which is cast in the dialogue form familiar to so many of his works, the characters of

Theogenes and Eusebius might well represent Wesley and his brother Charles, supposing him to have continued a little longer under his tutor, Theophilus, instead of breaking with him and setting up on his own account in 1738.[55]

Certainly the work dealt with the subject of righteousness, the wrath of God, and the need for an atonement which, as we shall see, were subjects of controversy between Law and Wesley.

Sometimes, however, the relation of Law to the Wesleys and to Methodism became a matter of contemporary comment and on more than one occasion this drew a protest from Wesley. Wesley's last publication in 1742 was entitled *The Principles*

---

[52] *William Law and Eighteenth-century Quakerism*, p. 242.
[53] *Journal*, Vol. III, p. 422.   [54] ibid.
[55] *Notes and Materials, etc.* p. 551.

of a Methodist,[56] and was occasioned by a pamphlet, *A Brief History of the Principles of Methodism*, from the pen of the Rev. Josiah Tucker in the course of which the author 'asserted that Mr. Law's system was the creed of the Methodists'.[57] In reply Wesley declared that he had been eight years at Oxford before he read any of Law's writings and, when he did, he was so far from making them his creed that he had objected to almost every page.[58] This retort, however, was obviously written in the heat of argument and is inconsistent with Wesley's other comments on the practical treatises, which we have already noticed.

But Josiah Tucker was not alone in alleging a connexion between Law and Methodism. Dr. Joseph Trapp, whose controversy with Law was, as has been noted, the occasion of two of the latter's publications during these years, is recorded to have accounted for the origin of Methodism thus:

When I saw these two books, *The Treatise on Christian Perfection*, and *The Serious Call to a Holy Life*, I thought, These books will certainly do mischief. And so it proved; for presently after up sprung the Methodists. So he (Mr. Law) was their parent.[59]

To this Wesley replied

Although this was not entirely true, yet there was some truth in it. All the Methodists carefully read these books, and were greatly profited thereby. Yet they did by no means spring from them, but from the Holy Scriptures; being 'born again' as St. Peter speaks 'by the word of God, which liveth and abideth for ever'.[60]

Yet another of Law's opponents, Bishop Warburton, declared that the Methodists were the offspring of Law and Count Zinzendorf jointly. This, too, Wesley countered in the same sermon by reaffirming Holy Scripture as the only foundation for the movement.

These are but outstanding examples of what was doubtless a frequent subject of comment and dispute at the time. Law was a very eminent writer and Churchman, the Methodist movement would be an inevitable topic of conversation in ecclesiastical circles, and the connexion between the two was

[56] *Wesley's Works*, Vol. VIII, pp. 359-74. The date 1740 given in *Wesley's Works* is wrong, as Tucker's pamphlet to which it was a reply only appeared in July 1742.
[57] ibid., p. 366.   [58] ibid.   [59] ibid., Vol. VII, p. 203.   [60] ibid., pp. 203-4.

naturally discussed. Overton, for example, gives amusing instances of sincere devotees of Law who were at great pains to demonstrate his complete freedom from the taint of Methodism, which was not considered quite respectable in orthodox circles.[61] Any confusion that arose in the matter was due in large measure to a failure accurately to define terms. If the expression 'Methodist' was used in its original sense of one who practises methodical self-discipline in matters of faith and practice, then Law was indeed a Methodist. There was the further fact that Law's distinguished opponents, Trapp and Warburton, were equally opposed to Methodism. But by this time Methodism had come to denote the growing movement which included other characteristics with which Law was by no means in sympathy, and in that sense Law could never have been termed a Methodist. In any event the real question should always have been, not whether Law was a Methodist, but how far the Methodists were followers of Law. In all this inquiry we find little evidence of Law being influenced by Wesley or the Methodists. Any influence that was exerted was by Law upon them. Similarly Wesley was fully justified in refuting the suggestion that the whole Methodist movement was created by Law and based on his teaching. We have already seen ample evidence to disprove that. However important the part played by Law up to 1738 there were obviously elements in the Methodism of 1756 which were entirely foreign to his outlook, and of which he strongly disapproved. The importance for our inquiry of the statements of Tucker, Trapp, and Warburton is that they afford contemporary evidence for the connexion between writings of Law and the beginnings of Methodism.

Before concluding the review of the years 1738-56 we should note that Wesley's earliest publications of extracts from Law's works took place during this period. It was characteristic of Wesley and a tribute to his sound practical common sense that he did not allow the estrangement that had grown up between them to prevent his making the fullest use of his old teacher's books for the benefit and instruction of his own followers.

The first such extract to be published by Wesley was in

[61] *Life and Opinions of the Rev. William Law*, pp. 389-90.

1740 and consisted of an abridgement of the first chapter of the *Christian Perfection* under the title *The Nature and Design of Christianity*. Fourteen years afterwards, in 1754, writing to Samuel Furly, Wesley advised him to recommend his tutor to read this, suggesting it would be more effective than engaging in a dispute with him.[62] In 1743 there appeared *A Practical Treatise on Christian Perfection*, which was Wesley's abridgement of the whole of Law's *Christian Perfection*, and this was closely followed in 1744 by an extract from the *Serious Call*. Then, more surprisingly, in 1749[63] Wesley reprinted a large part of Law's *Serious Answer to Dr. Trapp* including some of the mystical portions, guarding himself, however, by a footnote to the effect that such views are not supported by Scripture. As was his invariable custom when republishing the works of others, Wesley himself carefully edited them first.

[62] *Letters*, Vol. III, p. 122.
[63] All the authorities give 1749, but Harrison's of Cork, who printed it, clearly say 1748 (see *Wesley Bibliography*: by Richard Green, p. 56).

CHAPTER FOUR

1756 and After

THE QUARREL between Law and Wesley was publicly renewed by the latter when, nearly eighteen years after the previous correspondence in 1738, he issued an open letter to Law on 6th January 1756. The composition of this letter apparently took Wesley three weeks, as at the beginning it is dated 15th December 1755. The letter appears both in Wesley's complete *Works* and in the Standard Edition of the *Letters* in a slightly abbreviated form, which omits one of the warmest tributes Wesley ever paid to Law. Copies of the original are exceedingly rare, but happily the deficiency is remedied by Walton, who supplies us with the missing section.[1]

It will be easily allowed by impartial judges [writes Wesley] that there are few writers in the present age, who stand in any competition with Mr. Law, as to beauty and strength of language; readiness, liveliness, and copiousness of thought; and (in many points) accuracy of sentiment. [Wesley adds:] several of his treatises must remain, as long as England stands, almost unequalled standards of the strength and purity of our language as well as of sound practical divinity.[2]

Wesley's prefatory remarks were not all complimentary, as he proceeds with customary frankness to give his reasons for presuming to address the letter to Law, whom he acknowledges to be his superior in many respects. Among these reasons is this:

Being conscious of my own weakness and liableness to err, I am open to instruction from others, whereas it is a doubt, whether you think any man in Great Britain capable of instructing you.[3]

It is noteworthy, though not altogether surprising, that Law in his subsequent comments on the letter makes a similar remark about Wesley, describing him as being unwilling 'to give up his own Spirit'.[4] Wesley's later softening toward the mystics and his doctrinal modifications may be cited as

[1] *Notes and Materials, etc.*, p. 564. [2] ibid. [3] ibid.
[4] *Law's Works*, Vol. IX, p. 169.

justifying at any rate to some extent the claim he makes here to teachableness; Law, of course, only lived a few years after 1756, but there is no evidence of any tendency on his part to modify the rigidity of his position on the issues which divided him from Wesley, though we have already traced a steady development in his general outlook across the years.

The main body of the 1756 Letter consists of an attack on *The Spirit of Prayer* and *The Spirit of Love*. It ranges over a very wide field, falling naturally into two parts, concerned respectively with Law's 'philosophy'[5] and his 'divinity',[6] to use Wesley's own terms.

The first part, that is the attack on Law's 'philosophy', Wesley opens by reminding Law of an observation once made by himself.

You would have a philosophical religion; but there can be no such thing. Religion is the most plain, simple thing in the world. It is only 'We love Him because He first loved us'. So far as you add philosophy to religion, just so far you spoil it.

Wesley then charges Law with continually blending philosophy with religion more than any other writer in England, instancing in particular *The Spirit of Prayer* and *The Spirit of Love*, 'wherein from the titles of them one would expect to find no more of philosophy than in the Epistles of St. John'. Wesley is then a little obscure. He proceeds, 'Concerning which', but it is not altogether clear to what antecedent the pronoun 'which' relates. The general sense, however, is evident. It is Law's general position as expressed in these two works that Wesley assails on the following four grounds:

(1) That the whole of it is utterly superfluous: a man may be full both of prayer and love, and not know a word of this hypothesis.[7] (2) The whole of this hypothesis is unproved; it is all precarious, all uncertain. (3) The whole hypothesis has a dangerous tendency; it naturally leads men off from plain, practical religion, and fills them with the 'knowledge' that 'puffeth up' instead of the 'love' that 'edifieth'. And (4) It is often flatly contrary to Scripture, to reason, and to itself.[8]

[5] *Letters*, Vol. III, p. 333.
[6] ibid., p. 343.
[7] Wesley's mode of referring to Boehme's philosophical system.
[8] *Letters*, Vol. III, p. 332.

Over and above this philosophy which Wesley rejects as 'superfluous, uncertain, dangerous, irrational, and unscriptural', he alleges that Law had grieved many devoted Christians by advancing tenets in religion not only unsupported by, but even repugnant to, Scripture.

Then follows an examination of Law's exposition of the mystical philosophy of Jacob Boehme under four heads: (1) things antecedent to the creation; (2) the creation itself; (3) Adam in paradise; (4) the fall of man.[9] In a later chapter we shall discuss this criticism in so far as it is necessary to our subject to do so. Meanwhile, for our historical survey, we need only note first of all Wesley's failure fully to understand these theories, and, secondly, his complete disapproval of what he did understand. His two great objections to Boehme's mystical teaching, as interpreted by Law, were that it was contrary to Scripture and, moreover, that it was 'high-flown bombast' and 'unintelligible jargon'.[10]

At the conclusion of this attack on Law's exposition under each of the four heads mentioned above, Wesley suggests to him that he has done Boehme an irreparable injury, not by misrepresenting his sentiments (though that may be so) but by dragging him out of obscurity.

Men may admire the deepness of the well and the excellence of the water it contains; but if some officious person puts a light into it, it will appear to be both very shallow and very dirty.[11]

Wesley's excuse for writing at such length on 'so egregious trifles' is that they are mischievous trifles. Law's own case, he maintains, is a clear example of this, for he has been led astray on things of the greatest importance. Bad philosophy has 'paved the way for bad divinity'.[12] Wesley then embarks on the far longer and more important section of his letter which deals not with philosophical speculations but with the great religious truths. Law's acceptance of erroneous mystical beliefs has in Wesley's opinion led to deplorable consequences in this realm, and he accuses him on seven counts.

(1) He denies the omnipotence of God.[13]

[9] ibid., p. 333.   [10] ibid., p. 370.
[11] ibid., p. 342.   [12] ibid., p. 343.
[13] ibid., p. 343

(2) He denies the justice of God.[14] This section is largely devoted to a rebuttal of Law's statement that there is no wrath in God.
(3) He denies the Scripture doctrine of Justification.[15]
(4) His doctrine of the New Birth is wrong.[16] Under this head Wesley also attacks Law's doctrine of the profitableness of coldness over fervour.[17]
(5) His doctrine of Christ in every man.[18]
(6) His advocacy of the way of inward prayer, without an equal reliance on public worship and Bible reading.[19] This section includes a rejection of Law's culture of silence.
(7) His doctrine of hell as a state of soul.[20]

These disagreements between Law and Wesley will receive our consideration in Part Three of our inquiry, when the theological differences between the two men are reviewed.

In a brief concluding paragraph Wesley excuses his plainness of speech on the ground of the urgency of the matter. Law's later works may be more and greater than his first if only he will study Paul, James, Peter, and John, instead of Tauler and Boehme. Let him return to the plain religion of the Bible.[21]

Whatever we may think of Wesley's attack in detail, there can be no doubt that Overton is right when he attributes it to practical considerations.[22] Wesley had encountered a good deal of difficulty in the Methodist societies as a result of a tendency to 'stillness'. This quietistic attitude he thought Law's later writings were calculated to foster, and, as always, he was more than ready to take any action, however impetuous, to protect them. That such was his motive is shown by the fact that the substantial extract, which ultimately found its way into the complete edition of the *Works* and the Standard Edition of the *Letters*, was first published with other pamphlets in a Collection entitled: *A Preservative against Unsettled Notions in Religion*.[23] This had as its object the protection of

---

[14] *Letters*, Vol. III, p. 345. [15] ibid., p. 351. [16] ibid., p. 357.
[17] ibid., p. 360. [18] ibid., p. 361. [19] ibid., p. 364.
[20] ibid., p. 368. [21] ibid., p. 370.
[22] *The Life and Opinions of the Rev. William Law*, p. 383.
[23] *The Works of John and Charles Wesley: A Bibliography*, Richard Green, p. 105.

the Methodist societies against various seductive teachings which were producing disastrous results.

Nevertheless, Wesley was severely taken to task for this letter. Law himself did not answer the letter publicly. This was due partly to the fact that he did not think any answer was required,[24] and partly to a reluctance to administer any public rebuke. This latter reason he explained in a letter to Byrom dated 30th April 1757.

> I declined all thoughts of remarking upon Mr. Wesley's 'letter' myself, and discouraged others that would have done it for me, having no desire to help the world to see him and his spirit in a worse light than was done by his own pen.[25]

In private, however, Law exercised no such restraint. His earliest reference to Wesley's letter that has come down to us was in a letter to Mr. Langcake, a disciple of his. This letter, dated 24th January, less than three weeks after Wesley's letter was published, was not included in the *Collection of Law's Letters*, published in 1760, but is preserved for us by Walton. It seems that Mr. Langcake had been instrumental in procuring for Law a copy of the 1756 Letter (incidentally described by Walton as 'a rash and puerile effusion'). Law acknowledges this in these terms:

> I have much to thank you for in the zeal and diligence you have shown in sending me Mr. Wesley's letter. But am sorry you and Mr. Richardson (the publisher) should have wasted so many franks, for I was in no eagerness of seeing it soon, nor under any expectation of being obliged to take any notice of it.[26]

On 16th February Law wrote a letter to a lady described in the *Collection* as 'A Person of Quality',[27] whose identity is revealed as the Countess of Huntingdon by both Walton and Byrom, by the latter on the authority of John Wesley himself.[28]

> Mr. Wesley's letter [writes Law] did not at all disappoint me. I had no expectation of seeing a better, either with regard to the substance, or to the style and manner of it. If I knew of any kind of answer, that would

---

[24] *Law's Works*, Vol. IX, p. 167.
[25] *Remains of John Byrom*, Vol. II, Part II, p. 589.
[26] *Notes and Materials, etc.*, p. 561.
[27] *Law's Works*, Vol. IX, p. 165.
[28] *Remains of John Byrom*, Vol. II, Part II, p. 629.

do him any real good, I should advise it. But to answer it for the good of anyone else, seems to be quite needless. It does not admit of a serious answer, because there is nothing substantial, or properly argumentative in it. And to answer it in the way of ridicule, is what I cannot come into, being full as averse to make a mock of him in a religious garb, as to the doing the greatest bodily injury to his person. How far he has answered, or does answer any good ends of Providence, or is an instrument in the hands of God, is a matter I meddle not with; only wishing, that every appearance of good, every stirring of zeal, under whatever form it appears, whether in knowledge, or ignorance, in wisdom or weakness, may be directed, and blessed by God, to the best ends it is capable of.[29]

Later in the same letter Law returns to the subject of Wesley.

I was once a kind of oracle with Mr. Wesley. I never suspected anything bad of him, or ever discovered any kind, or degree of falseness, or hypocrisy in him.

But during all the time of his intimacy with me, I judged him to be much under the power of his own Spirit, which seemed to have the predominancy in every good thing, or way, that his zeal carried him to.[30]

It was to this 'unwillingness, or inability to give up his own Spirit' that Law attributed Wesley's censure of the Mystics.

Yet again in September of the same year Law wrote to Mr. Langcake a letter which began with a most unfair criticism of the Methodists in general.

Your strictures upon Messieurs of the Foundery, the Tabernacle, etc., are very just. These gentlemen seem to have no other bottom to stand upon, but that of zeal. I hope God will direct it for them, that more good may come from it, than the world is willing to believe.[31]

Looking back we can see how faulty was Law's judgement of the evangelical movement then gathering strength. The concluding part of the letter deals again with Wesley's 1756 Letter.

Mr. J. W. is an ingenious man; and the reason why his letter to me is such a juvenile composition of emptiness, and pertness, as is below the character of any man, who had been serious in religion but half a month, is because, it was not ability, but necessity, that put his pen into his hand.[32]

[29] *Law's Works*, Vol. IX, pp. 167-8.   [30] ibid., p. 168-9.
[31] ibid., Vol. IX, p. 198.   [32] ibid.

Wesley, Law proceeds to allege, in condemning Law's books and preaching much against them, had promised from time to time to write against them too. Therefore some answer had to be made and Wesley had in fact the same reasons and was under the same necessity as the Pope of 'condemning and anathematising the mystery revealed by God, in J. B.' (Jacob Boehme). Here, too, however, in the midst of this tirade, Law says of Wesley: 'Wish him God speed in everything that is good.'[33] In connexion with this letter Walton reveals an interesting fact; he describes how this *Collection of Letters* was prepared for publication:

The fact is, Mr. Ward and Mr. Langcake, both resident in London, manufactured (so to speak) a few of these letters, from originals or copies, which they had by them, cutting off certain portions from one letter, and appending them to another, according to their own taste and judgement; finally, perhaps, procuring Mr. Law himself to touch up the parts which did not well dove-tail in each other.[34]

It is further quite clear that this letter of September 1756, which we are now considering, owes its present form in the published *Collection* to this process. Originally it was not Wesley at all but Warburton who was coupled with the Pope as being under the same necessity of condemning Boehme. The original letter in which Warburton and the Pope were so coupled was written by Law in 1754 and is reproduced by Walton.[35]

On 11th July 1757 Law also wrote the letter '*In answer to a scruple*'.[36] This was presumably sent to Wesley, though the latter is not mentioned by name. The letter is Law's defence against Wesley's attack on his denial of wrath in God, and will receive consideration in Chapter Nine.

Law, however, was not alone in rebuking Wesley on account of the 1756 Letter. Whitefield characterized it to Lady Huntingdon as a most unchristian and ungentlemanly letter.[37] John Byrom twice remonstrated with Wesley personally on the subject. The story of the first occasion is told in two of Byrom's letters. Writing to John Lindsay on 1st August 1757 he says:

[33] ibid., p. 199. [34] *Notes and Materials, etc.*, p. 554.
[35] ibid., pp. 559-60. [36] *Law's Works*, Vol. IX, pp. 136-45.
[37] *Works of the Rev. George Whitefield*, Vol. III, p. 184.

This old acquaintance of mine [Wesley] was here not long ago and came to pay me a visit along with one of his preaching followers, to whom I had blamed that performance (the 1756 letter) much when it came out at first; ... to my urging him to repent of that wicked letter, I could get nothing from him but that—if he lived to publish another edition he would soften some expressions in it—which I did not accept of.[38]

Byrom amplified this in a letter to Bishop Hildesley on 8th October 1757 by adding to a similar description of the incident the fact that, when Wesley made the above-mentioned offer, Byrom insisted, not on alteration, but on obliteration, quoting: '*Multae non possunt, una litura potest.*'[39] Byrom's *Journal* for 2nd April 1761 records another visit from Wesley in the course of which, as he relates, 'We had again the talk about his Letter to Mr. Law, but to no other effect than two years ago'.[40] It will be noted that although Byrom says 'two years ago' the earlier visit was four years before. If there was an intermediate discussion of the subject between Byrom and Wesley, we know nothing of it and it is more probable that Byrom's 'two years ago' was a slip on his part. The evidence of Wesley's *Journal* is inconclusive on this matter. There is no mention of any visit to Manchester in 1757. The visit to Manchester at the beginning of April 1761 is recorded,[41] but no reference is made to Byrom. There is also a record of a visit of apparently three days in April 1759,[42] when Wesley would in all probability meet Byrom, and the subject might well have been discussed.

That brings us to the end of our account of the controversy concerning Wesley's 1756 Letter, but this was by no means the only subject of contention in which Law engaged with Wesley and the Methodists during these concluding years of his life. In 1756 Wesley issued *An Address to the Clergy*, a work addressed to clergy of all denominations, setting forth first of all the standard to be expected of ministers of Christ, then inquiring whether ministers do in fact attain this standard, and ending with an earnest appeal. The whole pamphlet is admirable alike in spirit and expression, and contains withal much that might have been expected to

---

[38] *Remains of John Byrom*, Vol. II, Part II.
[39] ibid., p. 599. The word 'litura' must be a mistake, though correctly quoted here.
[40] ibid., p. 629.   [41] *Journal*, Vol. IV, p. 446.   [42] ibid., p. 310.

commend it to the author of the *Christian Perfection*. How deeply Law had been provoked by the 1756 Letter can perhaps be gauged from the fact that, far from approving this new work of Wesley, he dismissed it in the postscript to a letter to Mr. Ward in terms of the utmost contempt as

empty babble, fitter for an old Grammarian, that was grown blear-eyed in mending dictionaries, than for one who had tasted the powers of the world to come, and had found the Truth as it is in Jesus.[43]

Law, presumably, based this criticism on Wesley's commendation of the languages of the Scriptures, Hebrew and Greek, and also secular branches of learning, as subjects in which it behoved a minister to be efficient. This was always a matter on which he and Wesley differed.[44] But there is much else in Wesley's pamphlet, notably the whole of the concluding section of the first part, where he shows how the grace of God should 'animate and govern the whole intention, affection, and practice of a Minister of Christ'.[45] (1) A minister should have one single intention: 'to glorify God, and to save souls from death'; (2) A minister should be 'endued with an eminent measure of love to God, and love to all his brethren';[46] and (3) A minister is called to be 'an example to the flock, in his private as well as public character'.[47] By no standard of fairness can Law's outburst be justified. Let us remember that, though originally added to a private letter, the letter with the postscript appeared in the published *Collection of Letters*. Especially in view of the editorial liberties which were taken with these letters it would have been a simple matter for Law to have omitted the postscript before publication, as it has nothing whatever to do with the letter to which it is attached. Well may Tyerman comment: 'Alas! William Law!'[48]

Wesley did not leave these various attacks of Law unanswered. That he felt their unfairness is clear from his letter to the *London Chronicle* on 17th September 1760.[49] This followed upon the publication of Law's *Collection of Letters*

---

[43] *Law's Works*, Vol. IX, p. 203.
[44] vide *infra*, pp. 92-4.
[45] *Wesley's Works*, Vol. X p. 486.
[46] ibid., p. 487.   [47] ibid., p. 488.
[48] *The Life and Times of John Wesley*, Vol. II, p. 269.
[49] *Letters*, Vol. IV, pp. 105-7.

containing the attacks on Wesley we have recounted. Wesley's letter opens with a review of the controversy to date. He refers to his own 1756 Letter and his *Address to the Clergy* in the same year, and then quotes Law's remarks as set forth above. He asserts that whether there was anything substantial in the 1756 Letter there was certainly, in spite of Law's remarks, something argumentative in it. The very queries relating to Boehme's philosophy were arguments in fact, if not in form. Wesley admits Law's claims to have been 'a kind of oracle' to him *once*, and speaks of him even at this stage in their relations as 'Mr. Law, whom I love and reverence *now*'.[50] Wesley then takes his stand squarely upon Scripture and declares that his censure of the Mystics sprang solely from his reverence for 'the oracles of God'. He takes exception to Law's reference to 'half a month' and claims to have been in some measure 'serious in religion' since he was six years old. He brushed aside as irrelevant Law's reference to the Pope and emphatically repudiates the suggestion that he was under any necessity of writing the 1756 Letter save that Mr. Law 'contradicts Scripture, reason, and himself'; and that he has seduced many souls from 'the Bible way of Salvation'. He recognizes that his espousal of learning was the cause of Law's displeasure with the *Address to the Clergy*, but pleads that a large part of it which insists on a single eye and a clean heart is what Christians cannot account or call 'empty babble'.[51]

Writing on the 28th of the same month to his brother Charles, Wesley again refers to Law's *Collection of Letters*, expressing his willingness to reread them but adding: 'I think I have answered them *quantum sufficit*. . . .' After a further consideration of the *Address to the Clergy* he states his conviction that it was plain Law never *read* it and doubtful whether he even *saw* it.[52] This letter, remarks Sugden, shows the importance the brothers attached to Law's strictures.[53]

This concluding period of our historical survey covers only the last five years of Law's life, which came to an end in 1761. During this time he published four works. Here are the titles with dates.

[50] *Letters*, Vol. IV, p. 106. [51] ibid., p. 107.
[52] ibid., p. 108. [53] ibid., Vol. IV, p. 108 (footnote).

1757. *A Confutation of Dr. Warburton's 'Divine Legation'.*[54]
1760. *A Dialogue on Justification.*[55]
1760. *A Collection of Letters.*[56]
1761. *An Humble, Earnest and Affectionate Address to the Clergy.*[57]

These works reveal no change in Law's ecclesiastical position. The important ones from our point of view in this inquiry are the *Collection of Letters* published in 1760, with which we have already dealt, and the *Dialogue on Justification* published in the same year. This *Dialogue* was Law's contribution to a controversy being waged in various quarters at the time. It seems to have been started by a certain Mr. Berridge, vicar of Everton. There was published in 1760 under the title of *A Fragment of True Religion*, the substance of two letters from Mr. Berridge (described as a 'Methodist Preacher in Cambridgeshire') addressed to a clergyman in Nottinghamshire. Wesley knew of these letters, for Byrom relates how at the interview between them on 2nd April 1761, to which we have already referred, Wesley informed him that the letters were not sent to Mr. Martin, but to Mr. Pointer.[58] These two letters of Mr. Berridge, of which the first was much the longer and more important, consisted of an attack on 'the doctrine that every man will naturally hold while he continues in an unregenerate state, viz. "That we are to be justified partly by our Faith and partly by our works"'.[59] Berridge claimed that the Doctrine of Justification by Faith was the distinctive mark of a Methodist, rather than a life of disciplined devotion. Describing his own spiritual pilgrimage, he says:

> During this time I was thought a Methodist by some people, only because I was a little more grave, and took a little more pains in my Ministry than some others of my brethren; but in Truth I was no Methodist at all, for I had no sort of acquaintance with them and could not abide their fundamental doctrine of Justification by Faith.[60]

[54] The full title of this work is: *A Short but Sufficient Confutation of the Reverend Dr. Warburton's Projected Defence (As he calls it) of Christianity, in his 'Divine Legation' of Moses.*
[55] Full title: *Of Justification by Faith and Works: A Dialogue between a Methodist and a Churchman.* See p. 58 *infra.*
[56] These letters though collected and published in 1760 were written at various dates between 1750 and 1757.
[57] This work appeared after the author's death.
[58] *Remains of John Byrom*, Vol. II, Part II, p. 630.
[59] *A Fragment of True Religion*, p. 2.   [60] ibid., p. 15.

He proceeds to attack the clergy of the last century whose sermons were full of a 'soul-destroying Doctrine that we are to be justified partly by our own works and partly by Christ's merits'.[61] This publication had already met with a rejoinder in the form of a pamphlet entitled *The Principles and Practices of the Methodists Considered*, by Dr. John Green, Bishop of Lincoln, wherein the author stressed the very great moral dangers attending the doctrine of 'free grace'.[62] Law now enters the lists. Walton suggests that the controversy afforded him an opportunity for which he had been waiting.[63] Certainly he opens by putting into the mouth of 'a Methodist' Mr. Berridge's words quoted above about the soul-destroying Doctrine of Salvation partly by Faith and partly by works.[64] Law then proceeds, however, to broaden the discussion, which develops into an attack by 'Churchman' on the opinions of 'Methodist', considered under three heads: (1) Faith without works; (2) A righteousness of Christ only outwardly imputed to us; (3) Absolute election and reprobation.[65]

The title page of this *Dialogue on Justification* describes it as a *Dialogue between a Methodist and a Churchman*. It must be recognized, however, at the outset, that the 'Methodist' is neither Wesley nor any of his followers, but a representative of the other wing of the Methodist movement, of which Whitefield was leader, and whose doctrines were those of a thorough-going Calvinist. For example, on the last of the three heads set forth above, Wesley would have emphatically agreed with Law. Similarly it is the 'Methodist' into whose mouth Law puts the words: 'Nothing more need be said against all your Doctrine, but that it is direct Arminianism.'[66] This nomenclature to a modern reader is most misleading if not entirely unintelligible. Certainly there were more Churchmen than Methodists among the Calvinists, and more Arminians than Calvinists among the Methodists.

So much has been said to make clear the occasion of Law's *Dialogue on Justification*. It is interesting to learn from Byrom that Wesley told him he had been asked to answer Law in this matter but replied that 'he had better business'. Byrom

---
[61] *A Fragment of True Religion*, p. 20. [62] pp. 25-6.
[63] *Notes and Materials, etc.*, by Christopher Walton. London 1854, p. 610.
[64] *Law's Works*, Vol. VIII, p. 217. [65] ibid., p. 239. [66] ibid., p. 240.

commented that in his view there was more justification for such an answer than for his 1756 Letter, because Methodism itself was now being attacked, but Wesley replied that he had answered Law in the newspapers.[67]

Law died in 1761, but Wesley survived him by thirty years, during which time his attitude toward his former spiritual director is marked by a definite softening and an increasing appreciation. In 1757 Wesley had written to Dorothy Furly to assure her that there was no need that we should ever lose the sense of God's love. In the course of the letter he remarks:

Mr. Law . . . speaking on this head, betrays deep ignorance, both of the Scriptures and the inward work of God. You are more liable to receive hurt from his late writings than from any others which I know.[68]

Five years later, at the interview with Byrom to which we have already alluded, Wesley still exhibited marked truculence where Law was concerned. Byrom brought up the subject of six men who had been 'read out' of the Methodist society for reading Boehme and Law. Wesley was 'warm' on the subject and declared that the men had been rejected,

not for reading the books, which was as indifferent as the colour of their hair, but if they would thrust their hair into other people's eyes, and trouble them with their notions—that was his reason.

When Mr. Philips, who was with Wesley, called the reading against the men 'an indiscreet thing', Wesley put the matter 'very magisterially upon his own authority', thereby causing Byrom to address him as 'Pope John' and 'Your holiness'.[69]

Beginning, however, in 1771, and at frequent intervals during the remaining twenty years of his life, we find Wesley cordially recommending Law's works to various of his followers. To Philothea Briggs in 1771 he recommends extracts from Law together with several of his own works.[70] He makes a similar recommendation to Elizabeth Ritchie in 1774,[71] while in 1783, writing to William Black, one of his followers whose story is told in the *Lives of the Early Methodist Preachers*,[72] he says:

[67] *Remains of John Byrom*, Vol. II, Part II, p. 630.
[68] *Letters*, Vol. III, p. 215.
[69] *Remains of John Byrom*, Vol. II, Part II, pp. 629-30.
[70] *Letters*, Vol. V, p. 241.
[71] ibid., Vol. VI, p. 125.
[72] ed. Jackson Vol. V, pp. 242-95.

I have sent you . . . two volumes of Mr. Law's works, which contain all that Mr. Allin would teach if he could: only it is the gold purged from the dross; whereas he would give you the gold and dross shuffled together.[73]

Highest praise of all came when Wesley wrote in 1787 to Ann Taylor: 'Next the Bible, the books you might profit by would be Mr. Law's *Works* and some of the *Sermons*.'[74]

Twice during these years it is recorded that Wesley held up as an example 'Miranda', the 'sober reasonable Christian', of Law's *Serious Call*, Chapter 8, who

does not divide her duty between God, her neighbour, and herself; but she considers all as due to God, and so does everything in His name, and for His sake.[75]

On the first occasion in 1774 this advice was given to Elizabeth Ritchie,[76] who evidently acted upon it, for seven years later in 1781, in a letter to Mary Bishop at her boarding school in Keynsham, Wesley enjoined: 'Make such Christians as "Miranda", as Miss Ritchie.'[77]

Side by side with this return of appreciation of Law on Wesley's part, his views appear to have been definitely modified. His intransigent attitude on the subject of Justification by Faith was moderated, as was also his attitude toward Mysticism, though Mr. Hobhouse is probably right in attributing this less to any change in Wesley's own views than to the fact that the danger to the Methodist societies from Moravian 'stillness' was largely past.[78] Be that as it may, mystical passages from several of Law's later works were reproduced by Wesley.

Other evidence of the softening attitude on Wesley's part is to be found in his commendation of Byrom's poems. Byrom, Walton tells us, had turned some part of Law's writings into poetry. Law had encouraged him in this, and Byrom writing to Law subscribed himself 'Your poet'.[79] Wesley writes thus of Byrom as a poet:

[73] *Letters*, Vol. VII, p. 182. [74] ibid., p. 374.
[75] *Law's Works*, Vol. IV, p. 63. [76] *Letters*, Vol. VI, p. 84.
[77] ibid., Vol. VII, p. 63.
[78] *William Law and Eighteenth-century Quakerism*, p. 318.
[79] *Notes and Materials, etc.*, p. 574.

He has all the wit and humour of Dr. Swift, together with much more learning, a deep and strong understanding, and, above all, a serious vein of piety.[80]

It is true that Wesley is constrained to protest against certain Behmenish elements, but he then continues:

> setting these things aside, we have some of the finest sentiments that ever appeared in the English tongue; some of the noblest truths, expressed with the utmost energy of language and the strongest colours of poetry. So that, upon the whole, I trust this publication will much advance the cause of God and of true religion.[81]

The sentiments so warmly commended were mainly those of Law, turned into verse by Byrom.

In 1783 Wesley had been staying in Dublin with Mr. Henry Brooke, and had uttered what the latter thought harsh and unfounded expressions about the Mystic writers. In a letter of 21st April Wesley frankly acknowledges his fault. 'The words you mention were too strong; they will no more fall from my mouth.'[82]

Finally it should be borne in mind that Wesley continued his practice of republishing parts of Law's writings. In 1768 he issued *An Extract from the Rev. Mr. Law's later works* in two volumes. These volumes contained extracts from: (1) *The Case of Reason*; (2) *The Serious Answer to Dr. Trapp*; (3) *Animadversions upon Dr. Trapp's Late Reply*; (4) *Confutation of Bishop Warburton's 'Divine Legation'*; (5) *The Spirit of Prayer*; (6) *The Spirit of Love*; (7) Mr. Law's *Letters*; and (8) *The Address to the Clergy*.[83] Among Law's later works only the *Appeal*, the *Way to Divine Knowledge*, and the *Dialogue on Justification* were passed over, and, in spite of Wesley's editing, a good many mystical passages remained. When Wesley and Coke instituted in 1782 a 'Society for the Distribution of Religious Tracts among the Poor', the first thirty works printed as tracts for free distribution included the *Serious Call* (which was given pride of place as Number One of the Series), the *Nature and Design of Christianity* (from Law's *Christian Perfection*), and the *Spirit of Prayer*.[84]

---

[80] *Journal*, Vol. V, p. 518.   [81] ibid., p. 521.   [82] *Letters*, Vol. VII, p. 174.
[83] *The Works of John and Charles Wesley: A Bibliography* Richard Green, pp. 142-3.
[84] ibid., p. 217.

This completes our historical survey of the relations between Law and Wesley. It outlines the story of the development of their careers and has enabled us to draw attention to the various incidents relevant to our inquiry. It provides the background against which to discuss those questions which require separate treatment.

PART TWO

Wesley's Indebtedness to Law

A

PRACTICAL
TREATISE

UPON

CHRISTIAN
PERFECTION.

By WILLIAM LAW, *A. M.*

Not as though I had already attained, either were already perfect. Phil. iii. 12.

LONDON,
Printed for WILLIAM and JOHN INNYS, at the West-End of St. *Paul's*. 1726.

Facsimile reproduction from the first edition

CHAPTER FIVE

The Ethical Ideal

WESLEY'S INDEBTEDNESS to Law was due to the part played by the *Christian Perfection* and the *Serious Call* (together with Taylor's *Rules of Holy Living* and à Kempis's *Christian Pattern*) in his moral awakening. From that time until the end of his life Wesley never ceased to aim at Christian Perfection[1] in his own life and summon others to join him in the same quest. It is no part of our purpose in this inquiry to add to the numerous expositions of the doctrine of Christian Perfection which already exist, but rather, having acknowledged our debt to them,[2] to confine ourselves to a treatment of the subject in so far as it concerns the relation between Law and Wesley.

Before proceeding to a detailed discussion of such questions as the similarities and differences between the doctrines, as accepted and proclaimed by the two men, stress must be laid (and it would be difficult to lay too much) on the *fact* of this revolutionary influence upon Wesley. As Dr. Cell remarks, Wesley was at this time 'seized of an idea that never after that let him go'.[3] Law's contribution in the *Christian Perfection* and the *Serious Call* was to act as a searcher of the consciences of men who for the most part were already practising Churchmen, and the conscience of Wesley was at this time awakened once and for all. We have already seen how this moral awakening needed the evangelical conversion of 1738 for its completion, but if we are to assess the importance of the earlier moral awakening at its true worth, we must further recognize

---

[1] 'Christian Perfection', 'Perfect Love', 'Scriptural Holiness', and 'Entire Sanctification' appear to be different ways of expressing the same idea by Wesley.
[2] I am especially indebted to Chapters 18 and 19 on 'William Law' and 'Methodism' respectively in Dr. R. Newton Flew's *The Idea of Perfection in Christian Theology*. Other discussions of the subject from the 'Wesley' angle which I have found valuable are contained in Dr. J. E. Rattenbury's *The Conversion of the Wesleys*. Dr. Henry Bett's *The Spirit of Methodism*. Dr. G. Croft Cell's *The Rediscovery of John Wesley*, O. A. Curtis's *The Christian Faith*, Dr. F. Platt's article 'Christian Perfection' in the *Encyclopædia of Religion and Ethics*, and articles by the late J. Agar Beet and the late W. J. Moulton in the *London Quarterly Review* for January 1920 and July 1925 respectively.
[3] *The Rediscovery of John Wesley*, p. 354.

that without it the 1738 conversion could never have happened. Every genuine evangelical experience must needs be preceded by a moral awakening. The very nature of conversion demands this. There can be no restored relationship without some sense of a broken relationship in need of restoration. Men are saved not only from something but into something. As Wesley said: 'If they are converted at all, they are converted from all manner of wickedness to a sober, righteous, and godly life.'[4] Otherwise the experience takes place in a vacuum and consists merely of a vague 'uplift' which cannot properly be termed conversion at all, and is unlikely to have permanent effects. Romans 8 is always preceded by Romans 7. It was an accurate description by Charles Wesley when he claimed that Law had been his schoolmaster to bring him to Christ, and the same could have been said with equal truth of John Wesley, for the part played by the Jewish Law in awakening the conscience of Paul was performed by William Law's practical treatises for the two brothers Wesley. Of course the experiences of moral awakening and evangelical conversion need not be separated by a long and painful period of impotence, amounting almost to despair, as happened with Wesley. There are many well-authenticated instances under the preaching of Wesley himself after 1738 of men being convicted of sin and in the course of the same sermon finding peace through God's forgiving and saving grace. But whether the interval be long or short, some moral awakening must precede a genuine evangelical conversion, and it is a fatal antithesis to set one against the other as is so often done in regard to Wesley.[5] Both are correctly understood only as they are recognized as the result of God's gracious activity in the human soul.

Furthermore, it is important to realize that not only did Wesley's moral awakening precede and make possible his evangelical conversion, but the influence of the ethical impulse so received persisted with unabated strength throughout his ministry. Wesley's own testimony is decisive on this point in his tract on *Christian Perfection*. The last edition he himself published of that work bears the full title: *A Plain Account of Christian Perfection as Believed and Taught by the Reverend Mr. John Wesley, from the Year 1725 to the Year 1777*.[6] In

[4] *Letters*, Vol. II, p. 136.   [5] e.g. by Dr. Piette.   [6] *Wesley's Works*, Vol. XI, p. 366.

this he recalls the stages by which he came to hold the doctrine beginning with his reading of Jeremy Taylor, à Kempis, and Law. He outlines the sermon on the subject entitled 'The Circumcision of the Heart',[7] preached by him before the University of Oxford in 1733, and remarks in this connexion:

It may be observed, this sermon was composed the first of all my writings which have been published. This was the view of religion I then had, which even then I scrupled not to term *perfection*. This is the view I have of it now, without any material addition or diminution.[8]

It is also worthy of note that this is the only sermon preached before 1738 which found a place in the *Forty-four Sermons* which together with Wesley's *Notes on the New Testament* were subsequently recognized as containing the doctrinal standards of the Methodist Church. As evidence of his remaining 'in the same sentiment', Wesley quotes portions of two hymns written before the conversion experience. The first of these, written in 1735, was a translation from Gerhard Tersteegen:

> *Is there a thing beneath the sun,*
> *That strives with thee my heart to share?*
> *Ah! tear it thence, and reign alone,*
> *The Lord of every motion there!*[9]

The other quotation dates from the beginning of 1738, when Wesley expressed his feelings in a hymn translated from Paulus Gerhardt:

> *O grant that nothing in my soul*
> *May dwell, but Thy pure love alone!*
> *O may Thy love possess me whole,*
> *My joy, my treasure, and my crown!*
> *Strange fires far from my heart remove;*
> *My every act, word, thought, be love!*[10]

Wesley comments:

Is not this the language, not only of every believer, but of every one that is truly awakened? But what have I wrote, to this day, which is either stronger or plainer?[11]

---

[7] *The Standard Sermons of John Wesley*, Vol. I, pp. 266 et sqq.
[8] *Wesley's Works*, Vol. XI. p. 369.
[9] ibid.   [10] ibid.   [11] ibid.

So far Wesley has been recalling his belief in Christian Perfection as he held it before 24th May 1738. A similar review is given by him in the celebrated letter to John Newton of 14th May 1765.[12] Then follows a series of extracts from Hymns, Sermons, *Minutes* of various Conferences, etc., written after 1738, beginning with the 1739 edition of *Hymns and Sacred Poems*.[13] But no mention whatever is made by Wesley of the 1738 conversion experience, a sure proof that, in his view, that experience, supremely important as it was for Wesley's religious life and the whole future course of his ministry, in no way modified his emphasis on Christian Perfection. The doctrine continued, as previously, to occupy a central place in his scheme of things. There was no further revision by Wesley of the *Plain Account of Christian Perfection* after 1777, but the theme continued to dominate his thought to the very end. On 15th September 1790, within a few months of his death, writing to Robert Carr Brackenbury of full sanctification, Wesley said:

> This doctrine is the grand depositum which God has lodged with the people called Methodists; and for the sake of propagating this chiefly He appeared to have raised us up.[14]

Thus Wesley affords an excellent illustration of the effect of God's gracious activity in a man's heart as described recently by Dr. John Baillie:

> When St. Paul and St. Augustine became Christians, the change that took place in them was indeed revolutionary enough and miraculous enough, yet we know well that, had God instead converted stones, or animal beings not already dowered with reason and conscience, and made good Christians and good apostles of *them*, we should be confronted with a miracle of a very different order. In spite of all that may and must be said about the radical nature of the conversion, there was clearly in the former case a continuity between what went before and what came after which there could not be in the latter.[15]

So it may be claimed that though Law was in no way directly responsible for the actual event of 24th May 1738, yet, by the dominant influence he exercised in the years preceding it,

---

[12] *Letters*, Vol. IV, p. 299.
[14] *Letters*, Vol. VIII, p. 238.
[13] *Wesley's Works*, Vol. XI, p. 370.
[15] *Our Knowledge of God*, p. 25.

he was a very important factor in deciding the sort of converted man Wesley became when from 1738 onward he proclaimed his message far and wide, and also the sort of message he proclaimed.

We have already observed in the historical survey that Law was no more content than Wesley with his position adopted in the *Christian Perfection* and *Serious Call* period, but moved forward, though along a very different road from that travelled by Wesley. We must accordingly next inquire what effect his acceptance of mysticism had upon his adherence to the doctrine of Christian Perfection. It can be unhesitatingly stated that a consideration of Law's later writings makes it abundantly clear that Dr. Flew is right in contending that there is no contradiction between the earlier and later periods of his writings as regards the centrality of 'Perfect Love' in the Christian ethic, but that a certain unity of message underlies the whole.[16]

It is true that under the influence of the mystical teaching he has a good deal to say that he had not said before. His main concern is now to explain man's need for salvation and how it can be met by regeneration and a consequent new life in God, but this in no way diminishes his emphasis on the importance of the ethical ideal. No clearer illustration of this can be cited than is afforded by his *Answer to Dr. Trapp*, written in 1740, the same year in which he wrote the *Appeal to All who Doubt the Truths of the Gospel*, a work saturated in mystical teaching. The theme of Dr. Trapp's discourse was 'the folly, sin, and danger of being righteous over-much', and it was aimed at the Methodists. In spite of Law's change of outlook, there is no question where he stands in this controversy. Nowhere are Dr. Trapp's readers told, complains Law,

> what Christian Perfection is, what a holiness of body, soul and spirit it requires, and what blessedness of life it gives; how powerfully all are called to it; how earnestly all ought to aspire after it; and how sadly they are mistaken, what enemies to themselves, who for the sake of any, or all the things in the world, die less purified and perfect, than they might have been.[17]

---

[16] *The Idea of Perfection in Christian Theology*, R. Newton Flew, pp. 293-304.
[17] *Law's Works*, Vol. VI, p. 5.

Again to no part of the world does Dr. Trapp represent or propose the perfection of the Gospel, or recommend it as that, which deserves all that they can do, or suffer for sake of it.[18]

On two occasions Law rebuts charges made by Dr. Trapp against Law's own practical treatises, once because in the *Christian Perfection* Law had urged Christians to seek comfort in God alone,[19] and once when Dr. Trapp by arbitrarily selected quotations from the *Christian Perfection* ignored the teaching of that work and the *Serious Call* to the effect that Christian Perfection consists in the holy and religious conduct of ourselves in every state of life.[20] The end of Salvation, says Law, is the restoration in us of that 'first Paradisaical Divine nature, which is the true image of God', which was lost at the Fall. 'When this begins, our salvation begins; as this goes on, our salvation goes on; when this is finished, our salvation is finished.'[21] Union with God is possible for all and this union is perfection.

> When we thus live wholly unto God, God is wholly ours, and we are then happy in all the happiness of God; for by uniting with Him in heart, and will, and spirit, we are united to all that He is, and has in Himself. This is the purity and perfection of life, that we pray for in the Lord's Prayer, that God's Kingdom may come, and His will be done in us, as it is in Heaven. And this we may be sure is not only necessary, but attainable by us, or our Saviour would not have made it a part of our daily prayer.[22]

The reason why 'we stand at this amazing distance from that state of perfection to which Christ has called us'[23] is in ourselves. Finally we may quote Law's unequivocal statement:

> the Christian religion has not had its proper effect, nor obtained its intended end, till it has so set up the Kingdom of God amongst us, that 'His will is done on earth, as it is done in heaven'. This is the perfection that every Christian, when advancing forward in the several degrees of holiness and purification, is to tend to, and aspire after.[24]

The foregoing extracts are taken from one of Law's works written in what we have called the intermediate stage of his thought. For evidence that the same emphasis on Christian

---

[18] *Law's Works*, Vol. VI, p. 6.   [19] ibid., p. 15.   [20] ibid., p. 48.
[21] ibid., p. 23.   [22] ibid., p. 33.   [23] ibid., p. 34.   [24] ibid., p. 40.

Perfection, as the goal of the Christian, persisted in the last stage, let us turn to the two parts of *The Spirit of Love*, written in 1752 and 1754 respectively.

In the first part Law speaks of God's immutable will for His creatures grounded in His nature, which consists of perfect love.

Whether, therefore, you consider perfection, or happiness, it is all included in the Spirit of Love, and must be so, for this reason, because the infinitely perfect and happy God is mere Love, an unchangeable will to all goodness. . . . Thus you see the ground, the nature, and perfection of the Spirit of Love.[25]

Similarly:

There is no peace, nor ever can be, for the soul of man, but in the purity and perfection of its first-created nature; nor can it have its purity and perfection in any other way, than in and by the Spirit of Love.[26]

In the second part of the work, where Law's general doctrinal position is farthest removed from that of Wesley, perfection still occupies a central position in his thought as the goal of God's purpose for man.

We find ourselves incapable of thinking any otherwise of God, than as the one only Good, . . . which can will nothing else to all eternity, but to communicate good, and blessing, and happiness, and perfection to every life, according to its capacity to receive it.[27]

Again, bound up this time with the doctrine of the Seed, where Law so nearly approaches Quakerism:

'Thou shalt love the Lord thy God with all thy heart, with all thy soul, and with all thy strength, and thy neighbour as thyself.' Now these two precepts, given by the written word of God, are an absolute demonstration of the first original perfection of man, and also a full and invincible proof, that the same original perfection is not quite annihilated, but lies in him as an hidden suppressed seed of goodness, capable of being raised up to its first perfection.[28]

These quotations from Law's later writings which are typical, though by no means exhaustive, make it clear that by his acceptance of the mystical teaching Law made the spiritual pilgrimage from νόμος to χάρις comparable in his experience

[25] ibid., Vol. VIII, p. 5. [26] ibid., p. 6.
[27] ibid., p. 38. [28] ibid., p. 50.

to the transition which for Wesley had its origin in the conversion of 1738.

Law came to recognize, as clearly as Wesley, the limitations of the ethical ideal and the need for some further dynamic if the moral transformation it involved is ever to be realized.[29] It is somewhat curious that Law himself in his later works describes the function fulfilled in the Christian life by external rules and precepts as laid down in the Scriptures in the same two ways as Charles Wesley had previously described the part played by Law in relation to the Wesleys. Charles Wesley called Law his schoolmaster to bring him to Christ,[30] and Law now writes:

> Virtue and goodness may be brought into us by two different ways. They may be taught us outwardly by men, by rules and precepts; and they may be inwardly born in us, as the genuine birth of our own renewed spirit.... Now this way of learning and attaining goodness, though thus imperfect, is yet absolutely necessary, in the nature of the thing, and must first have its time, and place, and work in us; yet it is only for a time, as the law was a schoolmaster to the Gospel.... But of all this outward instruction, whether from good men, or the letter of Scripture, it must be said, as the apostle says of the law, that it maketh nothing perfect; and yet it is highly necessary in order to perfection.[31]

Again, Charles Wesley had referred to Law as 'Our John the Baptist',[32] and Law also writes:

> What a folly would it be, to say that you had undervalued the office and character of John the Baptist, because he was not allowed to be the light itself, but only a true witness of it, and guide to it? Now if you can show, that the written word in the Bible can have any other, or higher office, or power, than such a ministerial one as the Baptist had, I am ready to hear you.[33]

So we may say, that in and after 1738 Law and Wesley travelled along parallel roads from νόμος to χάρις, separated however by an ever-widening doctrinal gulf, across which they never hailed each other. This will be the subject of our inquiry in a later chapter. Meanwhile let us note that, by however different a route it was to be achieved, Law continued

---
[29] *Law's Works* Vol. VII, p. 158. [30] *Journal of Charles Wesley*, Vol. I, p. 159.
[31] *Law's Works*, Vol. VIII, p. 104.
[32] *Life of Charles Wesley*, Moore, Vol. I, p. 107.
[33] *Law's Works*, Vol. VIII, p. 106.

THE ETHICAL IDEAL

to proclaim, as consistently as Wesley, the state of Christian Perfection as the goal of every Christian, a goal which he believed to be both essential and attainable.

So far we have considered the *fact* of Wesley's indebtedness to Law, showing how Law's influence in stimulating Wesley's devotion to the ethical ideal persisted throughout Wesley's life and also how the doctrine retained its central place in Law's thought despite the changes in his outlook. In the next chapter we shall be considering the extent to which that indebtedness is reflected in the practical outworkings of the doctrine in life and conduct. Before proceeding to this, however, it would be well to sketch the main similarities and differences in their understanding of the doctrine itself.

THE TRADITION OF THE CHURCH

Law never considered that in his practical treatises he was propounding something new, but rather that he was recalling his fellow Churchmen to a truth inherent in Christianity itself, originally in the New Testament, preserved in the main stream of Catholic piety, and also firmly rooted in the ideals and formularies of the Church of England.

If the doctrines of Christianity were practised, they would make a man as different from other people as to all worldly tempers, sensual pleasures, and the pride of life, as a wise man is different from a natural.[34]

Wesley was in hearty accord with this. It must be remembered that during the period that Law was Wesley's mentor, the latter studied the mystical divines and that to his death Wesley believed himself a faithful expositor of the true teaching of the Anglican Church. Dr. Bett[35] and Dr. Flew[36] have each given an impressive account of the debt Wesley consciously or unconsciously owed to the mystical tradition, and it is significant that in *A Plain Account of Christian Perfection* he not only quotes with approval Archbishop Usher's definition of a perfect man,[37] but also concludes the tract with the words of the pre-communion collect:

[34] ibid., Vol. IV, p. 14.
[35] *The Spirit of Methodism*, pp. 61-3.
[36] *The Idea of Perfection in Christian Theology*, p. 315.
[37] *Wesley's Works*, Vol. XI, p. 384.

Yea, we do believe, that He will in this world so 'cleanse the thoughts of our hearts, by the inspiration of His Holy Spirit, that we shall perfectly love Him, and worthily magnify His holy name'.[38]

GOD'S PURPOSE FOR ALL

Law and Wesley further agreed that Christian Perfection is the purpose of God for all. No clearer statement of this truth could be desired from Law than the opening words of the introduction to the *Christian Perfection*.

Christian Perfection will perhaps seem to the common reader to imply some state of life which everyone need not aspire after; that it is made up of such strictnesses, retirements, and particularities of devotion, as are neither necessary, nor practicable by the generality of Christians.

But I must answer for myself, that I know of only one common Christianity, which is to be the common means of salvation to all men.[39]

Law believed in the possibility of different degrees of glory in the world to come, but these are 'no objection against this doctrine, that all Christians are called to one and the same piety and perfection of heart'.[40] Nor do the existing differences between men in order and condition exempt any from the same demand.

Thus in all orders and conditions, either of men or women, this is the one common holiness, which is to be the common life of all Christians.[41]

Similarly:

If this devout state of heart, if these habits of inward holiness be true religion, then true religion is equally the duty and happiness of all orders of men.[42]

The reason for this is not arbitrary but rooted in the nature of God and man.

The necessities of a reasonable and holy life, are not founded in the several conditions and employments of this life, but in the immutable nature of God, and the nature of man.[43]

These quotations from the practical treatises present Christian Perfection as a universal demand. In Wesley, as we should expect, the approach is different, and the difference is

---

[38] *Wesley's Works*, Vol. XI, pp. 445-6. [39] *Law's Works*, Vol. III, p. 5. [40] ibid., p. 9.
[41] ibid, Vol. IV, p. 89. [42] ibid., p. 90. [43] ibid., p. 82.

characteristic. As Overton remarked, the *Serious Call* was 'more calculated to alarm than to attract';[44] whereas in Wesley's teaching, Christian Perfection is the gift of God, a glorious consequence of saving faith in Him. Sanctification is one of 'the things which are freely given us of God'.[45] Here too the universality of God's offer is central in the evangelical message. 'A Christian is so far perfect, as not to commit sin. This is the glorious privilege of every Christian.'[46] Such a liberating and transforming message perhaps finds its best expression in the Methodist hymns. Of many examples we may quote two. The first is from John Wesley's translation from Spangenburg:

> *We all in perfect love renewed*
> *Shall know the greatness of Thy power;*[47]

and the second from a hymn of Charles Wesley:

> *What is our calling's glorious hope*
> *But inward holiness?*
> *For this to Jesus I look up,*
> *I calmly wait for this.*
>
> *This is the dear redeeming grace,*
> *For every sinner free;*
> *Surely it shall on me take place,*
> *The chief of sinners, me.*[48]

In this belief Law and Wesley emphatically rejected Calvinism. In a letter written toward the end of his life, 'To a clergyman of Bucks', Law says:

Oh, the sweetness of God's election, cries out the ravished preacher! Oh, the sweetness of God's reprobation! might the hellish Satan well say, could he believe that God had made him a free gift of such myriads, and myriads of men, of all nations, tongues and languages, from the beginning to the end of the world, and reserved so small a number for himself.[49]

---

[44] *The Life and Opinions of the Rev. William Law*, p. 116.
[45] *Wesley's Works*, Vol. XI, p. 421.
[46] ibid., p. 376.
[47] *Methodist Hymn-book*. No. 784, verse 6.
[48] ibid., No. 557, verses 1 and 3.
[49] *Law's Works*, Vol. IX, p. 135.

And it is in reference to their failure always to stress the universality of redemption that this question and answer appear in the 'Minutes of some late conversations between the Rev. Mr. Wesley and others' under the date Monday, 25th June 1744.

Question 17. Have we not then unawares leaned too much towards Calvinism?
Answer. We are afraid we have.[50]

THE PLACE OF CONVERSION

We saw in the historical survey that Wesley found Law's ethical ideal impossible of attainment for himself and others until saving faith in Jesus Christ provided the dynamic which had been hitherto lacking. Justification must precede sanctification. His great complaint against Law was, as we have seen, that Law had never pointed him to this. It must be recognized, however, that, despite his failure to communicate the experience to Wesley, Law based his doctrine of Christian Perfection on conversion, as surely as did Wesley. Chapter 2 of the *Christian Perfection* is entitled: 'Christianity requires a change of nature: a new life perfectly devoted to God.'[51] In it he states:

Christianity is not a *school*, for the teaching of moral virtue. . . . It is deeper and more divine in its designs, and has much nobler ends than these, it implies an *entire change* of life.[52]

Again:

There is no alteration of life, no change of condition, that implies half so much, as that alteration which Christianity introduceth.[53]

He quotes great evangelical texts; for example: 'Except a man be born again, of the Water and the Spirit, he cannot enter into the Kingdom of God',[54] and he comments: 'These words plainly teach us, that Christianity implies some great change of nature.'[55] Finally:

---

[50] *Wesley's Works*, Vol. VIII, p. 278.
[51] *Law's Works*, Vol. III, p. 23. [52] ibid. [53] ibid., p. 24.
[54] John 35. [55] *Law's Works*, Vol. III, p. 25.

Nothing less than this *great change* of heart and mind can give anyone any assurance, that he is truly turned to God. There is but this one term of Salvation, 'He that is in Christ, is a new creature'. . . .

So that there is no religion that will stand us in any stead, but that which is the *conversion* of the heart to God.[56]

Indeed, Law could have joined with great fervour in the hymn, contained in *Hymns and Sacred Poems*,[57] which Wesley cites as 'strongly and explicitly' expressing his sentiments on Christian Perfection at that time.

> *Heavenly Adam, Life Divine,*
> *Change my nature into Thine;*
> *Move and spread throughout my soul,*
> *Actuate and fill the whole.*[58]

INTENTION

Great stress was laid by Wesley from the very beginning on the inward nature of Christian Perfection. When he first read à Kempis, he was greatly impressed by the need for 'simplicity of intention and purity of affection'. 'I saw,' he says, 'that giving even all my life to God . . . would profit me nothing, unless I gave my heart, yea, all my heart, to Him.'[59] A corresponding emphasis can be observed in Law, who speaks of 'the first and most fundamental principle of Christianity, viz., an intention to please God in all our actions'.[60] Also:

The fault does not lie here, that we desire to be good and perfect, but through the weakness of our nature fall short of it; but it is, because we have not piety enough to intend to be as good as we can, or to please God in all the actions of our life.[61]

GOD'S FREE GIFT

It is, of course, a fundamental evangelical truth that Salvation is a free Gift of God. Wesley's first standard sermon, preached shortly after his conversion, is in no way exceptional in this respect but states what he was ever proclaiming for the rest of his life.

[56] ibid., Vol. III, p. 35.
[57] *Hymns and Sacred Poems*, John and Charles Wesley, p. 122.
[58] *Wesley's Works*, Vol. XI, p. 370. [59] ibid., pp. 366-7.
[60] *Law's Works*, Vol. IV, p. 20. [61] ibid.

All the blessings which God hath bestowed upon man are of His mere grace, bounty, or favour; His free, undeserved favour; . . . and whatever righteousness may be found in man, this is also the gift of God.[62]

There is no language comparable to this in the *Christian Perfection* or the *Serious Call*, but in later life, in the *Spirit of Love*, Law expresses himself in terms which must satisfy the most ardent evangelical:

Consider only this, that to be angry at our own anger, to be ashamed of our own pride, and strongly resolve not to be weak, is the upshot of all human endeavours; and yet all this is rather the life, than the death of self. There is no help, but from a total despair of all human help. When a man is brought to such an inward full conviction, as to have no more hope from all human means, than he hopes to see with his hands, or hear with his feet, then it is, that he is truly prepared to die to self, that is, to give up all thoughts of having or doing any thing that is good, in any other way but that of a meek, humble, patient, total resignation of himself to God. . . . No repentance, however long or laborious, is conversion to God, till it falls into this state. For God must do all, or all is nothing; but God cannot do all, till all is expected from Him; and all is not expected from Him, till by a true and good despair of every human help, we have no hope, or trust, or longing after any thing, but a patient, meek, humble, total resignation to God.[63]

Could even Wesley have said it better?

We must next consider the subject of growth, progress, the time when Christian Perfection takes place, and related questions. In these matters there is both agreement and disagreement between Law and Wesley. For that matter Wesley himself is not always consistent, as those who have expounded his doctrine admit. The key to understanding the relation of the views of the men in these respects lies in the recognition that Wesley was much more interested in these matters than Law. This was due to the fact that he was constantly preaching the doctrine to great crowds of men and women and observing its effect. He was also the founder of hundreds of small societies devoted to the quest for Scriptural Holiness. Believing its truth with all his heart, Wesley was naturally anxious to see its logical and experimental outcome in the lives of his converts. Certain facts, however, can be definitely stated.

[62] *Sermons*, Vol. I, p. 37.   [63] *Law's Works*, Vol. VIII, pp. 126-7.

FALLING FROM GRACE

Wesley and Law agreed that Christian Perfection once attained might subsequently be lost. Commenting on the text, 'Whosoever is born of God, doth not commit sin, for His seed remaineth in him, and he cannot sin, because he is born of God',[64] Law remarks:

> This is not to be understood as if he that was born of God, was therefore in an absolute state of Perfection, and incapable afterwards of falling into anything that was sinful.
> It only means, that he that is born of God, is possessed of a temper and principle, that makes him utterly hate and labour to avoid all sin.[65]

Though Wesley at first dissented from this, he afterwards changed his view. He states in a letter to his brother in February 1767: 'Can one who has attained it fall? Formerly, I thought not; but you (with T. Walsh and Jo. Jones) convinced me of my mistake.'[66] A few weeks previously in his *Brief thoughts on Christian Perfection* he had similarly written: 'I do not include an impossibility of falling from it, either in part or in whole.'[67] Wesley's change of view is well reflected in a hymn of Charles Wesley, dealing with the possibility of falling from grace.

> *Ah! Lord, with trembling I confess,*
> *A gracious soul may fall from grace;*
> *The salt may lose its seasoning power,*
> *And never, never find it more.*
>
> *Lest that my fearful case should be,*
> *Each moment knit my soul to Thee;*
> *And lead me to the mount above,*
> *Through the low vale of humble love.*[68]

Here we should notice Wesley's insistence that such a fall from grace is inevitable, failing the continued exercise of faith. Wesley taught not only Justification but also Sanctification 'by faith'.

---

[64] 1 John 3₉.   [65] *Law's Works*, Vol. III, p. 27.   [66] *Letters*, Vol. V, p. 41.
[67] *Wesley's Works*, Vol. XI, p. 446.   [68] *Methodist Hymn-book*, No. 480.

> *Uphold me, Saviour, or I fall,*
> *O reach me out Thy gracious hand!*
> *Only on Thee for help I call,*
> *Only by faith in Thee I stand.*[69]

LIMITS OF PERFECTION

Wesley's own qualifications of the absoluteness of the Christian Perfection in which he believed are to be found in the *Plain Account of Christian Perfection*, where he explains that Christians are not perfect in knowledge, nor free from infirmities, including 'a thousand nameless defects, either in conversation or behaviour'. After adding that Christians cannot expect to be wholly freed from temptation he concludes:

> Neither in this sense is there any absolute perfection on earth. There is no perfection of degrees, none which does not admit of a continual increase.[70]

Whereas both men agreed that there was growth, Wesley went farther and insisted on some moment when Christian Perfection was instantaneously received. He makes many references to this, but the two ideas of growth and instantaneous reception are illustrated in the *Brief thoughts on Christian Perfection*:

> As to the manner. I believe this Perfection is always wrought in the soul by a simple act of faith; consequently, in an instant. But I believe a gradual work, both preceding and following that instant.[71]

Wesley was very definite on the entirety of perfection, which does not seem to have worried Law, who admitted different degrees in the matter. On one occasion, when Wesley suggested that the standard set forth by Law was too high to be attained, the latter replied: 'We shall do well to aim at the highest degree of perfection, if we may thereby, at least, attain to mediocrity.'[72] Whether Law ever moved from that position, Wesley, as we have seen, moved far from it. Law, on the other hand, never seems to have made any effort to

---
[69] *Methodist Hymn-book*, No. 478 (verse 7).
[70] *Wesley's Works*, Vol. XI, p. 374.
[71] ibid., p. 446.
[72] *Life and Opinions of the Rev. William Law*, J. H. Overton, p. 80.

schematize his faith, but ignored many points on which Wesley sought to be explicit.

Law seems from the first to have recognized varying 'degrees of goodness',[73] and in his latest writings stressed the supreme 'necessity of a continual inspiration of the Spirit of God, both to begin the first, and continue every step of a divine life in man'.[74] The early part of the *Address to the Clergy* is an exposition of this theme, reiterated again and again. The nearest approach to this in Wesley is recorded in the *Minutes of Conference* of 1770:[75]

Does not talking of a justified or a sanctified *state*, tend to mislead men? Almost naturally leading them to trust, in what was done in one moment? Whereas, we are every hour and every moment pleasing or displeasing to God, 'according to our works'. According to the whole of our inward tempers, and our outward behaviour.

Law would have heartily concurred.

COMMUNION WITH GOD

Finally, we may notice the complete accord between Law and Wesley in describing the goal of Christian Perfection as communion with God. In the *Christian Perfection* the former writes: 'This is the one sole end of Christianity, to . . . unite us to God, the true Fountain of all real Good.'[76] Nearly thirty years later he writes:

If all that is done without this love, whether in religious duties, of[77] common life, is but mere separation from God, then it must be the grossest blindness, to believe you can have any love of God, or goodness in any duties you perform, any further, or in any other degree, than as the Eternal, Holy Spirit of God, lives and loves in you.[78]

For the Wesleys also and their followers, as Dr. Flew emphasizes, ' "experience" did not mean merely a lofty moment in the soul's past, but a communion with God'.[79] The Wesley hymns testify to this again and again. We may cite the hymn quoted above which Wesley translated from Paulus

---

[73] *Law's Works*, Vol. III, p. 9.
[74] ibid., Vol. IX, p. 12.
[75] Vol. I, No. 26, p. 97.
[76] *Law's Works*, Vol. III, p. 12.
[77] 'of' is surely a misprint in the text for 'or'.
[78] ibid., Vol. IX, p. 162.
[79] *The Idea of Perfection in Christian Theology*, p. 316.

Gerhardt[80] or, as one of many such examples, the opening lines of Charles Wesley's well-known hymn:

> Love Divine, all loves excelling,
> Joy of heaven, to earth come down;
> Fix in us Thy humble dwelling,
> All Thy faithful mercies crown.[81]

Turning to the differences between the view of Christian Perfection held by Law and Wesley, we are immediately struck by the intense individualism of Law's outlook. This characteristic is especially noticeable when Law urges, as he frequently does, the necessity of Christian Perfection as affording the only chance of happiness hereafter. Knowing as we do to what an extent this selfish motive has spoiled the purity of the evangelical appeal on occasions in later generations, it is rather surprising to discover it in the writings of one whose personal character was as eminently unselfish as was that of Law.

> There are no enjoyments here that are worth a thought, but such as may make thee more perfect in those holy tempers which will carry thee to heaven.[82]

This passage in the opening chapter of the *Christian Perfection* is matched by a long exposition to the same effect, couched in even more vigorous language in the last chapter,[83] and by the graphic description of the scene at the death bed of 'Penitens' in the *Serious Call*.[84]

Many illustrations of this individualism are to be found in the intense mystical contemplations which characterize the speeches of Theophilus in the *Spirit of Prayer*. These are too long to quote in full, and we must content ourselves with one typical extract:

> The painful sense and feeling of what you are, kindled into a working state of sensibility by the light of God within you, is the fire and light from whence your Spirit of Prayer proceeds. In its first kindling nothing is found or felt, but pain, wrath, and darkness, as is to be seen in the first kindling of every heat or fire. And therefore its first prayer is nothing else but a sense of penitence, self-condemnation, confession, and humility.

[80] vide *supra*, p. 67.
[81] *Methodist Hymn-book*, No. 431.
[82] *Law's Works*, Vol. III, p. 23.
[83] ibid., pp. 244-7.
[84] ibid., Vol. IV, pp. 26-30.

THE ETHICAL IDEAL 83

It feels nothing but its own misery, and so is all humility. This prayer of humility is met by the divine love, the mercifulness of God embraces it; and then its prayer is changed into hymns, and songs, and thanksgivings. When this state of fervour has done its work, has melted away all earthly passions and affections, and left no inclination in the soul, but to delight in God alone, then its prayer changes again. It is now come so near to God, has found such union with Him, that it does not so much pray as live in God. Its prayer is not any particular action, is not the work of any particular faculty, not confined to times, or words, or place, but is the work of his whole being, which continually stands in fulness of faith, in purity of love, in absolute resignation, to do, and be, what and how his beloved pleases. This is the last state of the Spirit of Prayer, and is its highest union with God in this life.[85]

A particularly interesting example of this individualistic emphasis is in Law's denunciation of war where his main indictment is based on the fact that millions of young men are slain before they have the chance of salvation. After dwelling upon the social miseries and wrongs war brings in its train Law proceeds:

But there is still an evil of war much greater, though less regarded. Who reflects, how many hundreds of thousands, nay millions of young men, born into this world for no other end, but that they may be born again of Christ, and from sons of Adam's misery become sons of God, and fellow heirs with Christ in everlasting glory; who reflects, I say, what nameless numbers of these are robbed of God's precious gift of life to them, before they have known the one sole benefit of living; who are not suffered to stay in this world, till age and experience have done their best for them, have helped them to know the inward voice and operation of God's spirit, helped them to find, and feel that evil, curse, and sting of sin and death, which must be taken from within them, before they can die the death of the righteous; but instead of all this, have been either violently forced, or tempted in the fire of youth, and full strength of sinful lusts, to forget God, eternity, and their own souls, and rush into a 'kill or be killed', with as much furious haste, and goodness of spirit, as tiger kills tiger for the sake of his prey?[86]

This individualistic tendency, which led Law in his later writings to depreciate institutional religion, was one of the main issues between him and Wesley. A casual remark overheard by Wesley 'that a man could not go to heaven alone' had an

[85] ibid., Vol. VII, p. 128.   [86] ibid., Vol. IX, p. 87.

amazing effect on his mind,[87] and as early as 1739 in the celebrated Preface to the *Hymns and Sacred Poems*,[88] published in that year, which we shall consider in detail when dealing with mysticism, Wesley affirmed, 'The Gospel of Christ knows of no religion but social; no holiness but social holiness', moreover, the Methodist societies were founded on fellowship and regular observance of the means of grace.

The other great disparity lay in the doctrinal systems of Law and Wesley which radically affected their respective views both of the means whereby Christian Perfection is attained and indeed to an extent the nature of that Perfection. These doctrinal differences will form the subject of our consideration in Part Three, but should be briefly mentioned here to enable us to complete our survey of Christian Perfection. For Law the attainment of Christian Perfection was increasingly bound up with the mystical system as the fascination of that system grew upon him. His whole stress was laid on the necessity of the continuous inspiration of the Holy Spirit, and Christian Perfection came to be viewed in the light of the Behmenish doctrine of the Fall. The holiness to be attained is thus 'angelic holiness'. The whole doctrine is expounded at length in the *Way to Divine Knowledge* of which this is a typical extract:

See here, Academicus, the folly of your quarrelling with the word *angelic*, since the thing itself, angelic goodness, is absolutely necessary; it is the goodness of our first creation, and must be the goodness of our redemption. The falling from it has brought forth all the evils that we are surrounded with, and nothing can deliver us from the death of our fallen state, but a true and full resurrection of all that purity and goodness, which was living in the first creation of man.[89]

By Wesley, on the other hand, Christian Perfection was viewed in the light of his objective doctrine of the Atonement. As his acceptance of the ethical ideal had been a factor in making possible his evangelical conversion, so that conversion, centred in saving faith in the atoning death of Christ, now afforded a constant stimulus to moral and spiritual endeavour.

If Wesley rejected Calvinism, he rejected Antinomianism even more emphatically, as it 'strikes directly at the root of all

---

[87] *The Conversion of the Wesleys*, by J. E. Rattenbury, p. 45.
[88] John and Charles Wesley, p. viii.
[89] *Law's Works*, Vol. VII, p. 156.

holiness'.[90] The urge to Christian Perfection became an inevitable part of his response to the redeeming love of God in Jesus Christ. We have already seen how, at the beginning of the 1756 Letter, Wesley reproached Law for unfaithfulness to the plain central principle of Christianity: 'We love because He first loved us.'[91] This principle leads, says Wesley, to keeping God's commandments. 'As he loves God, so he keeps His commandments; not only some, or most of them, but all, from the least to the greatest.'[92] The attainment of Christian Perfection is constantly regarded in direct connexion with the experience of the cross of Christ. The best illustrations of this are again in Charles Wesley's hymns. For example:

> *First and last in me perform*
> *The work Thou hast begun*, . . .
> *Every moment, Lord, I want*
> *The merit of Thy death.*[93]

Or again we may cite Charles Wesley's well-known hymn, 'And can it be that I should gain',[94] where the wonder of God's immense and amazing mercy is revealed as the dynamic leading to new life and discipleship in the sinner liberated from the power of sin.

Other similarities and differences in relation to Christian Perfection will be best considered in the next chapter, where we deal with the ethical ideal, as reflected in its practical outworkings in life and conduct.

[90] *Wesley's Works*, Vol. VIII, p. 300.   [91] *Letters*, Vol. III, p. 332.
[92] *Wesley's Works*, Vol. VIII, p. 344.   [93] *Methodist Hymn-book* No. 459, verse 4.
[94] ibid., No. 371.

CHAPTER SIX

Practical Outworkings

IN THE LAST chapter we considered the relation of Law and Wesley in respect of Christian Perfection. We now proceed to a comparison of their teaching regarding the practical application of that ideal. This involves a consideration not only of certain specific principles of conduct, but also of certain qualities of character, which both men laid down as indispensable for the Christian. Law and Wesley in their writings always preserved a balance between character and conduct, which they regarded as interdependent. Christian Perfection must reside in the inward man, but must also find expression in word and deed at every point at which a man touches life. Law, for example, remarks:

Religion is no one particular virtue; . . . it does not consist in the fewness of our vices, or in any particular amendment of our lives, but in such a thorough change of heart, as makes piety and holiness the measure and rule of all our tempers.[1]

Similarly, although in the *Serious Call* he proposes a whole scheme of prayers on particular themes covering the various hours of the day, he also writes:

Devotion may be considered, either as an exercise of public or private prayers at set times and occasions, or as a temper of the mind, a state and disposition of the heart, which is rightly affected with such exercises.[2]

An example of a very different kind, but illustrating the same principle, is found in Wesley's letter to James Barry dated 26th September 1787. After advising preachers how to answer the question whether a man, who dances and plays cards, may be saved, Wesley continues: 'But I cannot advise them to speak this to unawakened people. It will only anger, not convince them. It is beginning at the wrong end.'[3] Similarly, of Christian Perfection he says: 'It is that habitual

[1] *Law's Works*, Vol. III, p. 34.   [2] ibid., p. 196.   [3] *Letters*, Vol. VIII, p. 12.

disposition of soul which, in the sacred writings, is termed holiness.'[4]

PERFECT LOVE TO GOD AND MAN

Christian Perfection consists in Perfect Love to God and man, and there is no text more often quoted, in whole or in part, by Law and Wesley than that on which our Lord Himself commented to a questioner, 'This do and thou shalt live';[5] namely: 'Thou shalt love the Lord thy God with all thy heart, and with all thy soul and with all thy strength and with all thy mind; and thy neighbour as thyself.'[6] This emphasis on the pre-eminence of love is common to both men throughout, but there is one passage where Wesley, though not quoting Law's exact words, so nearly does so, that his direct dependence on Law is beyond question. The passage concerned is in the sermon on 'The Marks of the New Birth', and it is interesting to place some of Wesley's remarks side by side with quotations from Chapter 20 of the *Serious Call:*

On loving our neighbour:
WESLEY: 'The necessary fruit of this love of God is the love of our neighbour.'[7]
LAW: 'The love therefore of our neighbour is only a branch of our love to God.'[8]
On loving our enemies:
WESLEY: '(love) of every soul which God hath made; not excepting our enemies; not excepting those who are now "despitefully using and persecuting us".'[9]
LAW: 'We should forgive all those injuries and affronts which we receive from others, and do all the good that we can to them.'[10]
On loving every man as ourselves:
WESLEY: 'A love whereby we love every man as ourselves; as we love our own souls.'[11]
LAW: '... till we look upon them with that love, with which we look upon ourselves'.[12]

[4] *Wesley's Works*, Vol. XI, p. 367. [5] Luke 11$_{27}$.
[6] e.g. *Law's Works*, Vol. III, pp. 42, 68, 72, etc., and *Wesley's Works*, Vol. XI, pp. 368, 371, 387, 390, 444.
[7] *Sermons*, Vol. I, p. 292. [8] *Law's Works*, Vol. IV, p. 220.
[9] *Sermons*, Vol. I, p. 293. [10] *Law's Works*, Vol. IV, p. 217.
[11] *Sermons*, Vol. I, p. 293. [12] *Law's Work*, Vol. IV, p. 216.

G

On loving as our Lord has loved us:
WESLEY: 'Our Lord has expressed it still more strongly, teaching us to "love one another, even as He hath loved us".'[13]
LAW: 'By the command of our Lord and Saviour, who has required us to love one another, as He has loved us.'[14]

SELF-DENIAL

Then, too, we observe a direct dependence of Wesley on Law in his teaching on the subject of self-denial. This theme is prominent throughout Law's practical treatises. Three chapters of the *Christian Perfection* are devoted to it, while Dr. Flew remarks: 'The *Serious Call* owes its greatness to the sense of the need for renunciation in every Christian life.'[15] Self-denial figures with equal prominence in Wesley, as, for example, when he places it prominently among the five heads to which he maintains Christian duty is reducible.[16] Like Law,[17] Wesley is fond of quoting our Lord's saying about cutting off a right hand or plucking out a right eye.[18] In the Sermon on '*The Circumcision of the Heart*', Wesley follows Law very closely, when illustrating the necessity of self-denial by the examples of St. Paul,

who, living 'in infirmities, in reproaches, in necessities, in persecutions, in distresses' for Christ's sake; who, being full of 'signs and wonders, and mighty deeds', who, having been 'caught up into the third heaven', —yet reckoned, as a late author strongly expresses it, that all his virtues would be insecure, and even his salvation in danger, without this constant self-denial. 'So run I,' says he, 'not as uncertainly; so fight I, not as one that beateth the air'; by which he plainly teaches us, that he who does not thus run, who does not thus deny himself daily, does run uncertainly, and fighteth to as little purpose as he that 'beateth the air'.[19]

The 'late author' referred to Law, not as deceased, but as having lately published the *Christian Perfection* and the passage, with one or two minor verbal alterations, is a quotation from that work.[20]

[13] *Sermons*, Vol. I, p. 293.
[14] *Law's Works*, Vol. IV, p. 222.
[15] *The Idea of Perfection in Christian Theology*, p. 296.
[16] *Wesley's Works*, Vol. XIV, p. 285.
[17] e.g. *Law's Works*, Vol. III, p. 109.
[18] e.g. *Sermons*, Vol. II, p. 289.
[19] *Sermons*, Vol. I, p. 278.
[20] *Law's Works*, Vol. III, p. 117.

PRACTICAL OUTWORKINGS   89

In view of this it is surprising to find Wesley five years later in his Sermon on 'Self-denial', severely criticizing as inadequate all previous treatises on the subject.[21] This is even more difficult to understand as Wesley's sermon is based on the text, 'If any man will come after Me, let him deny himself, and take up his cross daily, and follow Me',[22] a text which constantly recurs in Law and is the basis of his treatment of the subject. The only explanation, and one which is far from satisfactory, would seem to be that this sermon was first preached in February 1738 at a time when, as we have seen, Wesley was engaged in an inward struggle, and Law's writings had for the moment ceased to attract him.

HUMILITY

Again Law and Wesley agreed in insisting on humility. Law urged every devout person 'to begin every day in this exercise of humility',[23] while Wesley, in the sermon on 'The Circumcision of the Heart' gives it pride of place even over faith, hope, and charity.[24] In this passage Wesley's dependence on Law, though not so verbally exact, is too close to be accidental. Both stress the need for a right judgement of ourselves and for a recognition that we are not sufficient to ourselves to help ourselves, but are dependent on the power of God. Furthermore, Wesley's statement that riches constitute a hindrance to humility, by cutting a man off from faithful friends who might deal frankly with him,[25] is very reminiscent of Law's character 'Caecus', a rich man of good birth, who delights in the amiability of the humble and modest persons surrounding him.[26]

In respect of humility it is noteworthy that Wesley seems more satisfied with Law's teaching than with that of Jeremy Taylor, his disquiet with the latter's teaching on the question being voiced in a letter to his mother in 1725.[27]

[21] *Sermons*, Vol. II, pp. 282-3.
[22] Luke 923.
[24] *Sermons*, Vol. I, p. 268.
[26] *Law's Works*, Vol. IV, p. 168.
[23] *Law's Works*, Vol. IV, p. 164.
[25] *Wesley's Works*, Vol. VII, p. 216.
[27] *Letters*, Vol. I, pp. 19-20.

ATTITUDE TO 'THE WORLD'

These qualities of self-denial and humility were exalted by Law as being contrary to the whole spirit and temper of the world. This subject must next occupy our attention. Nothing could be more definite than Law's opposition to the world and all its works. As with self-renunciation, so also world-renunciation is the theme of three chapters in the *Christian Perfection*, and the subject recurs again and again in the *Serious Call*.[28] 'The gospel', writes Law,

> ... lays its first foundation in the renunciation of the world, as a state of false goods and enjoyments, which feed the vanity and corruption of our nature, fill our hearts with foolish and wicked passions, and keep us separate from God, the only happiness of all spirits.[29]

This opposition reaches its height in Law's interpretation of the parable of the Great Supper.

> This parable teaches us, that not only the vices, the wickedness and vanity of this world, but even its most lawful and allowed concerns, render men unable to enter, and unworthy to be received into the true state of Christianity.
> That he who is busied in an honest and lawful calling, may on that account be as well rejected by God, as he who is vainly employed in foolish and idle pursuits ...
> ... that Christianity is a calling that puts an end to all other callings; that we are no longer to consider it as our proper state, or employment, to take care of oxen, look after an estate, or attend the most plausible affairs of life, but to reckon every condition as equally trifling, and fit to be neglected, for the sake of the *one thing needful*.[30]

Law, however, is not consistent. The logical outcome of such an attitude would be complete withdrawal from the world. This conclusion, on the contrary, he rejects.

> (Christian Perfection) calls no one to a cloister, but to a right and full performance of those duties, which are necessary for all Christians, and common to all states of life.[31]

This is equally clear in the *Serious Call*:

> Again, let a tradesman but have this intention, and it will make him a saint in his shop; his every-day business will be a course of wise and

---

[28] See especially, *Law's Works*, Vol. IV, pp. 173-4.
[29] ibid., Vol. III, p. 36.   [30] ibid., p. 37.   [31] ibid., p. 5.

reasonable actions, made holy to God, by being done in obedience to His will and pleasure. He will buy and sell, and labour and travel, because by so doing he can do some good to himself and others.[32]

This principle is summed up by Law in the text he often quotes: 'Do all to the glory of God.'[33]

Wesley's attitude to the world is in part similar to that of Law, and in part a contrast. He too is fond of urging that men should do all to the glory of God.[34] There is also a marked resemblance between Law's argument in Chapters 12 and 13 of the *Serious Call* and Wesley's sermon on 'The Important Question'. Law's exposition is, as usual, much longer and more elaborate. Both men maintain, however, with equal vigour that the choice facing mankind is not between happiness here followed by misery hereafter, on the one hand, and misery here followed by happiness hereafter, on the other, but that here in this life, as surely as in eternity, it is the life of religion alone, which brings true happiness.[35] As we shall see, Wesley also joins with Law in condemning many worldly pursuits, and, like his followers, cultivated that asceticism which tends to draw a sharp distinction between the sacred and the secular. Writing from Savannah in 1737, he explicitly couples Law's name with his own in a letter couched in a more liberal vein. He refers to the pleasure to be derived from eating, and described his own endeavour to preserve a taste for all 'the truly innocent pleasures of life', refusing only what is 'a hindrance to some greater good or has a tendency to some evil'.[36]

In spite of these similarities, however, there is a definite difference between Law and Wesley in this connexion. There was no consciousness of it on the part of either in the earlier days, and indeed it probably only grew up as their careers led them along divergent paths. Law may have denied the necessity of a cloistered life, but in actual fact he did retire to Kingscliffe, and thereafter lived the life of a recluse. Wesley, on the contrary, plunged into a career of ceaseless activity, meeting men and women of all kinds and handling the myriad

[32] ibid., Vol. IV, p. 17.
[33] e.g. ibid., Vol. III, p. 109; Vol. IV, p. 33. Cf. 1 Cor. 10_{31}.
[34] e.g. *Wesley's Works*, Vol. XI, p. 373; *Sermons*, Vol. I, p. 279.
[35] *Law's Works*, Vol. IV, pp. 106-28; *Wesley's Works*, Vol. VI, pp. 504-5.
[36] *Letters*, Vol. I, p. 219.

problems of everyday living. Thereafter his attitude would be better described as world-transforming than as world-renouncing. He developed interests which were quite foreign to Law. The historian of the period must take account of him as a social and economic factor, and his contribution along these lines to the life of eighteenth-century England can be assessed without Law even being mentioned.[37]

ATTITUDE TO LEARNING

Even on subjects where the viewpoints of the two men were in general agreement, Wesley was less unbending than Law,[38] and in one respect, at any rate, their attitudes were diametrically opposed. We have already noted in the historical survey that the question of learning was a bone of contention between them. There are many illustrations of this, but perhaps the clearest is in a comparison of Law's *Address to the Clergy* with Wesley's work of the same title. Law regards religion and scholarship as necessarily opposed, and, in expounding this, displays a stubborn obtuseness which is surprising in such a master of reasoning. Dr. Flew suggests that Law's distrust of all human learning and human intellect may be due to his theory that the Fall was the result of a false curiosity.[39] We may agree and also add that the fact that Jacob Boehme, to whom Law owed the main influence which transformed his life, was unlearned in the technical sense,[40] would tend to confirm Law in his antipathy. He writes, for example:

When the holy Church of Christ, the Kingdom of God, came among men, was first set up, it was the apostle's boast, that all other wisdom or learning was sunk into nothing. 'Where', says he, 'is the wise, the scribe, the disputer of this world? Hath not God made them foolishness?' But now, it is the boast of all Churches, that they are full of the wise, the scribes, the disputers of this world, who sit with learned pomp in the apostle's chair, and have the mysteries of the Kingdom of God committed to them.[41]

[37] e.g. by Dr. Maldwyn Edwards in *John Wesley and the Eighteenth Century. A Study of his Social and Political Influence.*
[38] e.g. his attitude to the stage (vide *infra*, p. 97).
[39] *The Idea of Perfection in Christian Theology*, p. 306.
[40] *Spiritual Reformers in the Sixteenth and Seventeenth Centuries*, Rufus M. Jones, p. 152.
[41] *Law's Works*, Vol. IX, p. 65.

Again:

Happy, thrice happy are they, who are only the thus learned preachers of the Gospel, who through all their ministry, seek nothing for themselves or others, but *to be taught of God*; ... as unable to join with the diggers in pagan pits of learning, as with those that 'labour for the wind, and give their money for that which is not bread'.[42]

Wesley, on the other hand, writing of the indispensable equipment of a minister, asks: 'Can he take one step aright, without first a competent share of knowledge?'[43] This knowledge begins with a knowledge of the Scriptures but this, he insists, should include a knowledge of the original tongues. He continues:

Is not a knowledge of profane history, likewise, of ancient customs, of chronology and geography, though not absolutely necessary, yet highly expedient, for him that would thoroughly understand the Scriptures.[44]

Again he declares, 'Some knowledge of the sciences also, is, to say the least, equally expedient'; and 'Should not a minister be acquainted too with at least the general grounds of natural philosophy?' He even goes as far as to suggest that some knowledge of geometry is desirable, if a minister is to comprehend and explain to others such passages as 'The heavens declare the glory of God, and the firmament showeth His handiwork'.[45]

Wesley would, of course, have heartily agreed with Law's strictures on impure and impertinent books,[46] and indeed on one occasion sought the latter's advice as to how to deal with a student entrusted to his care who was spending too much time in secular reading to the detriment of his religious life.[47] Wesley's own practice coincided with his precept, and though more than once he styled himself *'homo unius libri'*,[48] that was only true in the sense that the Bible occupied the foremost position in his esteem; to the right understanding and interpretation of the Scriptures all else was subordinate and, indeed, ancillary. It is significant that Wesley has left behind not only his impressive collection of religious and theological

[42] ibid.
[43] *Wesley's Works*, Vol. X, p. 482.
[44] ibid., p. 483.
[45] ibid., Vol. X, p. 484.
[46] *Law's Works*, Vol. III, Chapter 10.
[47] *Letters*, Vol. I, p. 162.
[48] e.g. *Sermons*, Vol. I, p. 32; *Letters*, Vol. IV, p. 299.

writings, but grammars of English, French, Latin, Greek, and Hebrew,[49] as well as *A Compendium of Logic*[50] and a tract on *Primitive Physic*.[51] So we may conclude that, though Wesley's attitude to the world had a great deal in common with that of Law, his practical application of the injunction, 'Do all to the glory of God', was much more positive and enlightened.

Hitherto, we have been concerned with the ideal of Christian Perfection as it found expression in the temper and outlook which animated Law and Wesley. We now turn to specific principles of conduct. Though the ways of the recluse and the evangelist lay so far apart, an examination of their behaviour reveals many similarities.

SELF-DISCIPLINE

Outstanding among these is self-discipline. We have already referred to Law's *Rules for my Future Conduct* and it is well known that Wesley drew up similar sets of rules not only for his own observance, but also *Rules of a Helper* for his preachers, *Rules for the United Societies*, etc. For these, however, Wesley was chiefly indebted not to Law, but to Jeremy Taylor, and any correspondence between Wesley and Law must be regarded as due to their common dependence on Taylor, though illustrating doubtless that method of self-discipline which each practised and enjoined.

PRIVATE PRAYER

As regards the practice of prayer, however, Wesley followed Law closely. A large part of the *Serious Call* consists of a scheme of devotion, in the course of which Law recommends specific subjects for prayer at different hours of the day. Wesley expressly commends this in his Sermon on 'The more Excellent way'. Criticizing the tendency always to use the same forms, he suggests:

> But surely there is 'a more excellent way' of ordering our private devotions. What, if you were to follow the advice given by that great and good man, Mr. Law, on this subject?[52]

[49] *Wesley's Works*, Vol. XIV, pp. 1-160.
[51] ibid., pp. 320-31.
[50] ibid., pp. 161-89.
[52] ibid., Vol. VII, p. 30.

Law also advocated 'forms of prayer, at all the regular times of prayer'.[53] Wesley followed suit and published in 1733 *A Collection of Forms of Prayer*.[54] His scheme differed from that of Law, being arranged for every day in the week, instead of for various hours of the day, but there is a close correspondence between the topics suggested in the two schemes. Both include the love of God and our neighbour, humility, and resignation as suitable subjects on particular occasions.[55] Self-examination, which figures prominently in Law's scheme,[56] had been assiduously practised by Wesley from the days of the Oxford Methodists.[57]

REDEEMING THE TIME

This emphasis on self-discipline carried with it a high appreciation of the importance of time. 'It is never allowable to throw any time away',[58] writes Law, while the first injunction in Wesley's *Rules of a Helper* reads: 'Be diligent. Never be unemployed a moment. Never be triflingly employed. Never while away time. . . .'[59] In his Sermon 'On Redeeming the Time', Wesley writes: 'In how beautiful a manner does that great man, Mr. Law, treat this important subject!'[60] Then follows more than two pages of quotation from the *Serious Call*[61] (again with minor verbal changes and some omissions). A good deal of this is devoted to an insistence on early rising, which both men regarded as an elementary principle of self-discipline. To indulge in sleep 'gives a softness to all our tempers . . . and . . . silently . . . wears away the spirit of religion, and sinks the soul into dulness and sensuality'. It is not so much the fault of rising late but the irreligion of which that is evidence, which is to be deplored.

You must not therefore consider how small a fault it is to rise late; but how great a misery it is to want the spirit of religion, and to live in such softness and idleness as make you incapable of the fundamental duties of Christianity. . . .

We must blame it [wasting time in sleep], not as having this or that

[53] *Law's Works*, Vol. IV, p. 135. [54] *Wesley's Works*, Vol. XI, pp. 203-37.
[55] *Law's Works*, Vol. IV, pp. 164, 215, 241; *Wesley's Works*, Vol. XI, pp. 206, 211, 216, 225.
[56] *Law's Works*, Vol. IV, p. 252. [57] *Wesley's Works*, Vol. XI, p. 514.
[58] *Law's Works*, Vol. IV, p. 45. [59] *Wesley's Works*, Vol. III, p. 309.
[60] ibid., Vol. VII, p. 71. [61] *Law's Works*, Vol. IV, pp. 128-34.

particular evil, but as a general habit that extends itself through our whole spirit, and supports a state of mind that is wholly wrong.

FASTING

As a specific instance of self-discipline we should notice that Law and Wesley each enjoin the habit of regular fasting. While both men cite our Lord's Sermon on the Mount as authority for this, their expositions of the necessity of the practice appear otherwise independent, though quite in harmony. Law is more emphatic than Wesley, and terms the practice 'a universal duty',[62] while Wesley counsels a due sense of proportion.

How have some exalted this beyond all Scripture and reason; and others utterly disregarded it—as it were, revenging themselves by undervaluing as much as the former had overvalued it! Those have spoken of it as if it were all in all; if not the end itself, yet infallibly connected with it: these, as if it were just nothing; as if it were a fruitless labour, which had no relation at all thereto. Whereas it is certain the truth lies between them both. It is not all, nor yet is it nothing. It is not the end, but it is a precious means thereto.[63]

This is a striking example of that balanced judgement, so characteristic of Wesley, which Law was apt to lose on occasion.

AMUSEMENTS

Toward amusements in general, though Wesley was at pains to defend them when he regarded them as innocent,[64] his general attitude was very similar to that of Law, mainly on the ground of their futility and the waste of time involved, but sometimes on account of the evil inseparable from them. One passage in Wesley's *Earnest Appeal to Men of Reason and Religion* expresses, though with greater conciseness, Law's precise attitude defined at length in the *Serious Call*.

You eat, and drink, and sleep, and dress, and dance, and sit down to play. You are carried abroad. You are at the masquerade, the theatre, the opera-house, the park, the levee, the drawing-room. What do you do there? Why, sometimes you talk; sometimes you look at one another.

---

[62] *Law's Works*, Vol. III, p. 111.   [63] *Sermons*, Vol. I, p. 451.
[64] *Letters*, Vol. I, p. 219.

And what are you to do to-morrow, the next day, the next week, the next year? You are to eat, and drink, and sleep, and dance, and dress, and play again. And you are to be carried abroad again, that you may again look at one another! And is this all? Alas, how little more happiness have you in this, than the Indians in looking at the sky or water![65]

Yet in this matter also Wesley is prepared to make allowances, especially for those whom he regarded as less enlightened than the Methodists.[66] Another example of the more liberal strain in Wesley's thought is afforded by his attitude to the whole question of stage entertainments. Law condemns the stage and all connected with it root and branch, including those who defend or support it.

Let it therefore be observed, that the stage is not here condemned, as some other diversions, because they are dangerous, and likely to be occasions of sin; but that it is condemned, as drunkenness and lewdness, as lying and profaneness are to be condemned, not as things that may only be the occasion of sin, but such as are in their own nature grossly sinful.[67]

Again: 'It is a contradiction to all Christian holiness, and to all the methods of arriving at it.'[68]

Wesley, however, is prepared to make concessions to others if not to himself. Drawing a contrast with cockfighting and other amusements which he describes as 'foul *remains of Gothic barbarity*', he writes:

It seems a great deal more may be said in defence of seeing a serious tragedy. I could not do it with a clear conscience; at least not in an English theatre, the sink of all profaneness and debauchery; but possibly others can.[69]

It must be remembered that, as Wesley says, the condition of the contemporary English theatre was degenerate and disgusting beyond description, but it is significant that while Law metes out an indiscriminate condemnation on all plays and all actors, Wesley distinguished between the deplorable condition attending the production and performance of plays and the intrinsic merits or demerits of particular plays. But Wesley read and quoted Shakespeare.[70] Law certainly never quoted him. We have no evidence that he read him.

[65] *Wesley's Works*, Vol. VIII, p. 16; *Law's Works*, Vol. IV, pp. 106, 110, 111, etc.
[66] *Letters*, Vol. VIII, p. 12.   [67] *Law's Works*, Vol. II, p. 143.   [68] ibid.
[69] *Wesley's Works*, Vol. VII, p. 34.   [70] e.g. *Journal*, Vol. V, p. 431; Vol. VI, p. 69.

DRESS

The subject of dress was one to which Law and Wesley made frequent reference. They agreed in advocating plainness and simplicity and in condemning all gaiety, and foppery, and the wearing of ornaments or costly apparel of any kind. An examination of their various utterances, however, reveals no evidence of direct dependence of Wesley on Law in this matter, and beyond noticing their common interest and outlook, we need not dwell on this topic at length.

USE OF MONEY

Law and Wesley agreed in singling out money as both a responsibility and an opportunity for the practice of Christian Perfection. In 1736 Wesley preached a sermon on the text Matthew 6_{19-23}, which was based on Chapters 4 and 6 of the *Serious Call*. After urging that money should neither be laid up for posterity, nor laid out on oneself, Wesley embodied in his sermon a long extract from Law. The gist of this was that to waste money on oneself was to support a wrong temper and gratify a vain desire which all Christians should renounce. Money not spent in doing good to others must be spent to the hurt of oneself. 'It is spent to bad purposes and miserable effects; to the corruption and disorder of our hearts; to the making us unable to follow the sublime doctrines of the gospel. It is but like keeping money from the poor, to buy poison for ourselves.'[71]

Law and Wesley regarded money not as a bad thing but as a good thing which became corrupted unless expended in the exercise of Christian Philanthropy. It must be recognized that they practised what they preached. Law's benefactions to the poor of Kingscliffe have already been noticed. Wesley, speaking of himself in his Lincoln College days, says:

One of them (i.e. the Oxford Methodists) had thirty pounds a year. He lived on twenty-eight and gave away forty shillings. The next year, receiving sixty pounds, he still lived on twenty-eight, and gave away two and thirty. The third year he received ninety pounds, and gave away sixty-two. The fourth year he received a hundred and twenty pounds. Still he lived as before on twenty-eight, and gave to the poor ninety-two.[72]

---

[71] *Sermons*, Vol. I, p. 490; *Law's Works*, Vol. IV, p. 51.
[72] *Wesley's Works*, Vol. VII, p. 36.

In later years the thrifty habits of the Methodists caused them to accumulate wealth, which gave Wesley much anxiety.[73] He preached two further sermons on the subject in which he developed his view and evolved the celebrated threefold maxim: 'Gain all you can, save all you can, give all you can.'[74] He never departed, however, from the principles he had acquired from Law.

EDUCATION

One further point falls to be discussed before we conclude this review of the Practical Outworkings of Christian Perfection; namely, Wesley's indebtedness to Law in regard to the education of children. Law had introduced this theme into the *Serious Call*, because he regarded the customary education men were receiving as not being conducive to the practice of humility, and, therefore, as inimical to the attainment of Christian Perfection. In his sermon 'On the Education of Children' Wesley included a long extract from Law, in which the latter had laid down the way wherein a child should go and how he should be trained in it.

Had we continued perfect, runs the argument, the perfection of our nature would have rendered education unnecessary. But just as physical diseases require medicines for their cure, so the disorders of our rational nature require education, the purpose of which is to restore our rational nature in its proper state and supply the loss of original perfection.

This was the end pursued by Pythagoras, Socrates, and Plato in teaching youths what they believed to be the truth about man's nature and end, the soul, and God. Christianity has *now* new created the moral and religious world, and so one would have expected that it would have also mended the education of children. Every Christian country should abound with schools where children are trained in the sublimest doctrines of Christianity and the way of life involved in them. They should be taught the spirit of Christianity, including, of course, abstinence, humility, sobriety, and devotion as Christianity requires. This may as reasonably be expected

---
[73] ibid., Vol. VI, pp. 331, 332.
[74] Sermon on 'The Use of Money': *Sermons*, Vol. II, pp. 311 et sqq.

from a Christian education, as that diseases should be removed by physic.[75]

In this manner Law and Wesley, as with all the branches of human activity, which we have noticed in this chapter, relate the vast problem of education to these ideals of Christian Perfection which in their view constituted the only right goal of all living.

[75] *Law's Works*, Vol. IV, pp. 180-2; *Wesley's Works*, Vol. VII, pp. 87-8.

PART THREE

Wesley's Disagreement with Law

CHAPTER SEVEN

Wesley's Objection to Mysticism

'WESLEY'S hostility to William Law is only part of his rooted distrust of the mystical writers in general.'[1] So writes Mr. Hobhouse, and certainly the disagreements between the two men in the years following 1738 were closely bound up with the effect on Law of his acceptance of the mystical teachings, which Wesley as emphatically rejected. Accordingly, it seems expedient to set forth in this chapter the grounds of Wesley's objections to mysticism in general and the writings of Jacob Boehme in particular. Under the latter head we shall deal with Wesley's criticism, in the first part of the 1756 Letter, of Boehme's philosophical theories as interpreted by Law. We shall also notice to what extent, in spite of his pronounced and persistent opposition, there was common ground between the mystics and Wesley. Apart from mentioning them when completeness requires it, we shall reserve until Chapters 8 and 9 discussion of the doctrinal questions which were the occasions of specific controversy between Law and Wesley.

In approaching this question we are faced with the initial difficulty of defining mysticism. Few words are used with more variations of meaning. Dr. Rufus M. Jones writes:

(Mysticism) only means that the soul of man has dealings with realities of a different order from that with which the senses deal.... The mystic ... insists that his experience reveals the fact that the inner self has a spiritual environment in which it lives and moves and has its being.[2]

If this is so, assuredly all Christians are mystics, not least John Wesley. Indeed, a modern writer makes this very assertion:

Mysticism generally came back into Protestantism through the evangelical movement of the Wesleys and Whitefield. John Wesley's own story of his spiritual struggles reads strangely like a chapter from the old mystics.[3]

[1] *William Law and Eighteenth-century Quakerism*, p. 318.
[2] *New Studies in Mystical Religion*, p. 25.
[3] G. G. Atkins, *The Making of the Christian Mind*, p. 236.

We obviously need a narrower definition. The same writer remarks:

> Mysticism belongs to that totally useful family of words whose meanings are in their atmospheres and suggestions, rather than in their mathematical precision. Their meaning grows upon one gradually through long dealing with what they stand for.[4]

In view of this, our best course would seem to be to follow Wesley's own example, who offers no definition of mysticism, but is in no doubt as to what features of the system should be rejected. By summarizing these, and then observing, on the other hand, those elements in the mystical teaching which Wesley shared, we shall be in a better position to understand the part played by the system in the relation of Law to Wesley than by seeking at the outset some form of words whereby we might adequately define mysticism.

In the historical survey we noted that Wesley's first written renunciation of the mystical system was in a letter of 1736 written to his brother Samuel from Georgia.[5] How far had Wesley travelled along the road to mysticism before turning back? On two occasions in controversial letters he is concerned to maintain that neither he nor the Methodists had been committed to the mystical system. In December 1751, replying to Bishop Lavington's *The Enthusiasm of Methodists and Papists Compared*, Wesley writes:

> You observe, by the way, 'The Mystic divinity was once the Methodists' doctrine.' Sir, you have stepped out of the way only to get another fall. The mystic divinity was never the Methodists' doctrine. They could never swallow either John Tauler or Jacob Boehme; although they often advised with one that did.[6]

Twenty years later, in *Some Remarks on Mr. Hill's 'Farrago Double-distilled'* he asserts: 'I admired the Mystic writers. But I never was in their way.'[7]

From the time of his voyage home from Georgia, Wesley's depreciatory references to the mystics are frequent. On two occasions he expressed his opposition to them in a reasoned

---

[4] ibid, p. 217.
[5] *Letters*, Vol. I, p. 207. Cf. p. 14.
[6] ibid., Vol. III, p. 321. The reference, we may assume, is to Law.
[7] *Wesley's Works*, Vol. X, p. 438.

statement, and as these statements embody most of the objections which he brought against the mystics on other incidental occasions, it would be well to summarize them.

Wesley's most important statement on the subject of mysticism constituted the Preface to the volume of *Hymns and Sacred Poems*[8] published in 1739, and invests that work with very great interest.

The collection included some verses written upon the scheme of the mystic divines, 'whom', Wesley admits, 'we had once in great veneration, as the best explainers of the gospel of Christ'. In that respect, however, he now realizes that he erred 'not knowing the Scriptures, nor the power of God'. Lest others fall into similar error he proceeds to declare wherein he now apprehends those writers not to teach 'the truth as it is in Jesus'.

Wesley's objections are:

(1) They lay another foundation. While pulling down our own works, they establish instead our own righteousness. Virtuous habits or tempers are substituted for virtuous actions, but the ground of acceptance by God remains in ourselves. Whereas the truth is that neither inward nor outward righteousness is the cause of justification. Holiness of heart, as of life, is not the cause but the effect of it. 'The sole cause of our acceptance with God, ... is the righteousness and death of Christ, who fulfilled God's law, and died in our stead.' And the condition is our faith alone, as distinguished alike from holiness and good works.

(2) Even if they have laid the foundation right, the manner of building on it is opposite to that prescribed by Christ. 'He commands to build up one another. They advise, "To the desert! to the desert! and God will build you up".' While they counsel seclusion in order to purify the soul, our Lord and the apostles advocate fellowship. Wesley then quotes with effect the Scripture that no member can say to another member: 'I have no need of thee.' He recalls the sending out of the apostles *two by two* and the fact that the disciples were assembled together when they received the gift of the Holy Ghost. He concludes this section with references to the celebrated description of the ideal church in Ephesians 4.

[8] By John and Charles Wesley, pp. i ii-x.

(3) Wesley next attacks the superstructure which the mystics build. 'The religion these authors would edify us in, is solitary religion.' For them contemplation is the fulfilling of the law, even a contemplation that 'consists in a cessation from all works'. Whereas the gospel of Christ is directly opposite to this. 'It knows of no religion but social; no holiness but social holiness.' Faith working by love constitutes Christian Perfection. That love must be manifested by doing good to all men. Whosoever loveth his brethren must be 'zealous of good works'.

Wesley concludes the preface with an urgent appeal to his readers to walk in this way.

The abiding importance attached to this anti-mystical statement, not only by Wesley, but by Law, is evident from the fact that as late as 1756 Law referred to it in a letter as

that false and rash censure which he published in print against the Mystics: as enemies to good works, and even tending to atheism. A censure so false, and regardless of right and wrong, as hardly any thing can exceed it; which is to be found in a preface of his to a book of hymns.[9]

When Byrom asked him in 1761 if the preface still stood, Wesley answered 'that he knew of no alteration'.[10]

Wesley's other summary of his objections to the mystic writers is found in the *Journal* for 5th February 1764,[11] twenty-five years after the writing of the hymn-book preface. After reading a book in defence of the said writers, Wesley reaffirms his opposition to them on three grounds:

(1) Their sentiments. They have no conception of Church communion. 'They slight not only works of piety, the ordinances of God, but even works of mercy.' In spite of this most of them hold justification by works.

(2) Their spirit. 'Most of them are of a dark, shy, reserved, unsociable temper.' They despise those who differ from them.

(There is a remarkable resemblance here to Wesley's charge against Law at the end of the first of the May 1738[12] letters.)

(3) Their phraseology. This is unscriptural and affectedly

---

[9] *Law's Works*, Vol. IX, p. 169.   [10] *Remains of John Byrom*, Vol. II, Part II, p. 629.
[11] *Journal*, Vol. V, p. 46.   [12] *Journal*, Vol. VIII, p. 320.

mysterious. 'St. John speaks as high and as deep things as Jacob Boehme. Why then does not Jacob speak as plain as him?'

From these two statements it is clear that Wesley's objections to mysticism fall under the following heads:

(1) It strikes at the root of the central evangelical doctrine of Justification by Faith. In later years Wesley had to defend this doctrine not only against those who trusted in their own inward or outward righteousness, but against those who claimed that physical evil is the only means of curing moral evil. This principle, says Wesley, 'is one of those fundamental mistakes which run through the whole mystic divinity'.[13]

(2) Mysticism is prejudicial to good works.

(3) Mysticism enjoined solitariness, whereas Wesley believed in social love.

(4) Mystics slight the ordinances of God.

(5) Mysticism produces sourness and a contempt for others in its devotees.

(6) Mystics couch their teaching in mysterious and obscure phraseology.

To these we may add:

(7) Mystics deny 'imputed righteousness'. In this connexion Wesley especially cites Law.

One of the chief of these (mystics) in the present century, at least in England, was Mr. Law. It is well-known that he absolutely and zealously denied the imputation of the righteousness of Christ, as zealously as Robert Barclay, who scruples not to say 'Imputed righteousness!— imputed nonsense!'[14]

(8) Mystics teach that darkness is much more profitable than light.

So the mystics teach; so it is written in their books; but not in the oracles of God. The Scripture nowhere says, that the absence of God best perfects his work in the heart! Rather, His presence and a clear communion with the Father and the Son.[15]

It should be especially noted that in respect of every count in his indictment, Wesley takes his stand on Holy Scripture.[16]

[13] *Letters*, Vol. III, p. 108. [14] *Sermons*, Vol. II, pp. 435-6. [15] ibid., p. 261.
[16] e.g. *Letters*, Vol. IV, p. 234; *Journal*, Vol. II, pp. 494, 515; Vol. III, pp. 241, 289.

He is never tired of comparing St. Paul and St. John with the mystical writers to the detriment of the latter.[17]

How strongly Wesley felt upon these matters may be gauged from the violence of his language. As early as January 1738 he wrote:

> All the other enemies of Christianity are triflers; the mystics are the most dangerous of its enemies. They stab it in the vitals.[18]

As late as 1774, he referred to mystic divinity as 'this specious snare of the devil'.[19]

These were the characteristics Wesley had in mind when he attacked mysticism, and it is in that sense that we must understand the term as used by him.

The above sketch will serve as a background for our subsequent discussion of the doctrinal and practical aspects of the controversy between the two men, and, as far as they are relevant to our inquiry, they will come up for consideration in that connexion.

Before passing, however, from this preliminary sketch of mysticism we should pause to note the points of agreement between Wesley and the mystics, and also his own modifications of his attitude.

In spite of his intense hostility to their main tenets, Wesley's fairness evoked from him more than one tribute to the mystics, albeit in a qualified form. To his sister in 1773 he wrote:

> There are excellent things in most of the Mystic writers. As almost all of them lived in the Romish Church, they were lights whom the gracious providence of God raised up to shine in a dark place. But they do not give a clear, a steady, or an uniform light.[20]

Furthermore, in the previous year Wesley had retracted his former statement that the mystic writers were one great Antichrist, characterizing it as 'far too strong'.[21]

More important than this, however, as Dr. Workman reminds us,

> Mysticism and Methodism both built on the foundation, not of argument or observation, but of conscious spiritual experience. The doctrine of 'Assurance' is not far removed from a belief in the 'inner light'.[22]

---

[17] e.g. *Journal*, Vol. I, p. 440; *Letters*, Vol. III, pp. 332, 370.
[18] *Journal*, Vol. I, p. 420.   [19] ibid., Vol. VI, p. 10.   [20] *Letters*, Vol. VI, p. 43
[21] *Wesley's Works*, Vol. X, p. 395.   [22] *A New History of Methodism*, Vol. I, p. 55.

WESLEY'S OBJECTION TO MYSTICISM

The witness of the Holy Spirit with the believer's spirit, that the converted man is a child of God, is an essentially mystical teaching, and one with which Wesley and his followers have always regarded themselves entrusted as the guardians. That this is rooted in a faculty beyond reason is enshrined in one of Isaac Watts's hymns that the Methodist tradition has preserved:

> *Where reason fails, with all her powers,*
> *There faith prevails, and love adores.*[23]

John Wesley himself recognized the genuineness of the experience of the mystics. 'Will any one dare to affirm that all Mystics (such as Mr. Law in particular) . . . are void of all Christian experience!'[24] In the Sermon on 'The Means of Grace', in which he attacks the mystics for the neglect of the ordinances, Wesley nevertheless described some among them as

> men of love, experimentally acquainted with true, inward religion. Some of these were burning and shining lights, persons famous in their generations, and such as had well deserved of the Church of Christ, for standing in the gap against the overflowings of ungodliness.[25]

Finally Wesley declared quite unequivocally:

> A pious Churchman who has not clear conceptions of justification by faith may be saved; yea, a Mystic, (Mr. Law, for instance,) who denies justification by faith.[26]

When we remember, too, as we saw in the historical survey, Wesley's conscious or unconscious debt to the mystical tradition, and also his constant practice of including mystical works among his publications, we may agree with Dr. Workman that 'Wesley was more influenced by mysticism than he was aware'.[27]

We now turn to Wesley's especial strictures upon the writings of Jacob Boehme, which are of particular importance because of the dominant influence which we have seen Boehme exercised upon Law from about the year 1736 onward. Apart from one reference to Dionysius[28] and a few slighting mentions

---

[23] *Methodist Hymn-book*, No. 40, verse 4.
[25] ibid., Vol. I, p. 240.
[27] *A New History of Methodism*, Vol. I, p. 55.
[24] *Sermons*, Vol. II, p. 437.
[26] *Wesley's Works*, Vol. X, p. 391.
[28] *Journal*, Vol. II, p. 365.

of Tauler, when Wesley *attacked* individual mystics, it is either Boehme or Law whom he singles out, and the latter is clearly regarded by Wesley as Boehme's interpreter and disciple.

Boehme was born in Lusatia in 1585,[29] the son of a herdsman. His education in the conventional sense was of an elementary character and in due course he was apprenticed to a shoemaker. He was deeply shocked at the controversies raging within Protestantism and is reported to have received remarkable visions on several occasions. All his writings were composed between 1610 and 1624 in which year he died at the age of 39. As a result of revelations received, Boehme produced his philosophical system. Though this system has theological consequences concerning the way of salvation, it is mainly concerned with origins. Boehme goes back to the beginning, when the Divine Being first proceeded to manifestation. He expounds a theory of how there arose Three Principles; two eternal—darkness and wrath of the first, and light and love of the second—and this present world of the third Principle, which stands between the two and is qualified in good and evil. He also speaks of seven Forms of Nature, which he conceives as arising successively. Into this framework he fits the fall of Lucifer, on whom the whole blame is laid for the origin of evil, and of Adam, in whom, however, the light went not into extinction, as with Lucifer, but into hiddenness. This in turn paves the way for Boehme's exposition of the 'Way of Salvation', to which he relates the historic facts of the Christian revelation.

We are only concerned with the details of Boehme's system in so far as Law's acceptance and reinterpretation of them figured in his controversy with Wesley, but in view of Wesley's habit of coupling Law with Boehme, it would be well for us to note at this point Wesley's main objections to Boehme's system. These are chiefly contained in his *Thoughts upon Jacob Boehme*, published in 1780, and on examination are seen to be very similar to those he held against the mystics in general. We also note how again Wesley closely connects Law with Behmenism.

[29] For biographical details, etc., concerning Boehme I am indebted to the article by G. W. Allen in the *Encyclopædia of Religion and Ethics*, Vol. II, pp. 778-84, and to Dr. Rufus M. Jones' *Spiritual Reformers in the Sixteenth and Seventeenth Centuries*, Chapters 9-11

Wesley allows that Boehme was 'a good man' and 'wrote many truths', but denies anything new in that part of his writings. He objects most to Boehme's philosophy and phraseology. 'These are really his own; and these are quite new; therefore, they are quite wrong.'[30] Religion has been blended with vain philosophy, supported neither by Scripture nor reason.

I grant, Mr. Law, by taking immense pains, has licked it into some shape. And he has made it hang tolerably together. But still it admits of no manner of proof.[31]

Wesley proceeds to arrange his objections under five heads:
(1) The whole foundation is wrong. It is wrong to attempt to explain religion, which is the most simple thing in the world, by an abstruse, complicated, philosophical theory.

Either St. Paul and St. John knew this theory, or they did not. Mr. Law supposes, they did not know it; but that Jacob knew more than them both. I verily think this needs no confutation.[32]

On the theory itself Wesley then quotes a long extract from the beginning of the 1756 Letter to Law, which we consider below.
(2) Boehme 'builds no superstructure upon it, but what we knew before, either with regard to internal or external holiness'.[33] Wesley recounts the Christian doctrines of 'faith that worketh by love', the new birth, love of ·God and our neighbour, and claims that Boehme has added nothing to these.

(3) Boehme's language, however, is indeed new! It is novel and obscure, but unscriptural.[34] Concerning a remark that it needed to be read thrice to be understood, Wesley protests that it would crack any man's brain to brood so long over 'such unintelligible nonsense', and would be an unjustifiable waste of time.[35] It is doubtful if anybody understands it. 'I thought, if any man living understood Boehme, Mr. Law did. "No," says one who has been studying him these forty years, "Mr. Law never understood a page of him." '[36]

[30] *Wesley's Works*, Vol. IX, p. 509.   [31] ibid.   [32] ibid., p. 510.
[33] ibid., p. 511.   [34] ibid., p. 512.   [35] ibid., p. 513.   [36] ibid.

(4) The whole of Behmenism is useless, as it makes no eminent Christians.[37]

(5) It is not only useless, it is in a high degree mischievous. 'It strikes at the root of both internal and external religion, (suppose Mr. Law understood it,) by sapping the foundation of justification by faith.'[38]
It strikes at the root of humility.

> Never was a more melancholy proof of this than Mr. Law, who seriously believed himself the most knowing man in the kingdom, and despised all that contradicted him, even in the tenderest manner, as the mire in the streets.[39]

(This is an obvious reference to Law's treatment of Wesley.)
It strikes at the root of charity, and destroys zeal for good works; it discourages the use of men's talents, by declaiming against reason and learning. 'It strikes at the root of all revealed religion, by making men think meanly of the Bible.'[40]
Wesley concludes:

> Indeed it quite spoils the taste for plain, simple religion, such as that of the Bible is; and gives a false taste, which can relish nothing so well, as high, obscure, unintelligible jargon.[41]

Wesley appends a specimen of Boehme's syllabic method of interpreting Scripture. Boehme had taken the Lord's Prayer in German and made each syllable the basis of some mystical truth. e.g. '*Un* is God's eternal will to nature; *ser* comprehends in it the four forms of nature.'[42] Wesley reprints the whole prayer so interpreted, and tersely inquires:

> (1) Whether any man in his senses, from the beginning of the world, ever thought of explaining any treatise, divine or human, syllable by syllable. . . .
> (2) If any scripture could be thus explained . . . must it not be from the syllables of the original, not of a translation. . . .
> (3) Whether this explanation be any explanation at all . . . whether it does not reduce the divine Prayer . . . into an unconnected, incoherent jumble of no one can tell what!
> (4) Whether we may not pronounce with the utmost certainty, of one who thus distorts, mangles, and murders the word of God, that the

---

[37] *Wesley's Works*, Vol. IX, p. 510.   [38] ibid.   [39] ibid.
[40] ibid., p. 514.   [41] ibid.   [42] ibid., p. 515.

light which is in him is darkness; that he is illuminated from beneath, rather than from above; and that he ought to be styled a demonosopher, rather than a theosopher!⁴³

Certainly Wesley had not been slow in discovering Boehme's weak points!

Wesley's main criticism of the *details* of Boehme's system is contained in the first part of the 1756 Letter to Law, where Wesley challenges the validity of Boehme's philosophical speculations, which Law had taken over and embodied in the *Spirit of Prayer* and the *Spirit of Love*. This section of the letter occupies ten pages and Wesley's method is to quote some statement from one of these works, and ask several rhetorical questions concerning it, then proceeding to the next statement which he treats likewise. Any detailed analysis would clearly overweight our inquiry. We will accordingly summarize Law's teaching on each of the four subjects under which Wesley marshals his criticisms and state Wesley's main objections thereto.

I. THINGS ANTECEDENT TO THE CREATION⁴⁴

Wesley's attack here revolves around Boehme's teaching on nature and its seven properties.

These properties are attraction, resistance, whirling, fire, the form of light and love, sound or understanding, a life of triumphing joy.

Of the first three properties, attraction seeks change and new combinations, resistance is a conservative principle, and whirling arises out of the conflict of the first two. In modern terminology, we might call them heterogeneity, homogeneity, and strain.⁴⁵ Out of the strain arises fire, at which point self-consciousness arises and the possibility of choice. If the right choice is made fire passes into light and love, when self is thought of as made for the universe instead of the universe for self. Then follow sound, which includes all forms of understanding, and finally the life of triumphant joy.

Law had also stated: 'All that can be conceived is God, or

---

⁴³ ibid., pp. 517-18. ⁴⁴ *Letters*, Vol. III, pp. 333 et sqq.
⁴⁵ See G. W. Allen, loc. cit. (note 29, this chapter).

nature, or creature.' At other times he spoke of nature as a hungry, wrathful fire of life, and as only a desire.

Wesley attacks these definitions.

Is nature created or not created? It must be one or the other. If not created, is it not God? If created, is it not a creature? How, then, can there be three—God, nature, and creature—?

If nature is only a desire how can it also be, as Law maintained, 'the outward manifestation of the invisible glories of God'?

Wesley, then, inquires about the so-called seven properties of nature. 'The first three properties are attraction, resistance, and whirling', said Law. How can this be if nature is distinct from matter? This is a jumbling of dissonant notions.

II. THE CREATION[46]

This section is concerned with Law's views of the creation and especially the fall of the angels.

Law had said that 'a creation out of nothing is in no better sense than a creation into nothing'; and 'that all things were created out of nothing has not the least tittle of Scripture to support it'.

Wesley bluntly answers that a creation into nothing is a contradiction in terms, and that a creation out of nothing is tautology. Creation is equivalent with production out of nothing.

On Law's other point the first verse of Genesis provides the support Law denies.

This section is mainly concerned, however, with Wesley's criticism of the theory held by Boehme and Law of a prehuman fall due to the revolt of the angels. This theory is elaborated by Law in the *Spirit of Prayer* in long and vivid descriptions put into the mouth of God. As Mr. Hobhouse says,[47] it is impossible to believe that Boehme originated this myth, which has its roots in pre-Christian Jewish or Semitic tradition.

Wesley's criticism, at any rate, is lucid and concise. It is threefold: (1) He challenges the wisdom of taking liberties

---
[46] *Letters*, Vol. III, pp. 335-8.
[47] *William Law: Selected Mystical Writings*, pp. 310-11.

WESLEY'S OBJECTION TO MYSTICISM

with the Most High God and putting words into His mouth, especially when such words amounted, as Wesley thought, to nonsense. (2) He suggests that those who hold the theory are aiming at a wisdom wiser than the prophets and the apostles. (3) He flatly denies any vestige of proof of the theory.

Wesley renews his attack on the theory of the properties of nature at the end of this section.

III. ADAM IN PARADISE[48]

This section is a criticism by Wesley of Law's theory, whereby Adam was at first a being with a heavenly and an earthly body, both male and female in one person, which is the very perfection of the angelic nature. Law quotes: 'In the resurrection they neither marry nor are given in marriage, but are as the angels.'

Law thinks of the creation of Adam as God's means for the restoring of all things to their glorious state, lost by the revolt of the angels.

Wesley seeks to refute all this on direct scriptural authority. Confusing the two creations (Wesley of course only recognized one), Wesley declares that the restoration of all things was God's end in redemption, not in creation. With regard to the resurrection, the whole passage[49] makes it clear that men are equal to the angels not in being male and female, but in that they cannot die any more.

IV. THE FALL OF MAN[50]

Law's doctrine of the Fall of Man is here contrasted by Wesley with the Genesis account. 'Adam', said Law, 'had lost much of his perfection before Eve was taken out of him.' By letting in an adulterous love of the world, Adam lost his virginity and had no longer a power of bringing forth a birth from himself. So 'marriage came in by Adam's falling from his first perfection'. 'Had Adam stood, no Eve would have been taken out of him. But from Eve God raised that angelic man whom Adam should have brought forth without Eve, who is called the Second Adam, being both male and female.' 'The Second Adam is now to do that which the first should have done.'

[48] *Letters*, Vol. III, pp. 338-40.   [49] Luke 20_{35-6}.   [50] *Letters*, Vol. III, pp. 340-2.

Wesley rejects this root and branch. It was God who caused a deep sleep to fall upon Adam, and who made them at the beginning (with no word in Scripture of a previous fall), male and female. Law's account does no honour to the institution of marriage. Furthermore 'how does it appear (1) that Eve would not have been, had Adam stood, (2) that had he stood, he would have brought forth the Second Adam without Eve, (3) that Christ was both male and female, and (4) that He was on this account called the Second Adam?'

To suggest, as Law does, that the Second Adam is to do what the first should have done, is to dispense with any need of His being God. No one who believes the Christian revelation, says Wesley, can aver that Adam had the same spiritual power which Christ had, and could, had he not fallen, have brought to us the same benefit.

The section concludes with Wesley's ridicule of Law's idea that all the natural properties of man's creaturely life, which had been hidden in God, broke forth, when man fell, just as the natural qualities of darkness show forth their coldness and horror, when the darkness has lost the light. All this, maintains Wesley, is nonsensical speculation, incapable of proof.

So Wesley concludes his animadversions on Law's philosophical theories, which he found bewildering and indeed meaningless, and quite contrary to Scripture. It is not surprising that he found them such, especially Law's exposition of the seven properties of nature, which, as Mr. Hobhouse shows, is a difficult theory when treated by Boehme, but even more obscure when treated in the one-sided way in which Law dealt with it.[51]

As with other aspects of the Law-Wesley controversy, we must give due weight to the inevitable opposition which such speculative ideas would set up in the mind of one who at this time was engaged in an evangelical campaign of absorbing interest, requiring the application of the great truths of salvation to the urgent practical problems of everyday living.

[51] *William Law: Selected Mystical Writings*, pp. 344-5.

CHAPTER VIII

The Fundamental Doctrinal Issue

PART TWO of our inquiry revealed common ground between Law and Wesley concerning the spiritual union of the believer with Christ, freedom from sin, and Christian Perfection as the purpose of God for all men. Where they differed was in their conception of how men could attain to these things. Upon this their ultimate disagreement turned. It was Law's inadequate teaching in this respect that provoked the 1738 correspondence, and it was this same difference in theological outlook, with its unfortunate repercussions in some of the Methodist societies, which so profoundly disturbed Wesley, that he returned to the attack in 1756.

Accordingly, we now proceed to examine and compare the respective conceptions of the Atonement held by Wesley and Law; in the next chapter we shall review the various doctrinal issues raised in the 1756 Letter, and it will be seen that in the light of the fundamental difference between the views of the two men on the way of salvation, the remaining differences appear not only consequential but inevitable.

We state Wesley's position first, as it is altogether simpler to grasp, and, with Wesley's beliefs in mind, it will be easier to extract and present Law's views, which are largely dependent on and the result of his involved mystical theories.

Here we should note, what has often been remarked,[1] that Wesley was in no sense an original theologian. He sought neither to expound new dogmas, nor to overthrow existing ones. He himself insisted that what he preached was entirely scriptural and had been preached before by Paul in New Testament days, and by Augustine, Luther, and others in later times. Wesley's interests were practical rather than theoretical, and over against the prevailing tendencies of religious belief as variously represented by the Deists, the Calvinists, and the Mystics, he proclaimed the *fact* of the Atonement through the saving power of faith in Christ, as

[1] e.g. by Dr. H. B. Workman in *Methodism*, pp. 109-10.

experimentally verified in his own spiritual history. As late as 1778, in a Letter to Mary Bishop, Wesley at once stresses the vital importance of the Atonement and disavows comprehension of it:

> ... nothing in the Christian system is of greater consequence than the doctrine of Atonement. It is properly the distinguishing point between Deism and Christianity.... But it is true I can no more *comprehend* it than his Lordship (Lord Huntingdon); perhaps I might say than the angels of God, than the highest *created* understanding. Our *reason* is here quickly bewildered.... But the question is (the only question with me; I regard nothing else), What saith the Scripture? It says, 'God was in Christ, reconciling the world unto Himself'; that 'He made Him, who knew no sin, to be a sin-offering for us'. It says, 'He was wounded for our transgressions and bruised for our iniquities'. It says, 'We have an Advocate with the Father, Jesus Christ the righteous; and He is the atonement for our sins'.[2]

Wesley's teaching on the Atonement may be considered under five heads:

(1) Man's universal need.
(2) Salvation is God's free gift.
(3) Salvation is offered to all men.
(4) Faith is the condition of Salvation.
(5) Faith is centred in the atoning death of Christ.

1. MAN'S UNIVERSAL NEED

This springs from the fact of sin and universal guilt. Wesley's most comprehensive treatment of this theme is his work on *The Doctrine of Original Sin, according to Scripture, Reason and Experience*. This treatise was begun, significantly enough, a few months after the 1756 Letter to Law, and concluded in the following year. It occupies 270 pages in the Complete *Works*.[3] In order to establish the universality of original sin Wesley surveys the history of mankind, defending the scriptural account of the origin of sin, and reviewing the corrupt state of men in the pre-Christian era, both in Israel and in pagan lands. He then turns to the world of his own day and expounds the same doctrine with regard to his contemporaries all over the world. He examines in turn nations, professions,

[2] *Letters*, Vol. VI, pp. 297-8.   [3] *Wesley's Works*, Vol. IX, pp. 191-464.

families, and the individual, and everywhere detects the same unhappiness which he invariably attributes to sinfulness.

Universal misery is at once a consequence and a proof of this universal corruption. Men are unhappy . . . because they are unholy. '*Culpam pœna premit comes*': 'Pain accompanies and follows sin.' Why is the earth so full of complicated distress? Because it is full of complicated wickedness. Why are not you happy? Other circumstances may concur, but the main reason is, because you are not holy.'[4]

In a town, a corporation, a city, a kingdom, is it not the same thing still? From whence comes that complication of all the miseries incident to human nature,—war? Is it not from the tempers 'which war in the soul'? When nation rises up against nation, and kingdom against kingdom, does it not necessarily imply pride, ambition, coveting what is another's; or envy, or malice, or revenge, on one side, if not on both? Still, then, sin is the baleful source of affliction; and, consequently, the flood of miseries which covers the face of the earth,—which overwhelms not only single persons, but whole families, towns, cities, kingdoms,— is a demonstrative proof of the overflowing of ungodliness in every nation under heaven.[5]

There are many references scattered through Wesley's writings which are in harmony with the contentions of the treatise on Original Sin. Explaining, for example, the need for the new birth, in his Sermon on that subject, Wesley gives an account of the origin of sin along the lines of the account in Genesis 3.[6] In the Sermon on 'The Mystery of Iniquity' he stresses the universal extent of the fall: 'What, among so many thousands, so many millions, is there "none righteous, no, not one!" Not by nature.'[7] Rebutting the suggestion that the 'notions of the Methodists' were not the doctrine of the Church of England, Wesley states, in *A Farther Appeal to Men of Reason and Religion*, that part of the Ninth Article of the Church, which deals with original sin,[8] and there is an equally emphatic statement in the *Minutes of some Late Conversations*,

In Adam all die; that is, (1) Our bodies then became mortal. (2) Our souls died; that is, were disunited from God. And hence, (3) We are all born with a sinful, devilish nature. By reason whereof, (4) We are children of wrath, liable to death eternal. (Romans 6_{18}; Ephesians 2_3.)[9]

---

[4] ibid., p. 235.   [5] ibid., pp. 237-8.   [6] *Sermons*, Vol. II, p. 229.
[7] *Wesley's Works*, Vol. VI, p. 265.   [8] ibid. Vol. VIII, p. 52.   [9] ibid., p. 277.

No better evidence for John Wesley's doctrines can be found than Charles Wesley's hymns (and of course John Wesley's own translations of German hymns), for it was largely through their medium that the doctrines of the evangelical revival were popularized throughout the growing Methodist societies. We quote two examples from Charles Wesley, illustrative of the doctrines of sin, though it will be recognized that this theme is naturally not so frequent in the hymns as the doctrine of grace, and is often implicit rather than explicit. We may cite, however, the well-known couplet:

> *Show me, as my soul can bear*
> *The depth of inbred sin;*[10]

and again,

> *O let Thy love my heart constrain!*
> *Thy love for every sinner free,*
> *That every fallen soul of man*
> *May taste the grace that found out me.*[11]

II. SALVATION IS GOD'S FREE GIFT

This was so habitual an aspect of Wesley's thinking that it constantly found expression in his writings. Our purpose is best served by the classical instance in the Sermon on 'Salvation by Faith'. This sermon was preached in St. Mary's, Oxford, before the University on 11th June 1738, within three weeks of Wesley's evangelical conversion, and is placed first in the collection of the forty-four Standard Sermons. The sermon opens with an unequivocal statement of the doctrine of free grace.

All the blessings which God hath bestowed upon man are of His mere grace, bounty, or favour; His free, undeserved favour; favour altogether undeserved; man having no claim to the least of His mercies. It was free grace that 'formed man of the dust of the ground, and breathed into him a living soul', and stamped on that soul the image of God, and 'put all things under his feet'. The same free grace continues to us, at this day, life, and breath, and all things. For there is nothing we are, or have, or do, which can deserve the least thing at God's hand. 'All our works, Thou, O God, hast wrought in us.' These, therefore, are so

[10] *Methodist Hymn-book*, No. 465, verse 4. [11] ibid., No. 173, verse 4.

THE FUNDAMENTAL DOCTRINAL ISSUE 121

many more instances of free mercy; and whatever righteousness may be found in man, this is also the gift of God. Wherewithal then shall a sinful man atone for any the least of his sins? With his own works? No. Were they ever so many or holy, they are not his own, but God's. . . . If then sinful men find favour with God, it is 'grace upon grace!' If God vouchsafe still to pour fresh blessings upon us, yea, the greatest of all blessings, salvation; what can we say to these things, but, 'Thanks be unto God for His unspeakable gift!' And thus it is. Herein 'God commendeth His love toward us, in that, while we were yet sinners, Christ died' to save us. 'By grace' then 'are ye saved through faith.' Grace is the source, faith the condition, of salvation.[12]

This note of God's free grace in Jesus Christ is sounded continually in the Wesleys' hymns. From Charles Wesley we quote:

> *He left His Father's throne above—*
> *So free, so infinite His grace—*
> *Emptied Himself of all but love,*
> *And bled for Adam's helpless race.*
> *'Tis mercy all, immense and free;*
> *For, O my God, it found out me!*[13]

Or again,

> *Who can sound the depths unknown*
> *Of Thy redeeming grace;*
> *Grace that gave Thine only Son*
> *To save a ruined race?*
> *Millions of transgressors poor*
> *Thou hast for Jesu's sake forgiven,*
> *Made them of Thy favour sure,*
> *And snatched from hell to heaven.*[14]

III. SALVATION IS OFFERED TO ALL MEN

It is unnecessary to dwell at length on Wesley's belief in the universalism of free grace, as many of his controversies on the subject were occasioned by his opposition to the Calvinist doctrine of reprobation, to which Law was equally opposed. Furthermore, it has already been pointed out that Wesley

---

[12] *Sermons*, Vol. I, pp. 37, 38.
[13] *Methodist Hymn-book* No. 371, verse 3.
[14] ibid., No. 59, verse 3.

believed in Christian Perfection as God's free gift intended for all. *A fortiori* therefore he must have believed in the free gift of Justification which preceded Sanctification in Wesley's scheme.

This universalism of free grace, however, must be carefully distinguished from the unconditioned universalism taught by the Moravians which Wesley refutes at length in his correspondence with the Moravian church at Herrnhut,[15] and which, as we shall see, he attacked in Law. Wesley proclaimed God's free grace, available, indeed, for all men, but conditioned by faith. It is expounded, for example, in the Sermon on 'Free Grace' preached at Bristol in 1740. This sermon caused the first breach between Wesley and Whitefield. After writing of God's grace as 'free in all' Wesley asks: 'But is it free FOR ALL, as well as IN ALL?'[16] Then follows a carefully reasoned indictment of the doctrine of predestination, in which Wesley seeks to show that that doctrine makes void the ordinances of God, destroys several particular branches of holiness, destroys the comfort of religion, destroys our zeal for good works, and tends to overthrow the whole Christian revelation, which it makes contradict itself.[17]

Many of the most exultant hymns of the Wesleys are concerned with this theme, and are sung as heartily today by Methodists though the Calvinistic controversy has faded into obscurity in that communion. Notable among these is the hymn usually known as 'The Wesleys' Conversion Hymn', written by Charles Wesley on the day after his conversion.

> *Outcasts of men, to you I call,*
> *Harlots, and publicans, and thieves!*
> *He spreads His arms to embrace you all;*
> *Sinners alone His grace receives.*[18]

Nor can we forbear to quote, in this connexion:

> *Thy sovereign grace to all extends,*
> *Immense and unconfined;*
> *From age to age it never ends;*
> *It reaches all mankind.*[19]

---

[15] *Jcurnal*, Vol. II, p. 498.
[17] ibid., pp. 374-81.
[19] ibid., No. 77, verse 2.
[16] *Wesley's Works*, Vol. VII, p. 374.
[18] *Methodist Hymn-book*, No. 361, verse 4.

IV. FAITH IS THE CONDITION OF SALVATION

Here we come to the crux of the matter. Wesley's doctrine of Justification by Faith was closely woven into the texture of his religious thought and absolutely central in his theology. In the historical survey we noted that it was on this doctrine that the original breach with Law arose. We traced then the development of Wesley's spiritual struggle, as described by himself in the *Journal* for 24th May 1738. It is clear from that account that the evangelical conversion in 1738 was the culmination of a discontent that had been present in Wesley's mind for some years; for in or about the year 1730, long before the mission to Georgia, Wesley experimented with a kind of refinement of salvation by works. This took place as the result of conversations with 'a contemplative man'.

> Soon after, a contemplative man convinced me still more than I was convinced before, that outward works are nothing, being alone; and in several conversations instructed me how to pursue inward holiness, or a union of the soul with God. But even of his instructions (though I then received them as the words of God) I cannot but now observe (1) that he spoke so incautiously against trusting in outward works, that he discouraged me from doing them at all; (2) that he recommended (as it were, to supply what was wanting in them) *mental prayer*, and the like exercises, as the most effectual means of purifying the soul and uniting it with God. Now these were, in truth, as much my own works as visiting the sick or clothing the naked; and the union with God thus pursued was as really my own righteousness as any I had before pursued under another name.[20]

This experiment, however, completely failed to satisfy Wesley, who continues:

> In this refined way of trusting to my own works and my own righteousness (so zealously inculcated by the Mystic writers), I dragged on heavily, finding no comfort or help therein. . . .[21]

If, as some suggest,[22] the 'contemplative man' was Law himself, this incident has added significance for our comparison. But the identification is no more than an intelligent conjecture. Be that as it may, the incident serves to point us to the basic

[20] *Journal*, Vol. I, pp. 468-9 [21] ibid., pp. 469-70. [22] e.g. Curnock, ibid., p. 468, note 2.

doctrinal issue between the two men. For, as already outlined, the gravamen of Wesley's charge against Law in the first letter of 1738, reiterated even more emphatically in Wesley's second letter after Law's attempted evasion of the issue, lay in Law's failure to lead Wesley into a saving faith in Jesus Christ. After nearly twenty years, the same fundamental difference is Wesley's central point in the 1756 Letter.

One of Wesley's best expositions of Justification by Faith is in the sermon so entitled. In this sermon Wesley seeks to remove any wrong ideas of the nature of justification which may be in his hearers' minds. He is careful to distinguish between justification and sanctification. Justification

is not the being made actually just and righteous. This is *sanctification*; which is, indeed, in some degree, the immediate fruit of justification but, nevertheless, is a distinct gift of God, and of a totally different nature. The one implies, what God does for us through His Son; the other, what He works in us by His Spirit.[23]

This is important for our purpose, as Law held no such distinction between justification and sanctification. 'It is true,' comments Wesley in the Sermon 'On God's Vineyard',

a late very eminent author, in his strange *Treatise on Regeneration*, proceeds entirely on the supposition, that it [the New Birth] is the whole gradual progress of sanctification. No; it is only the threshold of sanctification, the first entrance upon it. And as, in the natural birth, a man is born at once, and then grows larger and stronger by degrees; so in the spiritual birth, a man is born at once, and then gradually increases in spiritual stature and strength. The new birth, therefore, is the first point of sanctification, which may increase more and more unto the perfect day.[24]

Nor, observed Wesley, is justification the 'clearing us from accusation', an opinion which he characterized as a 'far-fetched conceit'.[25] Least of all is it,

that God is deceived in those whom He justifies; that He thinks them to be what, in fact, they are not; that He accounts them to be otherwise than they are.[26]

[23] *Sermons*, Vol. I, p. 119.
[25] *Sermons*, Vol. I, p. 119.
[24] *Wesley's Works*, Vol. VII, p. 205.
[26] ibid., p. 120.

THE FUNDAMENTAL DOCTRINAL ISSUE   125

Wesley then states positively:

The plain scriptural notion of justification is pardon, the forgiveness of sins. It is that act of God the Father, whereby, for the sake of the propitiation made by the blood of His Son, He 'showeth forth His righteousness' (or mercy) 'by the remission of the sins that are past'.[27]

On faith as the condition of justification, Wesley writes:

But on what terms, then, is he justified, who is altogether *ungodly*, and till that time *worketh not?* On one alone, which is faith: he 'believeth in Him that justifieth the ungodly'. And 'he that believeth is not condemned'; yea, he is 'passed from death into life'.[28]

Faith, therefore, is the *necessary* condition of justification; yea, and the *only necessary* condition thereof.[29]

. . . it is the only thing without which no one is justified; the only thing that is immediately, indispensably, absolutely requisite in order to pardon. As, on the one hand, though a man should have everything else without faith, yet he cannot be justified; so, on the other, though he be supposed to want everything else, yet if he hath faith, he cannot but be justified.[30]

On the one relation of works to faith Wesley writes in the same sermon:

At what time soever a sinner thus believes . . . God . . . pardoneth and absolveth him who had in him, till then, no good thing. Repentance, indeed, God had given him before; but that repentance was neither more nor less than a deep sense of the want of all good, and the presence of all evil. And whatever good he hath, or doeth, from that hour, when he first believes in God through Christ, faith does not *find*, but *bring*. This is the fruit of faith. First the tree is good, and then the fruit is good also.[31]

Wesley's view of good works, rather slightly treated in this sermon, is clearly stated in *The Principles of a Methodist*:

Faith which brings not forth good works, is not a living faith, but a dead and devilish one. For even the devils believe that Christ was born of a virgin; that He wrought all kind of miracles, declaring Himself to be very God; that for our sakes He died and rose again, and ascended into heaven; and at the end of the world shall come again, to judge the quick and the dead. This the devils believe; and so they believe all that is written in the Old and New Testament: And yet still, for all this faith, they are

[27] ibid., pp. 120-1.   [28] ibid., p. 124.   [29] ibid., p. 126.   [30] ibid., p. 127.   [31] ibid., p. 125.

but devils; they remain still in their damnable estate, lacking the true Christian faith. The true Christian faith is, not only to believe the Holy Scriptures and the articles of our faith are true; but also, to have 'a sure trust and confidence to be saved from everlasting damnation by Christ', whereof doth follow a loving heart, to obey His commandments.[32]

Before concluding this section we should consider (what has already been mentioned in the previous chapter) Wesley's modification of his views in 1767. In the *Journal* for 1st December of that year, he records,

I was considering several points of importance. And thus much appeared clear as the day:

That a man may be saved who cannot express himself properly concerning Imputed Righteousness. Therefore, to do this is not necessary to salvation.

That a man may be saved who has not clear conceptions of it. (Yea, that never heard the phrase.) Therefore, clear conceptions of it are not necessary to salvation. Yea, it is not necessary to salvation to use the phrase at all.

That a pious churchman who has not clear conceptions even of Justification by Faith may be saved. Therefore, clear conceptions even of this are not necessary to salvation.

That a Mystic, who denies Justification by Faith (Mr. Law, for instance) may be saved. But, if so, what becomes of *articulus stantis vel cadentis ecclesiae*.[33] If so, is it not high time for us—'*Projicere ampullas et sesquipedalia verba*'; and to return to the plain word, 'He that feareth God, and worketh righteousness, is accepted with Him'?[34]

This was a great concession for Wesley to make, and it was seized upon by Mr. Hill in his *Review of All the Doctrines taught by Mr. John Wesley*, as an example of Wesley's inconsistency. Wesley, however, denies this in his *Remarks on Mr. Hill's 'Review'*:

It is certain here is a seeming contradiction; but it is not a real one. . . . Although Mr. Law denied justification by faith, he might trust in the merits of Christ. It is this, and this only, that I affirm, (whatever Luther does,) to be *articulus stantis vel cadentis ecclesiae*.[35]

---

[32] *Wesley's Works*, Vol. VIII, p. 363.
[33] Luther's description of the doctrine of Justification by Faith.
[34] *Journal*, Vol. V, pp. 243-4.
[35] *Wesley's Works*, Vol. X, p. 391.

THE FUNDAMENTAL DOCTRINAL ISSUE 127

That this modification is, as has been suggested earlier, an example of Wesley's breadth of Christian charity revealing an absence of anything approaching doctrinaire rigidity rather than any abandonment of his main doctrinal position, is clear from his letter in 1771 to the Countess of Huntingdon:

> ... I know your Ladyship would not 'servilely deny the truth'. I think neither would I; especially that great truth Justification by Faith, which Mr. Law indeed flatly denies (and yet Mr. Law was a child of God), but for which I have given up all my worldly hopes, my friends, my reputation—yea, for which I have so often hazarded my life, and by the grace of God will do again.[36]

V. FAITH IS CENTRED IN THE ATONING DEATH OF CHRIST

This proposition has been incidentally stated in the quotations already made from Wesley's writings and in the hymns cited. It is important, however, to make the point explicitly, as it is one great contrast between Wesley's outlook and that of Law. 'Justifying faith', writes Wesley,

> implies, not only a divine evidence or conviction that 'God was in Christ, reconciling the world unto Himself', but a sure trust and confidence that Christ died for *my* sins, that He loved *me*, and gave Himself for *me*.[37]

This direct relevance of the historic sacrifice on Calvary to the salvation of each individual sinner is an oft-recurring theme of Charles Wesley.

> *The God of love, to earth He came,*
> *That you might come to heaven;*
> *Believe, believe in Jesu's name,*
> *And all your sin's forgiven.*
>
> *Believe in Him that died for thee,*
> *And, sure as He hath died,*
> *Thy debt is paid, thy soul is free,*
> *And thou art justified.*[38]

Wesley's doctrine, as set forth above, is well summarized in *The Principles of a Methodist farther Explained*, written in 1746, of which summary we quote the first four propositions:

[36] *Letters*, Vol. V, p. 274.   [37] *Sermons*, Vol. I, p. 125.
[38] *Methodist Hymn-book* No. 372.

(1) Justification is the act of God, pardoning our sins, and receiving us again to His favour. This was free in Him, because undeserved by us; undeserved, because we had transgressed His law, and could not, nor even can now, perfectly fulfil it.

(2) We cannot, therefore, be justified by our own works; because this would be, to be justified by some merit of our own. Much less can we be justified by an external show of religion, or by any superstitious observances.

(3) The life and death of our Lord is the sole meritorious cause of this mercy, which must be firmly believed and trusted in by us. Our faith therefore in Him, though not more meritorious than any other of our actions, yet has a nearer relation to the promises of pardon through Him, and is the mean and instrument whereby we embrace and receive them.

(4) True faith must be lively and productive of good works, which are its proper fruits, the marks whereby it is known.[39]

When we turn from Wesley's exposition of the way of salvation to that of Law, our attention is immediately drawn to one aspect of the latter's outlook, which governed his whole approach to the question, and sharply distinguished it from that of Wesley. From the foregoing sketch of Wesley's doctrine it is clear that he was content with the account of the origin of the universe and of man, which is contained in canonical Scripture. He sought no further explanation of such matters, and speculations such as those of Boehme and Law he found both meaningless and obnoxious. He was entirely content to accept the Scriptural accounts and, with these as background, to apply the basic principles of evangelical Christianity to life as he found it.

Law, on the contrary, as a result of being engrossed in the philosophy of Boehme, regarded the Scriptural accounts as themselves posited against a remoter background, which afforded explanations of ulterior mysteries outside the scope of orthodox Christian theology. He followed Boehme along the labyrinthine paths of exploration into the timeless nature of God Himself. Such speculations, congenial enough to one living in detached seclusion at Kingscliffe, aloof from the practical problems of the masses of his fellows, were entirely foreign to Wesley, absorbed in the breathless excitement of his evangelical campaign.

[39] *Wesley's Works*, Vol. VIII, pp. 429-30.

It should be pointed out that Law's preoccupation with these concerns never affected his allegiance to the Church of England. There is an interesting parallel here to Wesley, who himself stoutly maintained his Anglican connexion, when for quite different reasons active opposition to his work might have caused one, whose roots were less deeply fixed, to renounce the church of his upbringing. Though Law moved from the rigidly High Church position of the Bangorian Letters, he remained a loyal Anglican in thought and practice, and was himself unconscious of any difficulty in reconciling his Behmenish beliefs with his position as an Anglican clergyman. Fresh evidence of this continued loyalty has recently come to light in a new work published in Germany.[40]

These philosophical speculations, however, though primarily concerned with pre-Scriptural events, did influence the approach of both Boehme and Law to the central truths of revealed religion. Wesley himself was quick to recognize this, when he alleged that Law's 'bad philosophy' had 'paved the way for bad divinity'.[41] We have already noticed this effect in the last chapter, in connexion with the Genesis teaching on creation and the fall of man, and we now proceed to examine Law's treatment of matters related to the atonement.

Behind all Law's theories on the way of salvation lies his cherished and tenaciously held belief in the essential unity of God, nature, and creature: '... as soon as we but begin to know', he writes in the *Appeal*,

> that the holy, triune Deity from eternity to eternity manifests itself in nature by the triune birth of fire, light, and spirit, and that all angels and men must have been created out of this nature; there is not a doctrine in Scripture concerning the creation, fall, and redemption of man, but becomes the most plainly intelligible, and all the mysteries of our redemption are proved and confirmed to us, by all that is visible and perceptible in all nature and creature.[42]

In the same work Law described the origin of evil as lying in the wrong choice made by creatures in the exercise of that self-motion with which they were necessarily endowed. God

---

[40] *Die Stufenfolge des Mystischen Erlebneisses bei William Law (1686-1761)*, by Konrad Minkner (Munich 1939), reviewed by Stephen Hobhouse, *Expository Times*, March 1941, pp. 237, 238.
[41] *Letters*, Vol. III, p. 343.   [42] *Law': Works*, Vol. VI, pp. 136-7.

could only bring any creature into existence by conferring on it 'the self-existent, self-generating, self-moving qualities of His own nature'. Hence every creature, being endowed with self-motion, must be capable of knowing right and wrong. God can therefore no more be held responsible for evil, than the sun for darkness.[43]

Also in the *Appeal* Law tells how the fall both of angels and men involved the breaking of the image of the Holy Trinity in the creature:

... in this consideration of God, as manifesting His Holy Trinity through nature and creature, lieth the solid and true understanding of all that is so variously said of God, both in the Old and New Testament with relation to mankind, both as to their creation, fall, and redemption. . . . All intelligent, holy beings were by God formed and created out of, and for the enjoyment of this kingdom of glory, and had fire, and light, and spirit, as the triune glory of their created being. . . . And thus they were creatures, subjects, and objects of the divine love; they came into the nearest, highest relation to God; they stood in, and partook of His own manifested nature, so that the outward glory and majesty of the triune God, was the very form, and beauty, and brightness of their own created nature. . . . Thus in this state, all angels and men came first out of the hands of God. But seeing light proceeds from fire by a birth, and the spirit from both, and seeing the will must be the leader of the birth, Lucifer and Adam could both do as they did, Lucifer could will strong might and power, to be greater than the light of God made him, and so he brought forth a birth of might and power, that was only mighty wrath and darkness, a fire of nature broken off from its light. Adam could will the knowledge of temporal nature, and so he lost the light and spirit of Heaven for the light and spirit of this world.[44]

The effect of this fall was fatal for Lucifer and the angels, but not for man, though pain and misery ensued for him.

This pain and misery, which is inseparable from the creature that is not in that state in which it ought to be, and in which it was created, is nothing else but the painful state of the creature for want of its own proper righteousness, as sickness is the painful state of the creature for want of its own proper health.[45]

The notable thing about this last pronouncement from the *Spirit of Love* is the entire absence of the slightest suggestion

---

[43] *Law's Works*, Vol. VI, p. 69.   [44] ibid., pp. 126-7.   [45] ibid., Vol. VIII, p. 78.

of punishment. This brings us to one of the main points of difference between the doctrinal systems of Wesley and Law, namely the latter's oft-repeated and strenuous denial of the possibility of wrath in God.

Describing in the *Spirit of Prayer* how Adam's fall and its consequences were the results of his own action, just as blindness follows the extinction of the eyes, Law proceeds:

... to charge his miserable state, as a punishment inflicted upon him by the severe wrath of an incensed God, is the same absurdity, as in the former supposed ... blindness.[46]

Not only so, but the nature of God Himself, maintains Law, excludes such a possibility.

For it is a glorious and joyful truth, (however suppressed in various systems of divinity) that from eternity to eternity, no spark of wrath ever was, or ever will be in the holy triune God.[47]

Years before, in the *Christian Regeneration*, Law had indignantly repudiated the doctrine of the wrath of God:

Some people have an idea or notion of the Christian Religion, as if God was thereby declared so full of wrath against fallen man, that nothing but the blood of His only begotten Son could satisfy His vengeance. ...

But these are miserable mistakers of the divine nature, and miserable reproachers of His great love, and goodness in the Christian dispensation.

For God is Love, yea, all Love, and so all Love, that nothing but Love can come from Him; and the Christian religion, is nothing else but an open, full manifestation of his universal Love towards all mankind.[48]

The wrath that needs removing resides not in God but in fallen man, declares Law.

There is no wrath that stands between God and us, but what is awakened in the dark fire of our own fallen nature; and to quench this wrath and not His own, God gave His only begotten Son to be made Man. God has no more wrath in Himself now, than He had before the creation, when He had only Himself to love. The precious blood of His Son was not poured out to pacify Himself (who in Himself had no nature towards man but love), but it was poured out, to quench the wrath, and fire of the fallen soul, and kindle in it a birth of light, and love.[49]

[46] ibid., Vol. VII, pp. 12, 13.
[48] ibid., Vol. V, p. 156.
[47] ibid., p. 14.
[49] ibid., pp. 156-7

This theme is developed in the *Spirit of Love*:

... the wrath, or resentment, that is to be pacified or atoned, cannot possibly be in the Deity itself.

For this wrath ... is, in its whole nature, nothing else but sin, or disorder in the creature. And when sin is extinguished in the creature, all the wrath that is between God and the creature is fully atoned. Search all the Bible, from one end to the other, and you will find, that the atonement of that which is called the divine wrath or justice, and the extinguishing of sin in the creature, are only different expressions for one and the same individual thing. And therefore, unless you will place sin in God, that wrath, that is to be atoned or pacified, cannot be placed in Him.[50]

That the removal of this wrath in man constitutes in Law's theology that universal need of salvation which, in Wesley's teaching, springs from original sin and universal guilt is clear from the following passage in the *Appeal*:

Neither reason nor Scripture will allow us to bring wrath into God Himself, as a temper of His mind, who is only infinite, unalterable, overflowing love, as unchangeable in love, as He is in power and goodness. The wrath that was awakened at the fall of man, that then seized upon him, as its captive, was only a plague, or evil, or curse that sin had brought forth in nature and creature: it was only the beginning of hell: it was such a wrath as God Himself pitied man's lying under it; it was such a wrath as God Himself furnished man with a power of overcoming and extinguishing, and therefore it was not a wrath that was according to the mind, will, and liking, or wisdom of God; and therefore it was not a wrath that was in God Himself, or which was exercised by His sovereign wisdom over His disobedient creatures: it was not such a wrath, as when sovereign princes are angry at offender , and will not cease from their resentment, until some political satisfaction, or valuable amends be made to their slighted authority. No, no; it was such a wrath as God Himself hated, as He hates sin and hell, a wrath that the God of all nature and creature so willed to be removed and extinguished, that seeing nothing less could do it, He sent His only begotten Son into the world, that all mankind might be saved and delivered from it.[51]

The contrast between this and the orthodox Catholic tradition is well drawn by Mr. Hobhouse:

To Wesley, as to Augustine, to Luther, to the Puritans and to the central tradition of the Catholic Church, forgiveness, atonement, meant primarily

[50] *Law's Works*, Vol. VIII, p. 70.   [51] ibid., Vol. VI, p. 140.

this removal of past guilt, including that of 'original sin'. To those who still move in this circle of ideas—guilt, righteous anger, retributive punishment, compensatory justice, sacrificial death, Law's teaching on the Atonement will probably seem unsatisfactory. For to him ... atonement is first and always at-one-ment, the recreating of the new sinless life in the soul and its reunion with God. Justification is swallowed up in Sanctification; past guilt, as distinct from present tendency to sin now victoriously overcome in Christ, is a harmful fiction that ought not to detain us.[52]

A clear statement of this is found in Law's *Collection of Letters*: 'What', he asks,

is God's forgiving sinful man? It is nothing else in its whole nature, but God's making him righteous again. There is no other forgiveness of sin, but being made free from it.[53]

How then, one may ask, does this God who is 'so all Love, that nothing but Love can come from Him'[54] seek to restore fallen man? Let Law himself make answer:

It may be proper to inquire, when, and how this great work is done in the soul?

The Mercy and infinite goodness of God, has chosen all mankind to salvation in Jesus Christ, before the foundation of the world. Now this eternal decree of God, took place upon the fall of Adam; and as he was admitted into the terms of Christian salvation immediately after his transgression, so all mankind, as being in his loins, were taken into the same covenant of grace, and what was then done to Adam, was done to him, as the common parent of mankind.

The bruiser of the serpent given to Adam, as his Saviour, was not a verbal promise of something only, that should come to pass in future ages to redeem him; ... but it was a redeeming power, which by the mercy of God, was treasured up in his fallen nature, which was to resist and overcome the wrath and death, and awakened nature of hell, that was in his soul; and from that time of God's accepting him to a salvation, through the seed of the woman, he was saved by the power of Christ within him, as really, as those that lived, and believed in Christ, after He had been incarnate. As nothing can save the last man, or become his righteousness, or redemption, but the divine nature of Jesus Christ, derived into his soul, so nothing else could be righteousness, redemption or salvation to the first man.

[52] *William Law: Selected Mystical Writings*, p. 299.
[53] *Law's Works*, Vol. IX, p. 144.
[54] ibid., Vol. V, p. 156.

All men therefore that ever were, or shall be descended from Adam, have Jesus Christ for their Saviour, as Adam had, they receive the promise made to him, and receive by that promise, that which he received by it, they have a seed of the woman, an incorruptible seed of life, springing up in the first essences of their life, which is to oppose and resist the seed of the serpent, or the diabolical nature that is in them also. And therefore no son of Adam is without a Saviour, or can be lost, or entirely overcome by the evil, that the fall has brought upon him, but by his own turning away from this Saviour within him, and giving himself up to the suggestions, and workings of the evil nature, that is in him.[55]

This conception of Christ as the second Adam undoing 'all the evil that the first Adam had done in human nature',[56] governs Law's thought of the work of Christ. In the *Spirit of Love*, for example, Law writes:

... there was an utter impossibility for the seed of Adam ever to come out of its fallen state, or ever have another, or better life, than they had from Adam, unless such a son of man could be brought into existence, as had the same relation to all mankind as Adam had, was as much in them all as Adam was, and had as full power, according to the nature of things, to give a heavenly life to all the seed in Adam's loins, as Adam had to bring them forth in earthly flesh and blood.[57]

This necessitated the whole process of our Lord's life and death. 'Therefore,' says Law in the *Appeal*, He

must enter into every state that belonged to this fallen nature, restoring in every state that which was lost, quickening that which was extinguished, and overcoming in every state that by which man was overcome.[58]

For this reason (and this reason only, be it noted) He must die:

... as eternal death was as certainly brought forth in our souls, as temporal death in our bodies, as this death was a state that belonged to fallen man, therefore our Lord was obliged to taste this dreadful death, to enter into the realities of it, that He might carry our nature victoriously through it. And as fallen man was to have entered into this eternal death at his giving up the ghost in this world, so the second Adam, as reversing all that the first had done, was to stand in this second death upon the Cross and die from it into that paradise out of which Adam the first died into this world.[59]

[55] *Law's Works*, Vol. V, pp. 163-4.
[56] ibid., Vol. VI, p. 145.
[57] ibid., Vol. VIII, p. 95.
[58] ibid., Vol. VI, p. 145.
[59] ibid., p. 145.

THE FUNDAMENTAL DOCTRINAL ISSUE 135

It follows that Law held every part of our Lord's life, death, resurrection, and ascension as having equal atoning efficacy. 'All these things', he writes in the *Appeal*,

> are so many equally essential parts of our Saviour's character, and He is the one atonement, the full satisfaction from sin, the Saviour and deliverer from the bondage, power, and effects of sin. And to ascribe our deliverance from sin, or the remission of our sins more to the life and actions, than to the death of Christ, or to His death more than to His resurrection and ascension, is directly contrary to the plain letter and tenor of the Scripture, which speaks of all these things as jointly qualifying our Lord to be the all-sufficient Redeemer of mankind.[60]

Similarly, in the *Collection of Letters*:

> The birth, the life, the death of Christ, though so different things, have but one and the same operation, and that operation is solely in man, to drive all evil out of his fallen nature, and delight the heart of God, that desires his salvation.[61]

This new birth of Christ in us is Law's whole conception of the atonement. As he remarks in the *Spirit of Love*:

> ... Christ is the atonement of our sins when by and from Him, living in us, we have victory over our sinful nature. ...
> The whole truth of the matter is plainly this, Christ given *for us*, is neither more nor less, than Christ given *into us*. And He is in no other sense, our full, perfect, and sufficient atonement, than as His nature and Spirit are born, and formed in us. ...[62]

Again, later in the same work he writes:

> All therefore that Christ does, as an atonement for sin, or as a satisfaction to righteousness, is all done in, and to, and for man, and has no other operation, but that of renewing the fallen nature of man, and raising it up into its first state of original righteousness.[63]

These extracts serve to bring out the irreconcilable difference between Law's entirely subjective doctrine and the objective theory of Catholic orthodoxy to which Wesley subscribed. Instead of a divine initiative expressing itself in an historical revelation, to which sinful man responds, the Atonement is represented as originating within man himself.

[60] ibid., p. 147.
[62] ibid., Vol. VIII, p. 74.
[61] ibid., Vol. IX, p. 140.
[63] ibid., p. 78.

This is even more definitely stated in the *Spirit of Prayer* where the sinner is urged to seek the union of the soul with God within his own heart.

Poor sinner! consider the treasure thou hast within thee, the Saviour of the world, the Eternal Word of God lies hid in thee, as a spark of the Divine Nature, which is to overcome sin and death, and hell within thee and generate the life of heaven again in thy soul. Turn to thy heart, and thy heart will find its Saviour, its God within itself. Thou seest, hearest, and feelest nothing of God, because thou seekest for Him abroad with thy outward eyes, thou seekest for Him in books, in controversies, in the Church and outward exercises, but there thou wilt not find Him, till thou hast first found Him in thy heart. Seek for Him in thy heart, and thou wilt never seek in vain, for there He dwells, there is the seat of His light and Holy Spirit.

For this turning to the light and Spirit of God within thee, is thy only true turning unto God, there is no other way of finding Him, but in that place where He dwelleth in thee. For though God be everywhere present, yet He is only present to thee in the deepest, and most central part of thy soul.[64]

In this scheme of things, faith does indeed play a part, but it is not, as in Wesley, called forth by and centred in the saving death of Christ on the Cross. It is rather an inward hunger, which finds its satisfaction within men's own nature. For example, in the *Christian Regeneration*, Law writes:

... when the seed of the new birth, called the inward man, has faith awakened in it, its faith is not a notion, but a real, strong, essential hunger, an attracting, or magnetic desire of Christ, which as it proceeds from a seed of the divine nature in us, so it attracts and unites with its like, it lays hold on Christ, puts on the divine nature, and in a living and real manner, grows powerful over all sins, and effectually works out our salvation.[65]

Indeed, it may be fairly claimed that this whole mystical outlook, which identifies Christ with the divine life of man, inevitably tends to depreciate the importance of the historical Incarnation, as is clearly revealed by the following passage in the *Spirit of Prayer*:

When therefore the first spark of a desire after God arises in thy soul, cherish it with all thy care, give all thy heart into it, it is nothing less

[64] *Law's Works*, Vol. VII, p. 28.   [65] ibid., Vol. V, p. 168.

than a touch of the divine loadstone, that is to draw thee out of the vanity of time into the riches of eternity. Get up therefore and follow it as gladly, as the wise men of the east followed the star from Heaven that appeared to them. It will do for thee, as the star did for them, it will lead thee to the birth of Jesus, not in a stable at Bethlehem in Judea, but to the birth of Jesus in the dark centre of thy own fallen soul.[66]

Similarly in the *Spirit of Love*, concerning the historical death of Christ:

The Christ of God was not then first crucified when the Jews brought Him to the cross; but Adam and Eve were His first real murderers; for the death which happened to them, in the day that they did eat of the earthly tree, was the death of the Christ of God, or the divine life in their souls.[67]

Finally, it must be observed that Law's theory of the Atonement led him to accept the doctrine of universal redemption. Wesley, as we have seen, proclaimed a universal gospel, but it was a universalism of God's offer and man's potential response. This was Law's original belief, as revealed, for example, in the *Serious Call*:

... when you die, this book will be laid open before men and angels, and according as your actions are there found, you will either be received to the happiness of those holy men who have died before you, or be turned away amongst wicked spirits, that are never to see God any more.[68]

So in his earlier treatises Law, like Wesley, taught a conditional salvation, but, as his outlook developed, his belief in the limitless love of God led him to an absolutely universalist position. In his last work, the *Address to the Clergy*, Law writes:

... all kinds of hellish wrath, hardened malice, fiery pride, selfish wills, tormenting envy, and earthly passions, which kept men under the power of Satan, must have their fulness of death, and fulness of a new life, from that all-powerful, all-purifying blood of the Lamb, which will never cease washing red into white, till the earth is washed into the crystal purity of that glassy sea, which is before the throne of God, and all the sons of Adam clothed in such white, as fits them for their several mansions in their heavenly Father's house.[69]

[66] ibid., Vol. VII, p. 47.
[67] ibid., Vol. VIII, p. 7.
[68] ibid., Vol. IV, p. 187.
[69] ibid., Vol. IX, p. 88.

This attitude of Law is the subject of a letter from his friend Langcake to Henry Brooke, in 1790, preserved for us by Christopher Walton. This letter contains the substance of remarks made by Law to Langcake, just before Law died. Langcake writes:

> With respect to this doctrine of universal redemption, I very well remember Mr. Law's speaking of it, upon my making him the last visit at Easter 1761, a few days before his death, for he died upon the 9th of April, and Easter Day was on the 22nd of March that year. He said that [it would seem as if] not only the whole human race, but even the fallen angels, would all be delivered out of misery, but not until the last judgement day. He said there would be a chasm in the creation without their being taken into happiness. But that that could not be, until they saw the whole creation made happy before them. When they saw this, and felt the eternal fire fully operating upon them, it would produce the blessed effect of [quickening or] awakening that [original root of] goodness which lay dormant in them. For though that goodness might be shut up in a sevenfold deeper or stronger compaction than fire is in a flint, yet as it was shut up [possibly not extinct and its essence destroyed, for what can die in eternity?], and preserved in them, it would come forth, and so they also would be made happy, to the full display of God's [wonderful wisdom and enravishing] love and goodness to all His creatures.[70]

As God's love manifestly does not triumph in all men in this life, Law inevitably found himself committed to a belief in purgatory. This finds expression in various of his writings. For example in the *Spirit of Love*:

> All the whole fallen creation, stand it never so long, must groan and travail in pain, this must be its purgatory, till every contrariety to the divine will, is entirely taken from every creature.[71]

Also, in the second part of the same work,

> ... these virtues are the only wedding garment; they are the lamps and vessels well furnished with oil.
>
> There is nothing that will do in the stead of them; they must have their own full and perfect work in you, if not before, yet certainly after the death of the body, or the soul can never be delivered from its fallen wrathful state.[72]

---

[70] *Notes and Materials*, p. 601. (The brackets in this quotation are Walton's.)
[71] *Law's Works*, Vol. VIII, p. 8.   [72] ibid., p. 131.

Again in a letter to Mr. T. L.: 'As for the purification of all human nature, either in this world, or some after ages, I fully believe it.'[73] Here, too, is yet another contrast with Wesley, who, as Dr. Rattenbury puts it in an illuminating phrase, 'believed in an ante-mortem purgatory but not in a post-mortem'.[74]

So we conclude this chapter, in which the respective doctrinal positions of Law and Wesley on the central truths of the Christian religion have been placed side by side. We are now in a position to consider Wesley's reaction to Law's views as those views are attacked in the 1756 Letter, which deals both with these questions and with other points of difference which sprang from their disagreement on the fundamental issue of the Atonement.

[73] ibid., Vol. IX, p. 191.   [74] *The Conversion of the Wesleys*, p. 196.

CHAPTER NINE

The 1756 Letter

IN THE LIGHT of the foregoing contrasted summaries of the doctrinal positions of Law and Wesley, we now proceed to review the specific charges which Wesley brings against Law in the latter part of the 1756 Letter.

I. THE OMNIPOTENCE OF GOD[1]

The subject matter of this section is more akin to that of the 'philosophic' questions with which Wesley dealt in the first part of the indictment than to the theological issues which subsequently arose. Moreover Wesley adopts the same method, as already described in the chapter on Mysticism, of quoting selected extracts from Law's writings and demolishing them either by rhetorical questions or by categorical denials.

No detailed analysis of this process would be possible without including here practically the whole section as it stands. Suffice it to say that the burden of Wesley's complaint against Law is that many things in the *Spirit of Prayer* and the *Spirit of Love* set bounds to God's omnipotence and 'abridge God of His power, after creation as well as before it'.

This is a very clear and interesting example of the way in which Law's acceptance of a system which had its roots in prescriptural and extra-scriptural theories of the origins of men and things, led him into consequent statements on matters within the scope of scriptural teaching. Such statements, innocuous enough and indeed logically necessary in his eyes, seemed almost blasphemous to Wesley, who was both contented with and insistent upon the scriptural account of such origins.

As an example, typical alike of Law's ideas and Wesley's rejoinders, we may cite the rather longer extract which Wesley reproduces (though not with complete accuracy) and refutes at the conclusion of the section.

[1] *Letters*, Vol. III, pp. 343-5.

Law's words are:

This is an axiom that cannot be shaken, Nothing can rise higher than its first created nature; and therefore an angel at last must have been an angel at first. Do you think it possible for an ox to be changed into a rational philosopher? Yet this is as possible as for one who has only by creation the life of this world to be changed into an angel of Heaven. The life of this world can reach no farther than this world; no omnipotence of God can carry it farther; therefore, if man is to be an angel at last, he must have been created an angel; because no creature can possibly have any other life or higher degree of life than that which his creation brought forth in him (*Spirit of Prayer*, Part II, p. 81).

Wesley's reply is:

I have quoted this passage at some length that the sense of it may appear beyond dispute. But what divinity! and what reasoning to support it! Can God raise nothing higher than its first created state? Is it not possible for Him to change an ox or a stone into a rational philosopher or a child of Abraham? To change a man or a worm into an angel of heaven? Poor omnipotence which cannot do this! Whether He will or no is another question. But if He cannot do it, how can He be said to do 'whatsoever pleases Him in heaven, and in earth, and in the sea, and in all deep places'? Thus does your attachment to a miserable philosophy lead you to deny the almighty power of God.

II. THE JUSTICE OF GOD[2]

Law, Wesley maintains, abridges the justice of God no less than His power. Wesley condemns this at greater length as being 'the one main hinge on which the controversy between Christianity and Deism turns'. To convert Deists by conceding this point, with the doctrine of Justification which is built on it, would be like converting Jews by allowing them the Messiah is not yet come, and would amount to establishing Deism while pretending to overturn it.

Wesley is clearly torn between his burning indignation against what he deems Law's false doctrine, and his reluctance to appear lacking in courtesy and respect to his former teacher. He would like

to forget who speaks, and simply consider what is spoken. The person I greatly reverence and love: the doctrine I utterly abhor, as I apprehend it to be totally subversive of the very essence of Christianity.

[2] ibid., pp. 345-51.

Wesley sees a cleavage between God's declaration that He will 'render to every man according to his works, whether they be good or evil', and Law's pronouncement in the *Spirit of Love*, 'there is no righteous wrath or vindictive justice in God', with its corollary that God never punishes. He, too, would like to prophesy these smooth things, but the Bible is an insuperable obstacle. He argues that to deny God's anger is to deny His justice, since anger is the passion which corresponds to the disposition of justice.

Wesley then sets forth Law's arguments under thirteen heads, culled from the *Spirit of Prayer* and the *Spirit of Love*, to which he appends characteristic comments of his own. These quotations, which represent Law's position, as stated in the last chapter, are well chosen and in no instance unfairly wrested from their context. One example will serve as illustration. Law had written: 'To say God ever punished any creature out of wrath is as absurd as to say, He began the creation out of wrath'; to which Wesley rejoins: 'I conceive not. It is not as absurd to say "God is angry at the guilty" as to say "God is angry at the innocent". Now, it is certain, when God began the creation of man, no guilty men were in being.'

Next, Wesley deals with Law's attempt to reconcile his position with the frequent references in Scripture to God's wrath, anger, etc. This attempt consisted largely of an explanation that, as everything ultimately owes its existence to God, there is a sense in which wrath, which resides in the creatures, can properly be termed God's wrath. Wesley quotes Law, for an example:

Devils are His as well as holy angels. Therefore all the wrath and rage of the one must be as truly His wrath and rage burning in them as the joy of the others is His joy.

'So it seems', commented Wesley,

the wrath of God in Scripture means no more or less than the wrath of the devil! However, this argument will not prove it. The joy of saints (not of angels, that I remember) is styled the joy of their Lord, because He prepared it for them and bestows it on them. Does He prepare and bestow the rage of devils upon them?

Law's denial of wrath led to a denial of punishment.

To say Adam's miserable state was a punishment inflicted upon him by God is an utter absurdity. His sin had not the least punishment of any kind inflicted upon it by God.

Wesley quotes freely in reply, especially Genesis 3, and asks:

Can any man read this and affirm, 'God did not inflict the least punishment of any kind either on Eve or Adam or the serpent'? With what eyes or understanding, then, must he read!

The final point seized on by Wesley is Law's statement on the Atonement, in relation to God's wrath.

The doctrine of Atonement made by Christ is the strongest demonstration that the wrath to be atoned cannot be in God.

'Who talks', demands Wesley,

of 'wrath to be atoned'? 'The wrath to be atoned' is neither sense nor English, though it is a solecism you perpetually run into: ... that the sin to be atoned cannot be in God we will allow; but it does not affect the question.

Wesley summarizes Law's teaching under the following three propositions.

(1) There is no vindictive, avenging, or punitive justice in God.
(2) There is no wrath or anger in God.
(3) God inflicts no punishment on any creature, neither in this world nor that to come.

Against these propositions Wesley marshals a formidable array of texts, forty-two in all, attributing to God justice, wrath, and the intention to punish, and then contents himself with the bare comment: 'Now, which am I to believe? God or man?'

This concluding question, so obviously decisive in Wesley's own judgement, furnishes the clue to the underlying cause of the difference between the two men on this issue. Law's teaching on the wrath of God was a direct consequence of his adherence to Boehme's philosophical system, and his interpretation of Scripture in harmony with that system was to him natural and indeed inevitable. Whereas for Wesley the plain words of Scripture carried an objective authority from which there could be no appeal. This was a clash concerning not merely conclusions, but premises, and there was no possibility of accommodation between the two ways of approach.

III. JUSTIFICATION[3]

This section reveals the fundamental difference between the theology of the two men. Law rejected the substitutionary theory of the Atonement, and propounded in its place what resembles in this respect the theory termed in modern parlance the 'moral influence' theory,[4] posited against the background of his mystical presuppositions.

Wesley opens his onslaught with a frankness which would have been objectionable in many writers but which was native to Wesley and therefore void of offence. He declares that Law seemed not to have the least conception of the matter, not even to know the meaning of the term 'Justification'. He then states Law's doctrine under what he calls 'seven peremptory assertions'.

(1) Salvation, which all divines agree includes both justification and sanctification, is nothing else but to be made like Christ (*Spirit of Prayer*, Part I, p. 53).

(2) Regeneration is the whole of man's salvation (Part II, p. 37).

(3) Redemption is nothing else but the life of God in the soul (Part I, p. 79).

(4) The one only work of Christ as your Redeemer is to raise into life the smothered spark of heaven in you (*Spirit of Love*, Part II, p. 45).

(5) He is our atonement and reconciliation with God, because by Him we are set again in our first state of holiness (Part I, p. 10).

(6) The atonement of the divine wrath or justice . . . and the extinguishing of sin in the creature are only different expressions of the same thing (Part II, p. 86).

(7) All that Christ does as an atonement has no other operation but that of renewing the fallen nature of man.

Wesley is content to comment on these assertions: 'Till they are fully proved, I cannot give up my Bible.'

Wesley then selects for specific criticism Law's passage

[3] *Letters*, Vol. III, pp. 351-7.
[4] *An Outline of Christian Theology*, W. N. Clarke, p. 320.

from the *Spirit of Love* where the latter inveighs against the orthodox explanation of God's relations with man under the analogy of 'debtor and creditor'.

The satisfaction of Christ is represented in all our systems of divinity as a satisfaction made to God, and the sufferings and death of Christ as that which could only avail with God to have mercy on man. Nay, what is still worse if possible, the ground and nature and efficacy of this great transaction between God and man is often explained by debtor and creditor; man as having contracted a debt with God which he could not pay, and God as having a right to insist upon the payment of it.

There is no wrath in God, no fictitious atonement, no folly of debtor and creditor.

'Folly of debtor and creditor!' exclaims Wesley. 'Surely I would not have spoken thus, unless I had been above the Son of God.'

Wesley quotes the petition in the Lord's Prayer, 'Forgive us our debts, as we forgive our debtors' (Matthew 6_{12}) and also, at length, the parable of the unmerciful servant (Matthew 18_{23-35}) as Scriptural authority for the analogy, and asks, 'Upon whom, then, lights the imputation of "folly", and "what is still worse"?' The intensity and depth of Wesley's feelings on this matter are denoted by the only comment he permits himself to make: 'Lord, lay not this sin to their charge! Forgive them; for they know not what they do.'

The matter, however, was not allowed to rest there, for Law makes it the subject of one of his published letters, dated 18th July 1757, and entitled *In answer to a scruple*. The whole letter is a restatement of Law's doctrine of the Atonement, in terms with which we are now familiar, with particular reference to the question of 'debtor and creditor'. In the course of it Law remarks:

I said 'Folly of Debtor and Creditor', because Christ's overcoming man's damnable death, by His victorious passage through it, has nothing in it that has any likeness to the transaction of a debtor paying his creditor; nothing was done in it by way of payment of a debt, any more than Christ paid a debt for Lazarus, when he raised him from the dead, or paid a debt for the man born blind, whom he helped to seeing eyes. For the good that is done us by the death of Christ is a good that relates solely to ourselves.[5]

[5] *Law's Works*, Vol. IX, pp. 142-3.

Law proceeds to challenge Wesley's citation of the two Scripture passages.

> You appeal to a parable of our Lord's, which has no more relation to the nature and efficacy of Christ's death, than the parable of the 'tares of the field'. . . .
>
> Read the whole parable, and you will be forced to see, that nothing else is intended to be taught by it, but that one conclusion: . . . 'So likewise shall my heavenly Father do unto you, if ye from your hearts forgive not everyone his brother their trespasses.'[6]

Indeed, Law urges, the parable teaches the very opposite of what is implied by 'debtor and creditor'. Instead of an authority of God which must have full satisfaction paid to it, it reveals a King frankly forgiving and not requiring any payment at all from the debtor or anyone else on his behalf. As for the petition from the Lord's Prayer,

> if God requires us to expect, and pray for the forgiveness of our debts, it is badly concluded from thence, that therefore full payment of them must be made.

So Law claims, in this letter, which is obviously aimed at Wesley, though he is not mentioned, that both the petition and the parable teach frank forgiveness and are incompatible with the doctrine of an infinite satisfaction, necessary to be made.[7]

Reverting to the 1756 Letter, Wesley's next question is, 'If', as Law suggests, 'the Son of God did not die to atone for our sins, what did He die for?' Wesley gives Law's answer to this in four statements, extracted from the *Spirit of Prayer*, adding to each statement his own rejoinder.

'(1) To extinguish our own hell within us (Law).'

Nay (says Wesley), the Scripture represents this not as the first but the second end of His death.

'(2) To show that He was above the world, death, hell, and Satan' (Law).

Where (says Wesley) is it written that He died for this end? Could He not have done this without dying at all?

'(3) His death was the 'only possible way of overcoming all the evil that was in fallen man' (Law).

[6] *Law's Works*, Vol. IX p. 143. [7] ibid.

This is true (acknowledges Wesley), supposing He atoned for our sins. But if this supposition be not made, His death was not the only possible way whereby the Almighty could have overcome all things.

'(4) Through this He got power to give the same victory to all His brethren of the human race' (Law).

(Wesley asks): Had He not this power before? Otherwise, how was He then ὁ ὤν. 'He that is', 'God over all, blessed for ever'?

So Wesley makes these four propositions the occasions of reasserting his own viewpoint, especially regarding the Omnipotence of God, the Divinity of Christ and the atonement wrought by His death. Wesley then with that naïve anxiety for Law's true welfare, that also characterized his first 1738 Letter, appends a long account of Justification written by 'a woman of the last century'; this woman was Anna Maria Van Schurman, a Quakeress, and the extract was from *Eukleria*, Part II.[8] We can only guess at the reasons which prompted Wesley to take this course, but it is significant that the woman was a Quakeress, and therefore might be calculated to impress Law, whose position at this stage was very near to that of the Quakers in some respects. Schurman's account is a comprehensive statement of the forensic theory of the Atonement, which would please Wesley both in its general form and by the frequent interspersion of passages of Scripture to drive home the argument. As we have already set forth Wesley's own doctrine, which is in complete harmony with this account, we may content ourselves by a very brief summary of the five divisions under which Schurman's account is arranged;

(1) Christ has acquired for us a right to eternal life by His satisfaction and merits alone.

(2) The surest way to the imitation of Christ is by faith in Christ crucified. This might be expected to appeal strongly to one who, like Law, believed so strongly in à Kempis.

(3) The origin and cause of our redemption must be sought in the divine initiative of God the Father who in His ineffable love willed to redeem us by the blood of His own Son. Many passages of Scripture are quoted in support of this, but especially Isaiah 53.

---

[8] *Letters*, Vol. III, pp. 353 et sqq.; *Journal*, Vol. I, p. 453.

(4) Consequently, Christ was not only a pattern, but first and foremost the surety of the new covenant—a sacrifice and a victim for the sins of His people.

(5) The substitution of the Messiah in the place of His people, to which the whole teaching of the Old Testament points, is confirmed by St. Paul (Galations 3_{13}), and St. Peter (1 Peter 2_{24}); by this He atones for the sins of His people and restores them to the favour of God.

Wesley concludes this crucial section of his attack on Law's doctrines:

> I have dwelt the longer on this head because of its inexpressible moment. For whether or no the doctrine of Justification by Faith be, as all Protestants thought at the time of the Reformation, *Articulus stantis vel cadentis Ecclesiae*, 'a doctrine without which there can be no Christian Church', most certainly there can be none where the whole notion of justification is ridiculed and exploded, unless it be such a church as includes, according to your account, every child of man, of which, consequently, Turks, Deists, and Pagans are as real members as the most pious Christian under the sun. . . .

IV. THE NEW BIRTH[9]

The fact that everyone that is justified is born of God leads Wesley to consider next Law's doctrine of the New Birth.

Here Wesley reverts to the practice of citing and contradicting various statements made by Law in the *Spirit of Prayer*. These successive statements and repartees deal with Law's theory of the two Adams, and the restoration of the divine life in man, with which we are familiar. An interesting feature of this section is the introduction of passages relating to the Sacraments of Baptism and the Lord's Supper; these serve to emphasize Wesley's orthodox beliefs in the Sacraments, and to suggest that Law's theories involve him inevitably in strange sacramental beliefs.

To Law's remark that only the Son of God could redeem us, because He alone could bring to life the celestial spirit and body which had died in Adam, Wesley protests that nothing of the sort was true. Rather He alone could redeem us because He alone, 'by that one oblation of Himself once offered',

[9] *Journal*, Vol. I, pp. 357-61.

could make 'a sufficient sacrifice and satisfaction for the sins of the whole world'.

Wesley then transfers the dialogue to the sphere of the other Sacrament. Law had maintained that a man must ' "be born again of the Spirit", because Adam's heavenly spirit was lost'. 'Nay,' replies Wesley, 'but because Adam had lost the inward image of God wherein he was created', and which only the Spirit of God could renew.

Law had interpreted being 'born of water' in relation to the 'heavenly materiality' of the mystical theory, which is called water, but Wesley interjects:

Vain philosophy! The plain meaning of the expression, 'Except a man be born of water', is neither more nor less than this, 'Except he be baptized'.

And that is necessary because God appointed it.

Turning again to the Lord's Supper, Wesley characterizes as unbiblical Law's suggestion that this is made necessary by the need of regaining our 'first heavenly body', and says it is necessary in order to 'strengthen and refresh our souls, as our bodies are by the bread and wine'.

To Law's doctrine that redemption is only the regaining our first angelic spirit and body, Wesley retorts: 'What an account is here of Christian redemption!' Law's other definition of redemption as 'nothing else but the life of God in the soul' had at any rate included an essential part, but this is 'no part at all; nothing else but a whim, a madman's dream, a chimera, a mere non-entity'.

Even Law himself knows better than that, says Wesley, quoting a passage concerning the restoration of the image of God. Law's confused and dark teaching, however, is not at all strange in view of his lack of conception of that 'faith whereby we are born again'. This affords Wesley another opportunity of stressing once more the nature of faith and insisting on the contrast between faith, which arises in the response to a divine initiative and that pseudo-faith which Law describes as 'the desire of turning to God'. Wesley employs here his favourite description of faith (which he had also used in the celebrated Sermon on Salvation by Faith, quoted in Chapter 8, *supra*). Faith is an ἔλεγχος, an 'evidence' or 'conviction' (which is totally different from a desire) 'of things not seen'. . . . of this in particular, that the Son of God hath loved me and given Himself for me. Whosoever hath this faith is born of God. Whosoever thus believeth is saved. . . .

Wesley, from his own accumulated experience of dealing with converted sinners, also challenges Law's description of the kindling of faith in the soul, especially the assertion that 'the first prayer of an awakening sinner is all humility'. 'On the contrary,' declares Wesley,

a sinner newly awakened has always more or less confidence in himself, in what he is, or has, or does, and will do; which is not humility but downright pride.

The letter thus passes to a description of that fervour of devotion which Wesley equates with the 'love of God shed abroad in the heart'. Law had written:

Then its prayer changes again, and continually stands in fullness of faith, in purity of love, in absolute resignation to do and be what and how his Beloved pleaseth. This is the last state of the spirit of prayer, and is our highest union with God in this life.

Wesley agrees, but challenges other statements of Law which appear inconsistent with this. For example: 'Fervour is good, and ought to be loved; but distress and coldness are better. It brings the soul nearer to God than the fervour did.' But how, asks Wesley, can it bring it to a union higher than 'the higher union with God'? Wesley will have none of this doctrine which he regards as 'inconsistent with that of St. Paul', and 'productive of the most fatal consequences'. Paul taught that the Kingdom of God in the soul is 'righteousness, and peace, and joy in the Holy Ghost'. Peace and joy are the divine means of preserving and increasing righteousness; accordingly distress and coldness are not better than fervent love and joy. To teach that it is better and more profitable for the soul to lose than to keep its sense of God's love, is to obstruct and destroy God's work in the heart. Indeed their loss is an indication that a man has grieved the Spirit of God. It behoves such to 'examine themselves, search out their spirit, cry vehemently to God, and not cease till He restores the light of His countenance'.

This inconsistency on Law's part, so unusual in him, is not confined to the passages in the *Spirit of Prayer* Wesley is now criticizing. Years before, in the *Christian Regeneration*, Law had viewed with disfavour certain accompaniments of the evangelical revival, especially the absolute assurance of salvation, and the emphasis on sudden conversion. He deplores the putting of such questions to others as:

Do you know and feel that all your sins are forgiven you? Do you know when and where, or at what time and in what place, you received this forgiveness? Do you know when and where you ceased to be one of those sinners called to repentance? ... Have you an absolute assurance of your salvation, and that you cannot possibly fall from your state of grace?[10]

Law suggests that this tends to make

this faith in the blood of Christ defective, and insufficient to my salvation, till a self-satisfaction, an own-pleasure, an own-taste, are joined with it. ... Is there not likely to be a more hurtful self-seeking, a more hurtful self-confidence, a more hurtful self-trust, a more dangerous self-deceit, in making faith to depend upon these inward workings and feelings, than in making it depend on outward good works of our own?[11]

These inward blessings of the spiritual life are

so many spurs, motives, and incitements to live wholly unto God; yet they may instead of that, fill us with self-satisfaction and self-esteem, and prompt us to despise others that want them. ...[12]

... these inward delights and enjoyments ... are not holiness, they are not piety, they are not perfection, but they are God's gracious allurements, and calls to seek after holiness and spiritual perfection. They are not to be sought for, for their own sakes; they are not to be prayed for, but with such a perfect indifference and resignation, as we must pray for any earthly blessings.[13]

Similarly, on sudden conversion Law writes:

It may freely be granted, that conversion to God is often very sudden and instantaneous, unexpectedly raised from variety of occasions. ... But then it is to be observed, that this suddenness of change, or flash

[10] *Law's Works*, Vol. V, p. 173.　　[11] ibid., p. 174.
[12] ibid., p. 177.　　[13] ibid., p. 178.

of conviction, is by no means of the essence of true conversion, and is no more to be demanded in ourselves, or others, than such a light from Heaven, as shone round St. Paul, and cast him to the ground.[14]

Still less, Law insists, is sudden conversion to be expected in others or to be regarded as evidence of our high state of a new birth in Christ. Then follows a passage where Law's insistence on regeneration as a process is most clearly contrasted with Wesley's teaching of justification as a single act to be followed by sanctification.

> Regeneration, or the renewal of our first birth and state, is something entirely distinct, from this first sudden conversion, or call to repentance; ... it is not a thing done in an instant, but is a certain process, a gradual release from our captivity and disorder, consisting of several stages and degrees, both of death and life, which the soul must go through, before it can have thoroughly put off the old man. . . .[15]

How are we to reconcile this hesitancy of Law to grant the validity of the initial evangelical assurance of forgiveness and subsequent inward experience, and his emphasis on the advantages of coldness over fervour, with his own stress on the inward joys which accompany the spirit of prayer?

Two factors probably contribute to the inconsistency. Firstly, his own temperament. He describes himself in 1739 in a letter to W. Walker, as a 'stranger to . . . divine illumination',[16] and secondly, his reluctance to be in any way associated with that 'enthusiasm' of which the Methodists were accused. As early as 1739, when Charles Wesley took John Bray to visit Law, the latter

> resolved all his (Bray's) feelings into fits or natural affections, and advised him to take no notice of his comforts, which he had better be without than with.[17]

Yet as a mystic, Law could not but describe that sense of God, which the true spirit of prayer produced. He seems to have been committed to an inconsistency, from which he never freed himself.

[14] *Law's Works*, Vol. V, p. 179.   [15] ibid., p. 180.
[16] *Remains of John Byrom*, Vol. I, Part II, p. 559.
[17] *Journal of Charles Wesley*, Vol. I, p. 159.

V. CHRIST IN EVERY MAN[18]

This doctrine, which follows from Law's teaching on the 'New Birth', provides an easy target for Wesley's thrusts. As the doctrine of the profitableness of coldness over fervour was a comfort to those who were sliding back, this doctrine of Christ in every man, Wesley asserts, is a comfort to those who never believed at all. It extends the bounds of the Catholic Church to include Jews, Mahometans, Deists, and heathens. Answering Law's theory that God spoke Christ into Adam after his transgression, Wesley protests that the Bible never mentioned the fact. The whole contention lacks the slightest proof. Paul ascribes the blessing of the indwelling Christ to believers only, and also wrote: 'If any man hath not the Spirit of Christ, he is none of His.' Summing up, Wesley writes:

> There can hardly be any doctrine under heaven more agreeable to flesh and blood; nor any which more directly tends to prevent the very dawn of conviction, or at least to hinder its deepening in the soul and coming to a sound issue. None more naturally tends to keep men asleep in sin and to lull asleep those who begin to be awakened. Only persuade one of this, 'Christ is already in thy heart; thou hast now the inspiration of His Spirit; all the peace and joy of God are within thee—yea, all the holy nature, tempers, and Spirit of Christ'; and you need do no more: the siren-song quiets all his sorrow and fear. As soon as you have sewed this pillow to his soul, he sinks back into the sleep of death.

Nowhere is the distinction between the mystical and evangelical approaches to the Atonement revealed in sharper contrast.

VI. STILLNESS AND THE MEANS OF GRACE[19]

Law's doctrine of Christ in every man led logically to the advocacy of quietism and consequent neglect of the Scriptures and the outward ordinances of the Church. Wesley regarded this as sheer disobedience to God, and assails it in this next section of his letter. Law advised as a first step 'to turn wholly from yourself and to give up yourself wholly unto God'. Wesley retorts 'from the experience of a thousand souls, as

---

[18] *Letters*, Vol. III, pp. 361-4.   [19] ibid., pp. 364-8.

well as from Scripture and the very reason of the thing', that many desire this but none can attain it without first having saving faith, which alone makes possible this and the acquisition of the other virtues Law enjoins. Law's culture of stillness is rejected by Wesley with equal firmness.

I read nothing like it in the oracles of God. I cannot find one word there of 'refraining from all conversation, from writing and reading, for a month'.

'Stop all self-activity (urged Law), be retired, silent, passive, and humbly attentive to the inward light.' 'Open thy heart to all its impressions, wholly stopping the workings of thy own reason and judgement.'

I find no such advice in the word of God (counters Wesley). And I fear they who stop the workings of their reason lie the more open to the workings of their imagination.

Wesley deals next with the deplorable consequences which, in his judgement, ensue from this mistaken quietism. First of all, it leads to the disregard of learning from other men and from books. ' "Seek", say you, "for help no other way, neither from men, nor books; but wholly leave yourself to God." ' Law contrasted two ways of attaining goodness: 'one by books or the ministry of men, the other by an inward birth. The former is only in order to the latter.' Wesley allows that the externals of religion are only a means to the soul's inward renewal, but strongly asserts that the two should not be set asunder. Inward grace is received through the outward means appointed by God.

More serious still he regards the fact that Law appeared to include the Bible in the books which could be dispensed with. By comparing the Bible with John the Baptist, Law 'set Christ and the Bible in flat opposition to each other!' But by keeping the Bible rather than going from it, we are taught of Him.

Wesley proceeds to quote Law's celebrated passage:

Christ is the church or temple of God within thee. There the supper of the Lamb is kept. When thou art well grounded in this inward worship, thou wilt have learned to live unto God above time and place. For every day will be a Sunday to thee, and wherever thou goest thou wilt have a priest, a church, and an altar along with thee.

The plain inference is (remarks Wesley): Thou wilt not need to make any difference between Sunday and other days. Thou wilt need no other church than that which thou hast always along with thee; no other supper, worship, priest, or altar. Be well grounded in this inward worship, and it superseded all the rest.

Once again Wesley opposes to Law's position the plain teaching of the Bible and the commandments contained in it. This is another Gospel, 'which leads quite wide of the Gospel of Christ'.

This is the climax of a long-standing quarrel. Though Law's absorption in mysticism undoubtedly aggravated his tendency to disregard the Means of Grace, even in the *Serious Call* he had incurred Charles Wesley's displeasure[20] by writing:

It is very observable, that there is not one command in all the Gospel for public worship; and perhaps it is a duty that is least insisted upon in Scripture of any other. The frequent attendance at it is never so much as mentioned....[21]

And in the same work, as Mr. Hobhouse observes,[22] the character of Ouranius, the model country clergyman, is drawn with no reference to the functions of the administration of the Sacraments or even the conduct of public services.[23]

Wesley, on the other hand, as early as 1739, had to combat stillness in the Societies,[24] of which Molther, the Moravian, was the instigator. It was at this time that Wesley preached his sermon on the 'Means of Grace', in which he expounds more fully the views expressed in the 1756 Letter.[25] It may be remarked that Wesley's strictures were of no effect. A few weeks after the 1756 Letter was published, Law wrote the Letter 'To Mr. J. L.', emphasizing even more strongly than before the true inwardness of churchmanship and the efficacy of the Sacraments in the inward spirit.[26]

[20] *Remains of John Byrom*, Vol. II, Part 1, p. 182.
[21] *Law's Works*, Vol. IV, p. 10.
[22] *William Law and Eighteenth-century Quakerism*, p. 264.
[23] *Law's Works*, Vol. IV, pp. 229 et sqq.
[24] *Journal*, Vol. I, p. 430.
[25] *Sermons*, Vol. I, pp. 238 et sqq.
[26] *Law's Works*, Vol. IX, pp. 109 et sqq.

VII. HELL[27]

The final count in Wesley's indictment of Law's theology concerns Law's denial of the existence of hell. Here Wesley is briefer, contenting himself with three excerpts from Law's writings: 'Hell is no penalty prepared or inflicted by God'; 'Damnation is only that which springs up within you'; and 'Hell and damnation are nothing but the various operations of self.'

Instead of arguing the case in his own words, Wesley prefers to quote against Law a fairly long statement of the current orthodox belief, published by Dr. Peter Browne, Bishop of Cork. This consisted of four main points, of which the following is a very brief summary.

Concerning future punishments, we learn from revelation only:

(1) That they are both for soul and body; . . . in hell the wicked will be subject to extreme torments of both together.

(2) That the chief cause of their eternal misery will be an eternal exclusion from the beatific vision of God. . . .

(3) That one part of those punishments will be by fire, than which we have not any revelation more express and positive. . . .

(4) The eternity of these punishments is revealed as plainly as words can express it. . . .

Wesley then supports the Bishop's contentions with Scripture passages chosen by himself and asks: 'If the case is not so, why did God speak as if it was?' It is unthinkable that this should be an act of guile on the part of the God of truth. Accordingly, concludes Wesley:

If there be 'no unquenchable fire, no everlasting burnings', there is no dependence on those writings wherein they are so expressly asserted, nor of the eternity of heaven any more than of hell. So that if we give up the one, we must give up the other. No hell, no heaven, no revelation!

How shrewd a reasoner Wesley was, is shown by the fact that when years afterwards the doctrine of a materialistic hell did lose its hold on the popular mind, it was not long before the emphasis was also shifted from the hereafter altogether, and Protestant Christendom still awaits a popular presentation of the truths about eternity, that shall restore that supremely

[27] *Letters*, Vol. III, pp. 368-70.

important doctrine to its rightful place in the minds of believers.

After a brief reference to Law's vain attempts to meet the situation with his doctrine of purgatory, the very passing nature of which reveals Wesley's scorn for the belief, the letter closes with a final appeal to Law to renounce the unintelligible jargon of the mystic writers and return to the plain religion of the Bible: 'We love Him because He first loved us.'

As we have passed under review the various issues raised, it has become increasingly clear that the fundamental difference between Law and Wesley on the Atonement has lain at the root of all their subsidiary differences (except possibly that concerning coldness and fervour, where, as we saw, Law himself is inconsistent). We have been examining two systems of doctrine, each coherent within its own framework, but starting from such conflicting premises that many opposite conclusions were bound to be reached.

Begin with Law's mystical preconceptions, and his subjective theory of the Atonement inevitably follows, and with equal logic his Doctrine of the New Birth, the new man in Christ, Universalism, and Purgatory; these in turn could only result in emphasis on the inner life, the absence of any sharp distinction between Justification and Sanctification, with a correspondingly diminished regard for the historical Christ and the observance of external ordinances.

Wesley's acceptance, on the other hand, of the absolute authority of Scripture and the objective theory of the Atonement based on the historic facts recorded therein, ensured his adherence to a doctrine of saving faith, springing not from within man, but in response to God's manward initiative in history. Hence, too, his rejection of all universalist theories to include those who made no response. The historic act of redemption retains the central place in his scheme, and this involved consequent reading of the Bible, and observance of those means of grace, where the historical facts are brought to mind and symbolized.

The inevitable outcome was a cleavage between the views of the two men of the means whereby holiness was to be attained, as complete as their views on the necessity and possibility of its attainment by every Christian were identical.

The Science of Religious Truth, fundamentally and fully elucidated, in Theory and Practice.

A GUIDE

TO THE PECULIAR SCIENTIAL AND EXPERIENTIAL KNOWLEDGE

OF THEOLOGY, NEEDFUL, TO COMPOSE AN

ADEQUATE AND SUITABLE BIOGRAPHY

OF THE ACCOMPLISHED ENGLISH SAGE

AND CHRISTIAN PHILOSOPHER,

WILLIAM LAW,

(*The Author of the "Serious Call to a Devout and Holy Life," &c.,*)

OUT OF MATERIALS TO BE PROVIDED.

FOR WHICH AN EDITOR IS REQUIRED.

The groundwork qualifications of mind presumed to be in the candidate, upon which the above described knowledge is to be superinduced, are these following—

1. The possession of sound classical learning, luminous common sense, acute ironical wit, and masculine strength of reason and judgment.
2,—of high rhetorical art, and pure Saxon simplicity of verbiage.
3,—of *skeleton-leaf* exactness of logical power and demonstration.
4,—of easy, natural aspiration of thought, as to length and cadency of periods, with great practice in argumentive composition.
5,—of a devout and serious spirit, or mental complexion. And,
6,—as to religion, of the ancient Methodist views, of the necessity and blessedness of earnest devotion to God, and the attainment of perfect sanctity or holiness of spirit, and outward practical life.

LONDON:

THEOSOPHIAN LIBRARY, LUDGATE STREET.

Free. First issue, 5000.   *Christmas, 1856.*

N.B.—*The more this read and considered, with its Scripture and other references, the yet higher and deeper found, and better and better liked.*

Facsimile reproduction

PART FOUR
Law and the Beginnings of Methodism

TO THE CHRISTIANITY, THE PHILOSOPHY, THE ERUDITION, SCIENCE, AND NOBLE INTELLIGENCE OF THE AGE.

NOTES AND MATERIALS

FOR AN ADEQUATE

BIOGRAPHY

OF

THE CELEBRATED DIVINE AND THEOSOPHER,

WILLIAM LAW.

COMPRISING AN ELUCIDATION OF THE SCOPE AND CONTENTS OF

THE WRITINGS OF JACOB BÖHME,

AND OF HIS GREAT COMMENTATOR,

DIONYSIUS ANDREAS FREHER;

WITH A NOTICE OF THE MYSTICAL DIVINITY AND MOST CURIOUS AND SOLID SCIENCE OF ALL AGES OF THE WORLD. ALSO AN INDICATION OF THE TRUE MEANS FOR THE INDUCTION OF THE INTELLECTUAL "HEATHEN," JEWISH, AND MAHOMEDAN NATIONS INTO THE CHRISTIAN FAITH.

The time is born for Enoch to speak, and Elias to work again.

The manifestation of the "mystery of Christ"—of Deity, Nature and all things, (and universal refinement of philosophy and theology,) was the *Elias* mission of Behmen, Freher, and Law, and God's last dispensation to mankind.

PRINTED FOR PRIVATE CIRCULATION.

FIVE HUNDRED COPIES.—LONDON. A.D. 1854.

Facsimile reproduction

CHAPTER TEN

The Testimony of Christopher Walton

ONE OF THE main sources on which we are dependent for our knowledge of Law is Christopher Walton, who compiled a volume entitled: *Notes and Materials for an Adequate Biography of the Celebrated Divine and Theosopher William Law.*

It has seemed best (while quoting this work for historical facts as our inquiry has proceeded) to reserve for presentation at this stage our discussion of his theories on the various aspects of our study. Some such discussion must find a place in our inquiry as Walton is the only writer who has hitherto set forth, albeit amid much extraneous matter, any detailed account of the relation between Law and Wesley, and our investigation could not be complete unless we at any rate examined his conclusions and sought to form a judgement upon them. The inclusion of the discussion at this point seems appropriate as it provides a link between our consideration of John Wesley and of the beginnings of Methodism, for although he reviews and comments on many of the aspects of the relationship of the two men, Walton's main concern is to establish the connexion between Law's writings and Methodism as he himself knew it in the nineteenth century. Walton's volume, of which only five hundred copies were printed, and these for private circulation, appeared in 1854, bearing on its cover the legend: 'Elucidation of the Sublime Genius and Theosophian Mission of William Law.'

Later writers on Law, such as Overton, Alexander Whyte, and Mr. Stephen Hobhouse have drawn freely from Walton's *Notes and Materials*, and seem to have regarded him as a reliable authority.[1] Walton's information is, however, relatively inaccessible, not only because of the rarity of the volume, but also because of the extraordinary fashion in which he has presented his material. The work is a long one of nearly seven hundred pages, printed exceedingly small, without an

[1] *The Life and Opinions of the Rev. William Law*, by J. H. Overton, Preface, p. vi. *Characters and Characteristics of William Law*, by Alexander Whyte, pp. xx, xxx. *William Law and Eighteenth-century Quakerism*, by Stephen Hobhouse, p. 13.

index or a table of contents. There is no division into chapters, and there are no subject headings. Often one or two lines of text are at the head of a page, the rest of which consists of footnotes; one such footnote occupies 294[2] pages. There are innumerable digressions, reminiscent of Herodotus, the resultant effect being one of indescribable confusion, so that, as Mr. Hobhouse remarks, the information contained is 'as good as lost to the general reader'.[3]

It is important to distinguish between Walton's reliability as narrator and as critic. As an historiographer (rather than an historian) his accuracy has not been questioned by later writers, and we may regard him as generally trustworthy, though even here he is not without blemish. He is guilty of an extraordinary mistake in dating John Wesley's conversion before that of his brother Charles.[4]

This error is quite unaccountable and leads one to suspect that his acquaintance with the biographical details of the Wesleys is less thorough than with those of Law. Another mistake is that when referring to Wesley's statement to Law that he preached 'after the model of your two practical treatises', he applied the statement to the period of Wesley's sweeping evangelistic campaigns,[5] whereas Wesley so described his preaching during the two years preceding 1738. The explanation of this is simply Walton's passionate enthusiasm for Law and all his works, which betrayed him into this historical inaccuracy, as it also was the principle which governed all his judgements. Our estimate of Walton's opinions must be formed in the light of this fact. Overton referred to him as 'that most indefatigable investigator of everything relating to William Law'[6] and as 'that devoted Law-worshipper whose information about everything which concerned his hero is most extensive',[7] and there can be no question that Walton's critical faculty was entirely submerged by his boundless admiration for Law. This does not mean that his conclusions are necessarily faulty, but it is a factor constantly to be borne in mind. Walton was a lifelong

[2] pp. 334-628. (See facsimile on p. 184 infra.)
[3] *William Law and Eighteenth-century Quakerism*, p. 16.
[4] *Notes and Materials, etc.*, p. 568. [5] ibid., p. 569.
[6] *The Life and Opinions of the Rev. William Law*, p. 239. [7] ibid., p. 369.

Methodist,[8] and made his first acquaintance with Law's works as a result of an accidental meeting with Wesley's publication, *Some extracts from Mr. Law's writings*.[9] Walton's regard for Wesley was second only to his regard for Law. He never criticizes Wesley, except where the latter disagrees with Law, and then he is indiscriminately scathing in his condemnation. This in no way diminished his allegiance to Methodism, since, as we shall see, it was his unshakable conviction that Methodism was the logical and inevitable outcome of Law's teaching.

As illustrations of Walton's attitude, let us consider his treatment of the two main clashes between Law and Wesley in 1738 and 1756 respectively.

THE 1738 CORRESPONDENCE

He attributes the 1738 correspondence to the mischievous intervention of Böhler,

> Böhler, whose knowledge and experience of Christian truth had doubtless impressed him with a just opinion of the unprofitable, ungospel character of Marsay's views and writings, might have hastily concluded that Law, who had been previously represented to him as attached to the Mystics, was of a similar turn of mind; and so, as common with zealous sticklers for exciting interpretations of gospel doctrines, he would peremptorily judge him accordingly, and not hesitate to express his opinion to such of his friends as desired it. Whence may be accounted for, those groundless and injudicious letters that, shortly after this interview, were addressed to Law by his quondam pupil ... and which, however sincere and right meaning, betray the uncertainty and imperfection of the writer's theological science at the time when he wrote them.[10]

This, however, is entirely to ignore Wesley's own internal spiritual struggle, which led him in the first place to seek Böhler's advice and help.

Walton further defends Law by advancing the view that Law's failure to lead Wesley to an experience of saving faith was a deliberate exercise of restraint on the part of Law, so as not to hasten Wesley's spiritual development before a sufficient

---
[8] *Dictionary of National Biography*, Vol. XX, p. 728.
[9] *Notes and Materials, etc.*, Preface, p. ii.
[10] ibid., p. 370.

scriptural foundation was laid. It is typical of Walton's style that all this is casually inserted in a parenthesis:

Friday, June 4th, 1742. [This was about four years after the period when, see his letter to Mr. Law of May 14th, 1738, he considers he had discovered he was but a 'child of hell', 'having the faith of a devil', etc., though for thirteen years previous he had been a most sincere, devoted Christian. The fact was, he was just emerging out of the legal into the gospel state; but the popular character of his religious education, not having made him master of the rationale and scope of mystic theology, he had not understood his true state and position in the experience of Christianity. But now that he had passed through the 'legal' state and also that 'in the flesh' and farther had entered into the new birth of the Spirit, or 'spiritual state' of Christianity, he fancied,—as almost all new converts do fancy,—that he ought to have been in this state from the very first; and thereupon flies at Mr. Law, his spiritual preceptor, in the letter referred to, for not having taught him this at first. But Mr. Law knew his business too well ever to lead souls imperfectly: he, like his Master, knew the absolute necessity of a deep Scriptural foundation for a high superstructure of holiness, and therefore in his first works he keeps his scholars under the ministration of the law, and of Christ in the flesh, until they are grown naturally ready, by a conscious inwardly felt want of a radical change, yea in their very essences, in order to a full deliverance from their present bondage into the glorious liberty of the light of God! And so it occurred in this individual's case, in God's own time and way, because he was pressingly desirous, earnest, and diligent. But Mr. Law is as free from blame as Kempis or the Holy Spirit Himself, in regard to this individual's experience; on the contrary as the instrument of the Latter,—regarding the amazing results of this individual's subsequent career,—'to him it endless honour brings', as will be shown in the biography, when demonstrating the former part of the Elias-Baptist character of his mission.][11]

To this contention it may be replied that there is no shred of evidence to support it. If it were true, why did not Law himself say so? It may also be fairly remarked that thirteen years is a long time to be compelled to wait, until the 'superstructure' could be imposed, especially for one who, like Wesley, had been a devotee of the Scriptures long before he met Law. And we may doubt whether anything further would have happened even then, if Wesley had been content to remain Law's disciple.

[11] *Notes and Materials, etc.*, p. 92.

Elsewhere Walton seeks to justify Law, by extolling the merits of the *Demonstration of the . . . errors of 'A plain Account . . .'*, maintaining that that work contained all the evangelical instruction that Wesley complained was lacking in Law.

Do but imagine a poor, broken down penitent, well informed in the language of the gospel, conscious of the high requirements of God's righteousness, finding after repeated experiments no ability to live up to the gospel commands, and seeing no way for a deliverance from the weight and burden of his sins, in short, in a total despair of self and all creaturely help; do but imagine such an one in this state, (which it is the direct natural tendency of the *Christian Perfection* and *Serious Call* to bring their faithful student unto,) and then say if anything more suitable, more edifying, more evangelical, in the whole nature of gospel instructions can possibly be placed before such a character, or, in Law's words, can be better timed. . . .

Take all the cherished conceits and imaginations of the modern evangelical doctrines together, and, if reduced to pure essential truth, we repeat they do not contain one particle more of solid evangelical instruction for a penitent to induce and enable him to 'lay hold of Christ' in the importunity, simplicity, and full assurance of faith, than is contained in this following extract if duly apprehended; which is from Law's *Review of an Account of the Nature and End of the Sacrament of the Lord's Supper*.[12]

Then follows a long extract, in which we search in vain for any exposition of the doctrine of 'saving faith' as Wesley came to understand it.

This is, of course, merely a reiteration of Law's own plea in the 1738 correspondence. The simple answer is the one Wesley gave, that, though, in his opinion, an excellent work, Law's answer to *The Plain Account* did not affect the question.[13] In actual fact it did not lead, and never would have led, Wesley to a knowledge of saving faith.

Walton, we may add, severely criticizes Wesley for omitting to insert the 1738 correspondence in his diary.[14]

THE 1756 LETTER

Walton makes frequent allusions to the 1756 Letter, but he has no special theories of his own to advance, as he has concerning the 1738 correspondence. He contents himself with pouring

[12] ibid., pp. 227-8.   [13] *Letter*, Vol. I, p. 241.   [14] *Notes and Materials, etc.*, p. 94.

scorn upon it, and eulogizing Law by contrast. He quotes with approval the opinion of an anonymous lady, a Wesleyan like himself, to whom he submitted the letter;

> It is not worth reading: there is no argument in it. It is like an ignorant person quoting an author's words he does not understand, and saying, 'Isn't that absurd? Whoever thought of that? Where do we find that or that in the Bible?' Poor man! he meant well; he was a good man, but he couldn't reason. Mr. Wesley was not made for philosophy; his talent was only practical.[15]

This view coincided with Walton's own, who wrote:

> The Letter indeed, is nothing but an incongruous selection of sentences or parts of ideas out of Mr. Law's works, without the slightest apprehension or conception of the ground or principles of the author.[16]

It is perhaps a sufficient answer to this to remind ourselves that Wesley himself insisted even more emphatically that Law was in these matters beyond his comprehension, but for a different reason!

More serious is Walton's allegation that, in the 1756 Letter and also in the 1760 Letter to the *London Chronicle*, Wesley actually misrepresented Law. In the first instance it is not only Walton, but Law himself, who makes this charge in a private letter to Langcake which Walton quotes and accepts as accurate. The passage in question follows an extract cited by Wesley from the *Spirit of Prayer*.

> I will here give you an infallible touchstone, that will try all to the truth. It is this: Retire from the world, and all conversation, only for one month; neither write, nor read, nor debate anything in private with yourself; stop all the former workings of your heart and mind; and, with all the strength of your heart, stand all this month as continually as you can, in this following form of prayer to God.[17]

Wesley omits the word 'following' and continues the quotation: 'If your heart cannot give itself up in this manner to prayer be fully assured you are an infidel.'[18] Law calls this 'a most flagrant piece of forgery' and continues:

---

[15] *Notes and Materials, etc.*, p. 565. [16] ibid.
[17] *Law's Works*, Vol. VII, p. 124. [18] *Letters*, Vol. III, p. 365.

The above words from whence this charge against me is drawn, are enclosed between inverted commas as mine, and the page referred to, where they are. And yet they are no more in my book, than in the gospel of St. John, nor were ever any more in my thoughts than the most foolish frantic thing in the world.[19]

But what are the facts? It is true that in the *Spirit of Prayer* the words complained of were separated from the first part of the quotation, but the intervening section is almost wholly made up of Law's suggested form of words for the prayer concerned. It is also true that Wesley did not quote the exact words as they appear in the *Spirit of Prayer*. Law actually wrote: 'Now if you dare not, if your hearts will not, cannot give themselves up in this manner to the spirit of this prayer, then the touchstone has done its work, and you may be as fully assured, both what your infidelity is, and from what it proceeds, as you can be of the plainest truth in nature.'[20] Wesley has followed his customary practice of making verbal alterations and some omissions, but in no way has he altered the sense of what Law wrote. If there was wilful misrepresentation in this matter, it was Law who was guilty of it, nor can Walton evade his share of responsibility, for, with both men's works available, he neglected to verify Law's accuracy.

The second instance of Wesley's alleged misrepresentation is less serious and concerns only Walton, not Law. Walton suggests that Wesley's summary of Law's objections to the 1756 Letter is misleading, omitting altogether 'those passages which constitute the gravest reflexions on his character'.[21] But there was surely no need for Wesley to quote Law's strictures *in extenso*. A summary was much more suitable, and he has certainly included some very offensive passages, such as the one about the 'empty babble, fitter for an old grammarian . . . etc.'[22] Indeed it may be urged that it would have defeated Wesley's purpose in writing to the Press to have concealed the extent of Law's attack.

Regarding Wesley's opposition to the mystics in general and to Boehme in particular, Walton seeks to establish that, for his own evangelical doctrines, Wesley was indirectly indebted to Boehme's *Way of Christ*, which influenced the Moravians,

[19] *Notes and Materials, etc.*, p. 566.
[20] *Law's Works*, Vol. VII, p. 124.
[21] *Notes and Materials, etc.*, p. 564.
[22] *Letters*, Vol. IV, p. 105.

who in turn influenced Wesley.[23] On this score we may reply that although it is possible that some indirect influence was exercised, Law's philosophical and doctrinal position was very much more directly and closely dependent on Boehme, and it was that position which Wesley was assailing. Nor is Walton convincing in his suggestion that Law's *Confutation of Dr. Warburton's 'Divine Legation'* embodies all needful evangelical doctrine.[24] While that work contained much that met with Wesley's hearty agreement, it nowhere sets forth Wesley's doctrinal position as we set it forth in Chapter 8.

From these examples of Walton's theories we may fairly conclude that, no more than Law, did he ever understand Wesley's position or appreciate the true significance of Wesley's 1738 conversion and the consequent reorientation of his theological outlook.

Before passing on, it is pleasant to notice, by contrast, Walton's outspoken tributes to Wesley. Even concerning the 1738 controversy he writes:

there can be no doubt that his publication was the offspring of a sincere regard to what he conceived to be the interests of truth and Christianity, ... thinking that Mr. Law was really unacquainted with the true and simple nature of the gospel, and therefore that he was in duty bound to try to set him right.[25]

Again, dealing with Bishop Lavington's attack, Walton remarks:

The personal charges, implied and expressed in Lavington's work, were ... harsh and far from merited; for, weak as Mr. Wesley may be considered in regard to his judgement of recondite topics, yet his motives in religion were indisputably fervent and sincere, and his intention to do good pure and simple.[26]

Walton concludes his review of the 1756 Letter with a comprehensive appreciation of Wesley and his work, too long to be quoted in full. The introduction, however, admirably illustrates Walton's regard for Wesley, which, as we have seen, was subordinated only to his unmixed veneration for Law.

[23] *Notes and Materials, etc.*, p. 93. [24] ibid., p. 565.
[25] ibid., p. 563. [26] ibid., p. 567.

In writing a work like this, we have of course felt bound to speak of things as they occurred, and not according to the ordinary lights of a fifty year's beatification, or the views of partial and biassed sectarians. Thus, while holding in as high esteem as anyone, Mr. Wesley's character of sincerity, devotedness to God, and usefulness to the church, it has been our business immediately to point out the distinguishing characteristics of Mr. Law, as a mystic prophet of God, a theologian, and man of erudition and genius . . . and this more especially when the course of our narrative rendered it necessary to remark on the irrational attacks made upon the general tenor of his later writings. Having said thus much then of an uncomplimentary character, in justice to the subject of our memoir, and to the general object of edification which we have in view, it will now afford us equal pleasure to take the other hand of justice and truth, and to glance at the inner spirit of Mr. Wesley, as he doubtless stood before God.[27]

LAW'S INFLUENCE ON METHODISM

With this sketch of Walton's view of the relation between Law and Wesley in our minds, we turn to Walton's oft-expressed conviction that the real origin of Methodism, as he knew it, was to be found in Law's practical treatises.

First of all, it is significant that, in stating the qualifications necessary for the writer of the biography of Law, for which Walton's compilation was intended as a storehouse of material, Walton stipulates that the candidate shall have been brought up among the Methodists.[28] He also includes Wesley's *Sermons* and *Hymn-book* among the preliminary works to be read.[29] One very important result Walton expected from the proposed work was the

refinement and exaltation of the genius of Methodism, which is undeniably the most advanced system of popular evangelism that this country and the continent of America, with the world at large, have ever witnessed.[30]

Methodism's pre-eminence, according to Walton, was entirely due to its foundation in Law's teaching. He describes Wesley in an amusing simile, as one

who, if Law might be considered the perfecter of the steam-engine, and inventor of locomotives, might himself be considered as the managing director of the first English railway company and chief engineer.[31]

[27] ibid., p. 568. [28] ibid., p. 371. [29] ibid., p. 4.
[30] ibid., Preface, p. xxxiii; also pp. 633-5. [31] ibid., p. 92.

'Methodism itself', Walton assures us,

is nothing more than a superstructure, of which the chief foundation is Mr. Law's *Serious Call* and *Christian Perfection*, as the true spirit and interpretation of the fundamental obligations and duties of the gospel; which are to precede, give birth to, and then to be the fruits of, and strengthen the regenerate life.[32]

The only original thing in Methodism was the directing talent of its founder, for

all the sober groundwork of ascetic and devotional piety is that of the Church of England, as illustrated by Law, Jeremy Taylor, and other of her divines.[33]

Deploring the spiritual lethargy in Germany at the time, Walton asks how the regeneration of that nation is to be effected and makes reply:

As that of England was effected, viz., by Law's *Christian Perfection*, and *Serious Call*, by Taylor's *Holy Living and Dying*, and the three vols. of 'Kempis', falling upon and enkindling the spirit of a young, ardent, devout, Wesley-Ignatius.[34]

To this combination of Law's inspiration and Wesley's practical genius, Walton attributes the overthrow of Deism, the 'last effort of human vanity', which was

swept away by the action of the spirit of Methodism—that being the direct offspring of the Elias-Baptist ministration of Law, and, though remotely, of the spirit of Boehme.[35]

Walton described Methodism as the great moral discovery of the previous century, referring to it as

the form and aggressive spirit of simple Bible Christianity (and the call and qualification of all the lay members of the mystical body of Christ to activity in the evangelical work, as local preachers, . . . as leaders of bands and classes, etc., all without exception being employed in doing good, and promoting the success of the gospel) . . . —which was originated by Mr. Law's practical treatises providentially falling upon rightly-prepared minds, to put their purified principles into working effect.[36]

[32] *Notes and Materials, etc.*, p. 563. [33] ibid., p. 568.
[34] ibid., p. 127.   [35] ibid., p. 88.   [36] ibid., p. 498.

In one notable passage Walton recognizes the continuing centrality of Christian Perfection in the Methodist movement. After speaking of Wesley's own allegiance to that ideal, he continues:

> The original principles of Methodism are nothing more than the methodical and evangelical principles of Law's *Call* and *Christian Perfection* carried into practical operation by a number of united Christian brethren collected together here and there and over the land. And though admitting the ignorance, erroneous views, and disorder that have occasionally characterized their doctrines and practices, which, however, was hardly avoidable; yet the principles, the practice, and discipline of Methodism may be justly considered as embracing the machinery for the entire Christian and political regeneration of a country, yea, and with the supervention of the lights indicated in this treatise, of the intellectual, as well as the illiterate world.—Thus Wesley practised and led others to practise the science which Law in so masterly a manner has taught: thus he proceeded and upon such a foundation; (N.B.)[37] *ever retaining the original practice* of Law's books, he went on from weakness to strength, from one degree of experience and evangelical ministration to another; always having before his eye the high perfection of Christ, which through the development of the Spirit of Christ in him by regeneration, he knew to belong to him and to be the privilege of all, as believers, to attain unto: wherefore he so publicly enforced the doctrine of Christian Perfection or 'entire Sanctification'; as knowing, moreover, that the soul must ever be pressing forward in grace, by prayer and self-denial, or it will inevitably retrograde into the rational animal nature of the world.[38]

On another occasion, Walton, advocating the establishment of a college, where the science and practice of Christ-like perfection might be professedly taught, claimed that Methodism was already performing that function for large numbers of people.[39]

In Walton's view, despite Wesley's opposition to mysticism, that element was now embedded in Methodism. For example, after a summary of mystical books in German, French, and English, he concludes:

> These were all to centre in William Law, and be reproduced in a new, pure, practical form, as the spirit of Methodism, with its action and reaction, for the renovation of Gospel Christianity.[40]

---

[37] *Notes and Materials, etc.*, Walton's own parenthesis.
[38] ibid., p. 176.   [39] ibid., p. 252.   [40] ibid., p. 128.

He even regarded contemporary Methodism as in some sense a popularization of Boehme's views,[41] though doubtless he would have in mind Boehme's *Way of Salvation* rather than his abstruse philosophical theories.

Walton was especially an admirer of a Methodist minister, then recently dead, named William Bramwell, of whom he invariably spoke in terms of extreme admiration, often as 'the holy Bramwell'.[42] He regarded him as a 'classic illustration of Mr. Law's grand doctrine of "regeneration" and "spirit of love" ', and averred that 'Bramwell's letters ought to constitute an inseparable appendix to Mr. Law's evangelical doctrinal works'.[43]

CRITICISM OF WALTON'S THEORIES

These extracts from Walton's work, though by no means exhaustive, suffice to illustrate his attitude and outlook. We note in this last section, dealing with his conviction concerning Methodism's origin in Law's treatises, the same uncritical reverence for his hero. He is even prepared to give Law the credit for those features of Methodism, such as lay preaching and class meetings for fellowship, of the former of which Law definitely disapproved,[44] and in the latter of which he never evinced the slightest interest, this being, as we have seen, one great difference between Law and Wesley.

To sum up, we may say that Walton's attribution of the Methodist movement in its entirety to the influence of Law, is hopelessly wide of the mark, and merely reflects the subordination of any critical judgement he may have possessed (and there is evidence of little) to his personal predilections. Walton, of course, had no special equipment which would enable him to arrive at sound conclusions on such a matter. He was a Methodist tradesman, who made a hobby of the study of William Law.

Even when he is on sound ground in pointing out the connexion between Law's practical treatises and the beginnings of Methodism, his verdict is far too sweeping in singling out those treatises as the origin of Methodism, while only making

---

[41] *Notes and Materials etc.*, Preface, p. x.   [42] ibid., p. 443.
[43] ibid., p. 569.   [44] *Journal of Charles Wesley*, Vol. I, p. 159.

passing mention of Jeremy Taylor, à Kempis, and no mention at all of Wesley's mother Susanna, perhaps the greatest influence of all. More serious, however, is the way in which Walton ignores the other side of Methodism, which may have been, as he says, 'the great moral discovery' of the previous century, but was certainly very much more. Walton's apparent unawareness of the deep cleavage between the evangelical and mystical systems makes one wonder whether the hymns of the Wesleys were sung in the church he attended! To this unbalanced view we need make no further reply in view of investigations in Part Three of this inquiry.

Notwithstanding this, the fact that Walton, already a loyal Methodist, stumbling accidentally on Law's writings, was able to perceive so definite a connexion between Law and Methodism is significant. And it may justifiably be argued that Walton's ability to gloss over those elements in Methodism which either had no connexion with Law, or were directly contrary to his system, is additional reason for accepting his testimony in respect to that strain in Methodism, where our inquiry has already led us to emphasize Law's influence, namely the centrality in the life of Wesley himself first of all, and then in the movement he founded, of the ethical ideal of Christian Perfection as the attainable goal of every Christian.

The contemporary evidence for a definite connexion between Law's treatises and the rise of Methodism, afforded, as we saw, by Trapp and Warburton, is now reinforced by the testimony of Christopher Walton in the succeeding century.

CHAPTER ELEVEN

The Influence of Law on Methodist Belief and Practice

IT HAS GROWN increasingly clear in the course of our inquiry that, as far as Wesley was concerned, it was not only his own individual spiritual history with which we were dealing, but also the inception and growth of the Methodist movement founded by him. We noticed how his mission as the leader of the great evangelical campaign and director of the Methodist societies, which were its fruits, profoundly affected his own religious development and was partly responsible for the widening of the gulf between Law and himself. All his views were continually being experimentally tested, as he dealt with the problems of sin and salvation among the multitudes who came to regard him as their father in God.

It must now be recognized that his position in relation to Methodism during his lifetime, and indeed subsequently, was such that any influence exerted on Wesley did not cease with him but was carried over and became a factor in the great religious revival, which he initiated. Wesley was an autocrat, who imposed his views and his methods on his willing followers, and it might perhaps be said that, not forgetting John Knox and William Booth, no religious denomination bears more distinctly the impress of its founder than does Methodism. It must be remembered that Wesley lived for more than fifty years after his conversion in 1738, and exercised complete authority to the end. In some remarkable ways that authority is exercised to this day. For example, the doctrinal standards of Methodism were laid down during Wesley's lifetime as being contained in his *Notes upon the New Testament*, and the first four volumes of his *Sermons*,[1] and they remain so today.[2] Further, Charles Wesley's hymns contain John Wesley's teaching. 'Methodism', writes a modern authority,

[1] *Wesley's Works*, Vol. VIII, p. 331.
[2] *Minutes of the Methodist Conference*, 1939, p. 337.

'was born in song and ... sang its own hymns because no others would do',[3] and those hymns have maintained their pre-eminent position in Methodism worship.

Almost exactly one-quarter of the hymns in the present book (1933) are by Charles Wesley. Adding the twenty translations of John Wesley, and the three original hymns attributed to him, we have no fewer than 265 hymns by the two brothers out of a total of 984; and quite half this number—say 150—are in common use all over Methodism.[4]

(It may be added that this is a lower proportion than in any of the preceding Wesleyan Methodist books.) This is no accident, but because Methodism retained its close adherence to its original tradition, in the framing of which Charles Wesley in his own sphere played as essential a part as John.

We have seen that John Wesley's indebtedness to Law consists mainly in the devotion to the ethical ideal of Christian Perfection for which Law was largely responsible. The centrality of this has been preserved in Methodism. Wesley insisted on this throughout his life and even as late as November 1790, only a few weeks before his death, gave instructions how to treat opponents of the doctrine within the societies.

If we can prove that any of our Local Preachers or Leaders, either directly or indirectly, speak against it, let him be a Local Preacher or Leader no longer. I doubt whether he shall continue in the Society. Because he that can speak thus in our congregations cannot be an honest man.[5]

The *Sermons*, which are held to contain the doctrinal standards of Methodism, forty-four in number, include not only those on 'The Circumcision of the Heart' and 'Christian Perfection', but no fewer than thirteen on the Sermon on the Mount, so that by the very charter of its existence Methodism is pledged to the maintenance of both Christian doctrine and Christian ethics. Moreover, while many of Charles Wesley's hymns deal with the evangelical experience, Christian Perfection was one of his chief themes. Many successive Wesleyan *Hymn-books* contained a section 'for believers seeking full redemption', which title has given way to 'Christian Holiness' in the 1933

---

[3] *Praises with Understanding*, by A. S. Gregory, pp. 63-4.
[4] ibid., p. 63.   [5] *Letters*, Vol. VIII, p. 249.

book, a section of twenty-eight hymns, twenty-four of which Charles Wesley wrote.

How completely the ideal of Christian Perfection was implanted in the beginnings of Methodism by its founder may be judged by the persistence of the ideal, as the Methodist Church grew and spread. There is no better exposition of this than that delivered at the Methodist Centenary Celebration in New York in 1866.

(Methodism) takes the old theology of the Christian Church, but it takes one element which no other Christian Church has dared to put forward as a prominent feature of theology. In ours it is the very point from which we view all theology. Now listen; I want that to be understood. Knowing exactly what I say, and taking the full responsibility of it, I repeat, we are the only Church in history, from the apostles' time until now, that has put forward as its very elemental thought—the great central pervading idea of the whole Book of God from the beginning to the end—the holiness of the human soul, heart, mind, and will. Go through all the confessions of all the Churches, and you will find this in no other. You will find even some of them that blame us in their books and writings. It may be called fanaticism, but, dear friends, that is our mission. If we keep to that, the next century is ours; if we keep to that, the triumphs of the next century shall throw those that are past far into the shade. Our work is a moral work—that is to say, the work of making men holy. Our preaching is for that, our church agencies are for that, our schools, colleges, universities, and theological seminaries are for that. There is our mission—there is our glory—there is our power, and there shall be the ground of our triumph. God keep us true.[6]

Nor has this prominence of the ethical ideal disappeared from present-day Methodism. Woe betide any candidate for the Methodist ministry who approaches the various tests to which he is subjected, without being prepared to expound the doctrine of 'Entire Sanctification' and its place in the scheme of evangelical doctrine in relation to Justification. It is significant too, that the *Serious Call* retains its place in the books officially recommended by the Methodist Conference to be read by 'Preachers on trial'.[7]

So Law, in his practical treatises, was helping to set in motion a process which was to extend far and wide beyond

[6] John McClintock, the first president of the Drew Theological Seminary, quoted by O. A. Curtis in *The Christian Faith*, p. 372.
[7] *Minutes of the Methodist Conference*, 1939, p. 236.

anything which in his wildest dreams he could have imagined. It is not claimed, of course, that any but a small fraction of those who have thus come indirectly under his influence have been conscious of their debt to him. The vast majority probably never heard of him.

This applies equally to the practical outworkings of the doctrine. As with Wesley himself the ideal and its practical consequences in daily life have been inseparable from the earliest days of Methodism. Some of the first examples are to be found in *The Lives of Early Methodist Preachers*[8] and *Wesley's Veterans*.[9] An examination of these volumes yields no direct evidence of conscious dependence on Law. Yet we know that they read Law. 'All the Methodists carefully read these books', said Wesley of the *Christian Perfection* and the *Serious Call*, 'and were greatly profited thereby.'[10] It is significant that these two works were also included in the curriculum of Kingswood School, which Wesley founded for the sons of Methodist preachers.[11] One of the 'Early Methodist Preachers', whose autobiography has come down to us,[12] was sent these works by Wesley himself in 1783,[13] though it is Wesley, and not Black, who tells us so. Wesley's own expositions of Christian Perfection were so adequate, and his influence on his followers so dominant, that there was no need for them to go behind Wesley to Law.

Yet whether directly or indirectly, consciously or unconsciously, these men displayed traits of character entirely consistent with what Law enjoined. As an illustration, taken at random, we may cite the tribute to John Pawson paid by Adam Clarke.

Mr. Pawson's deportment was at all times grave, dignified, and recollected. He had not a variety of forms for different occasions; his character was fixed and permanent, so that he was the same in spirit, whether in the pulpit, in his family, or among his friends. Sacred things were ever treated by him with that honour and reverence which are their peculiar due. . . . Family prayer he never omitted, nor slightly passed

---

[8] Edited by Thomas Jackson: Fourth edition, with additional lives, in six volumes.
[9] Edited by Rev. John Telford: Two Vols. (selected from above).
[10] *Wesley's Works*, Vol. VII, p. 203.
[11] *John Wesley and the Advance of Methodism*, by J. S. Simon, p. 83.
[12] 'Life of Mr. William Black, (*Early Methodist Preachers*, Vol. V, pp. 242 et sqq.).
[13] *Letters*, Vol. VII, p. 182.

over, however fatigued; judging that nothing but the overwhelming power of disease could be a sufficient excuse for the neglect of this most important duty.[14]

Again:

The doctrines of the witness of the Spirit, and salvation from all sin in this life, he considered a depositum entrusted by the special mercy of God to the care of the Methodists; and was greatly distressed when he found any among ourselves denying them, or attempting to fret them away by far-fetched refined speculations.[15]

He never trifled; he never impaired his authority or respectability as a minister of God by any lightness or improper compliances. He could not, he would not, accommodate himself to any kind of company.[16]

'... he had no end in view but the glory of God; and was always ready to sacrifice his ease, property, health, and life itself to the promoting the religion of Christ among men.[17]

As he was a strict economist, and lived by rule, he was never hurried; everything was referred to its own place and time.[18]

As it was with these earliest of Wesley's helpers, so also the rank and file of Methodists observed a discipline, laid down by Wesley, which embodied many of those features of Christian Perfection, which, as we have seen, were common ground between him and Law as practical applications of that ideal. The various sets of 'Rules' drawn up by Wesley for the United Societies in 1743, and for the Band Societies in 1738 and 1744 are, as has been pointed out, culled mainly from the works of Jeremy Taylor, yet on examination the correspondence between them and Law's directions in the two practical treatises is most marked. Here again is no conclusive proof of direct dependence on Law, but a very suggestive indication, not only of common dependence on Jeremy Taylor, but also of a similarity of temperament in Wesley and Law at this stage which found its expression in the system of discipline laid down for the Methodist people.

These 'Rules' are collected on pages 269-74 of Volume VIII of *Wesley's Works*, and it is illuminating to place extracts side by side with Law's own injunctions:

RULES: Avoid 'putting on of gold or costly apparel' (p. 270).

---

[14] *Lives of Early Methodist Preachers*, Edited by T. Jackson, Vol. IV, p. 92.
[15] ibid., p. 96.   [16] ibid., p. 98.   [17] ibid., p. 100.   [18] ibid. ,p. 101.

'To wear no needless ornaments, such as rings, ear-rings, necklaces, lace, ruffles' (p. 274).

LAW: In his advice to Flatus (*Serious Call*, p. 106),[19] Feliciana (p. 111), Matilda (p. 194), and in many other passages, Law inveighs at considerable length against jewels, fine clothes, etc.

RULES: Avoid 'softness, and needless self-indulgence' (p. 270).

LAW: 'The world abounds with people who are weakly and tender merely by their indulgences' (*Christian Perfection*, p. 112).[20]

RULES: Avoid 'laying up treasures on earth' (p. 270).

LAW: In this connexion Law contrasts Flavia and Miranda in the *Serious Call*, Chapters 7, 8, and 9.

RULES: Avoid 'reading those books which do not tend to the knowledge or love of God' (p. 270).

LAW: Classicus is criticized on this account in the *Serious Call* (p. 143), and there is a long exposition of the same theme in the *Christian Perfection*, Chapter 10.

RULES: Avoid 'drunkenness, buying or selling of spirituous liquors, or drinking them, unless in cases of extreme necessity' (p. 270).

LAW: Advocates temperance and even abstinence (*Christian Perfection*, pp. 127 et sqq.).

RULES: Avoid 'the profaning the day of the Lord' (p. 270).

LAW: Assumes the importance of Sunday observance (*Christian Perfection* p. 162).

RULES: To use private prayer every day; and family prayer, if you are at the head of a family. To read the Scriptures, and meditate therein, at every vacant hour (p. 274).

LAW: Devotes a large part of the *Serious Call* to advocating private devotion at various hours.

RULES: Emphasis on fasting and abstinence (pp. 271, 274).

LAW: Assumes fasting in the *Serious Call* (p. 157) and the *Christian Perfection* (pp. 105, 111).

RULES: Advocate members of the Societies 'denying themselves and taking up their cross daily' (p. 271).

[19, 20] The references on this page to the *Christian Perfection* and *Serious Call* are to Volumes III and IV respectively of *Law's Works*.

LAW: Chapters 6, 7, and 8 of the *Christian Perfection* are all concerned with self-denial, and this text as authority for it.

RULES: 'Do you desire to be told of all your faults, and that plain and home?' (p. 272).

LAW: Susurrus is changed, when rebuked for his outstanding fault (*Serious Call*, pp. 239-40).

RULES: 'Not to mention the fault of any behind his back, and to stop those short that do' (p. 273).

LAW: The whole incident of Susurrus is a commentary on this rule (*Serious Call*, pp. 239-40).

The practical side of Sanctification is expounded by one of Methodism's foremost nineteenth-century theologians, in words which, making allowance for changes of vocabulary and style, might have come straight out of Law:

> Entire sanctification means the sanctification of everything. The sanctification, for example, of the daily work; that is, doing it to the Lord, and, therefore, doing it as well as we can. If a ploughman be entirely sanctified, he will plough a straight furrow—or at least try his best to do so. If he be a mason, he will put no bad work into his walls; if a doctor, he will care more about curing his patients than about getting large fees; if he be a minister of religion, he will strive to serve the people of his charge to the utmost of his ability. . . . Entire sanctification means dedicating all our property to God. When Christians ask themselves, 'How much of my money shall I devote to religious purposes?' they do not consider rightly. There ought to be no question of 'how much'; all must be devoted to God. . . . Entire sanctification means simply this: spending all our time in the Lord's service; making our religion our life, our life our religion.[21]

Throughout its history Methodism has jealously safeguarded the moral and doctrinal integrity of its preachers. An inquiry on these points is still made concerning each minister at the May Synod every year,[22] and concerning each Local Preacher at every quarterly Local Preachers' Meeting.[23]

These examples serve to establish the fact that the ideal and the practice of Christian Perfection, instilled into Wesley in no small measure through Law's instrumentality, were faithfully reproduced in the doctrines and discipline of Methodism.

---

[21] *Life of Benjamin Hellier*, edited by his son and daughter, pp. 311-12.
[22] *Minutes of the Methodist Conference*, 1939, p. 318.   [23] ibid., p. 280.

There is a similar reflection of Law's outlook, as shared to a lesser degree by Wesley, observable in the tendency in Methodism to set up an arbitrary division between the sacred and the secular, especially in regard to art and literature, and to an even greater degree to entertainments and recreation. John Pawson, whom we have already instanced as a man of outstanding devotion, even burnt Wesley's copy of Shakespeare;[24] and the studied plainness to the point of ugliness of many Methodist chapels bears its unmistakable witness. The present writer well remembers his own father describing how in his boyhood on the Sunday prior to the advertised visit of a circus to the town where he lived, it was publicly announced from the pulpit that any member of society, proved to have visited this entertainment, would have his name removed from the class book. In regard to literature this prejudice has now disappeared, and the architecture of many modern Methodist churches testifies to the change of attitude in that respect. In other matters greater liberty of thought and action is now permitted to the individual Methodist, but the Standing Orders of the Methodist Church still embody regulations restricting the use of Methodist Trust premises for purposes of entertainment, framed with a stringency unequalled in the corresponding regulations of any of the large Protestant denominations.[25]

There are other traits in Wesley's post-conversion beliefs and practices, where Wesley and Law were on common ground. His 'solid Anglican training and attachment'[26] kept Wesley faithful in many respects to the traditions and customs of the national Church, with the result that Methodism, in spite of the eventual breach, has always occupied a position nearer to the Church of England than have the other Nonconformist communions of England. It would be fanciful, however, to attribute this in any way to Law's influence.

Mysticism, too, found its way into Methodism to a moderate degree, in spite of John Wesley's opposition to mystical teaching, but it was mainly through Charles Wesley's hymns that this occurred and indeed through the translations of German hymns made by John Wesley, who, as we have

[24] *The Idea of Perfection in Christian Theology*, by R. Newton Flew, p. 339.
[25] *Minutes of the Methodist Conference*, 1939, pp. 334-6.
[26] *The Conversion of the Wesleys*, by J. E. Rattenbury, p. 173.

noticed, was not entirely consistent in this matter. Here, however, Law's influence can be clearly detected on occasions. The conception of 'the new man in Christ', which recurs so often in Charles Wesley's hymns,[27] is, of course, a central idea of Boehme, as interpreted by Law, but, most clearly of all, Charles Wesley borrowed from Law and included in his hymns the thought that the regenerate soul is a 'Transcript of the Trinity'. This was Law's definition of man before the fall and of man restored to the divine image, and illustrations of Law's use of the idea, and Charles Wesley's adoption of it have been fully recorded by Dr. Henry Bett.[28]

This conception of Law's, which we have already noticed in the doctrinal section, appears in passages like the following:

How could the Holy Trinity be an object of Man's worship and adoration, if the Holy Trinity had not produced itself in man?[29]

Our redemption consists in nothing else but in the bringing forth this new birth in us ... that, being thus born again in the likeness of the Holy Trinity, we may be capable of its threefold blessing and happiness.[30]

So Charles Wesley writes:

And when we rise, in love renewed,
Our souls resemble Thee
An image of the Triune God
To all eternity.[31]

Besides this and other hymns quoted by Dr. Bett, there are many similar examples, such as the following:

O that we now, in love renewed,
Might blameless in Thy sight appear;
Wake we in Thy similitude
Stamped with the Triune character.[32]

The borrowing of this idea from Law was conscious and intentional for in a letter to his wife Charles Wesley writes:

[27] e.g. *Methodist Hymn-book*, Hymns 550 (verses 4-5); 557 (verse 5); 431 (verse 3), etc. It is, of course, likely that Charles Wesley derived this conception directly from St. Paul, independently of Boehme and Law.
[28] *The Hymns of Methodism in their Literary Relations*, pp. 68-9.
[29] *Law': Works*, Vol. VI, p. 78 (quoted by Dr. Bett, loc. cit.).
[30] ibid, Vol. VI, pp. 80, 81.
[31] *Wesley's Hymns and New Supplement*, No. 256 verse 6 (quoted by Dr. Bett, loc. cit.).
[32] ibid., No. 261, verse 4.

'A transcript of the One in Three' is the definition of man unfallen, and of man restored to the divine image. The expression is Mr. Law's, not mine; who proves a trinity throughout all nature.[33]

Such traces of Law's influence in Methodism, however, are few and incidental. They arose in spite of the gulf between the mystical and evangelical systems of doctrine, not because of any similarity, let alone dependence, and did not in any way affect the main stream of Methodist development. Where the influence of Law may fairly be discerned in Methodist faith and practice is in the ethical emphasis which characterized the movement, as it characterized its founder, in whom much of its original impetus was due to the profound effect of Law's practical treatises on a mind already prepared for it by the training received from his mother, and by a study of the works of à Kempis and Jeremy Taylor.

[33] *Journal of the Rev. Charles Wesley*, Vol. II, p. 207.

lustre, before the first desire. This is more according to Behmen's sense than that, and I think it is no less intelligible than that; and what in the answer is further added, for an illustration from outward nature, may illustrate this so well as that, if not better, as to my thinking.

Page 53. Q. 1. Grace and peace from the one divine essence, or threefold Spirit only, considered as in himself alone without the creature, cannot be profitable unto man. Man hath broken or disharmonised in himself the seven properties of the divine nature, is fallen thereby into misery, strife and restlessness, and wants now grace and peace. All the grace without him, cannot profit him, if there be not peace made within him; this peace therefore dependeth upon that grace, and from that grace this peace must be brought into man. But it cannot be brought into him except by an actual reconciling and reharmonising of the disordered properties of his human nature. And seeing this human nature is an offspring of the Divine nature, or of God as manifested in his eternal nature, unto this disharmonised nature therefore is rightly wished, not only grace, but also peace, and not only (1.) from God, as the only original of all grace and peace, but also (2.) from the seven Spirits before his throne, as the seven Divine open Fountains, out of which the human nature was flown forth, and unto which it must be brought back again, if man shall be partaker again of the Divine nature, as he was in the beginning. And (3.) also from Jesus Christ as the King and Head of men, in whom all this reconciliation was first effected, and by whom it is to be effected further in all his members. And in this consideration (as might be made out sufficiently), lyeth certainly the true ground of this Apostolical wish. But that it is not used so by any of the other Apostles, nay even not by St. John himself, except only in this mystical and prophetical book of his, doth shew us sufficiently, that it was not then the time for the opening and understanding this mystery, but that this book was written only for the future ages and generations then to come.

Page 53. Q. ult. Instead of the words *flowing out from them*, I would rather say—flowing out through them, or being unfolded, displayed, or manifested by them. For that former, as to my thinking, seems to make the seven properties an original of the Divine attributes, when their original (if we may so speak, for properly they have none) is in the abyssal Unity or central Allsufficiency before and without the properties of nature, and by them they are only unfolded out of their centre.

Page 55. Q. 1. Here I think it would be needful to say something, though never so little, concerning this expression, *before*. Not that an understanding reader should have need thereof, but only for to remove a stumbling-block from the sight of the ignorant.

Q. 2. A little more relation between this Q. and *A*. would there be, if in the answer to the words *to know and perceive*, were added, *distinctly*. And here might be considered also, what Behmen frequently objects himself, and answers also sufficiently, viz., Whether all the foregoing consideration of God in general, and this question of his distinct knowledge in particular, doth not import a beginning of the Divine Triune Being, or at least of the manifestation thereof. And whether Behmen's expression of an *eternal beginning* might not be so represented, that no man of sense could find a contradiction therein.

☞ As a relief to the uniformity and matter of these pages, we present currently therewith, the following Notes and Memoranda, relating to the personal history, birth-place, family and friends of the subject of the proposed biography; which, though belonging more appropriately to that work, may not be unacceptable to the readers of this preliminary treatise.

And here we take occasion to say, in reference to the compilation and authorship of the Biography, that what is WANTED in short, as the sum and the object of the present treatise, and as necessary in the nature of the thing, is AN EDITOR, who, whilst proving himself an exact historian, a solid universal scholar, a just thinker, a profound philosopher, and a deeply-experienced, enlightened christian, shall produce a masterly picture, or biography of the individual, in all the features and developments of his mind and character;——interweaving the scanty incidents of his life that have been preserved, with such tender and manly reflections, and filling up the vacancies in his history with such elevated and charming natural conceptions and observations, and interspersing the whole with such dashes and reliefs of sublime instruction, though popularly expressed, as shall irresistibly inspire the reader with a fervent admiration of true wisdom and piety, and also *fire* him with an ardent and indomitable resolution, to immediately commence the pursuit of evangelic perfection, and the imitation of so perfect a model of a learned and accomplished English gentleman, philosopher and christian. The whole to be rendered as captivating, by the dignity and importance of the diversified subjects upon which it treats, in so uniformly felicitous and masterly a manner, as, by the condescending tenderness, nobility and wisdom of its sentiments, and the classic purity, elegance and *sweeping* rhetorical and strictly logical *power* of its composition:——all which qualifications, a solid duly-constituted ordinary genius may engraft upon itself, by diligence and a close study of the models referred to, and through the directions and specifications interspersed throughout the present treatise. In a word, as none but a Law could design and execute a perfect biography of a man, a scholar, a philosopher, and a Christian; so this treatise aims solely at creating another Law, possessed of all the talents of the former, with all the highest practical experiences, discoveries, and divine manifestations in the human nature, that have distinguished these last ages, superinduced thereupon: for without a beau-ideal or model of a perfect man in all his characteristic features and particulars, how shall mankind be elevated to their proper redeemed perfection, how shall the Gospel produce its full results. To proceed.

The town of King's Cliffe is situate in the northern part of the county of Northampton, at about equal distances from the counties of Huntingdon, Lincoln, and Rutland, and is a place of great antiquity. Though now of small extent, and secluded from the great highways intersecting the country north and south, it has anciently been famous as a royal residence of the monarchs of England; but in later ages, it has obtained a much greater honour and celebrity, by being the birth-place of the individual who is to form the chief subject of the proposed biography, the justly celebrated, oracle of wisdom, truth, and goodness, WILLIAM LAW.

The proper name of this place is Clive, meaning a town on a slope. Indeed, the word cliff is

Summary and Conclusion

Summary and Conclusion

'NEVER, elsewhere, except in the apostles themselves, and in the sacred books they have left, were the true foundation and the sublime superstructure of Christianity so effectually united.'[1] So Alexander Knox, his younger contemporary and follower, wrote of Wesley. The verdict is confirmed by one of Wesley's most recent biographers, Dr. G. Croft Cell, who writes: 'The most important fact therefore about the Wesleyan understanding of the Gospel in relation to the Christian ethic of life is that the early Protestant doctrine of justification by Faith and the Catholic appreciation of the idea of holiness or Christian perfection—two principles that had been fatally put asunder in the great Church conflicts of the sixteenth-century—reappeared in the comprehensive spirit of Wesley's teaching fitly framed together in a well-balanced synthesis.'[2]

Our own inquiry into the relation of Law to Wesley has served to show how these two strains of Christian tradition, which had often existed separately and sometimes even in opposition, were combined in Wesley's teaching and consequently in the faith and practice of the Methodists.

Moreover these two elements of Catholic holiness and evangelical conversion express respectively Wesley's indebtedness to Law and his reaction against him.

In Part Two of our inquiry we sought to show how the dominant influence, exercised for some years by Law and his writings, kindled in Wesley that passion for the ethical ideal, which remained unimpaired by his rejection of the mystical system. This zeal for holiness was in turn communicated by him to his converts, becoming one of the characteristic features of the Methodist movement.

Wesley's evangelical conversion in 1738, on the other hand, following a period of frustration and struggle, during which he came to feel his situation beyond Law's power to help, led him to suspect the soundness of Law's own religious basis and

[1] *The Works of Alexander Knox, Esq.*, Vol. I, p 83
[2] *The Rediscovery of John Wesley*, pp. 359-60.

provoked the breach between them which was never healed. It may be assumed that the quarrel was constantly smouldering in the minds of both men from that time forward, although it only burst into flame in 1756, when Wesley returned to the attack.

During the intervening years Law's increasing absorption in Boehme's mysticism, and Wesley's ceaseless evangelical activity had been confirming them more strongly in their divergent theological views, and the effect of this process was revealed in their irreconcilable doctrinal positions which we have attempted to set forth in Part Three.

The intensity of Wesley's attack and the bitterness of Law's comments indicate how deep was the cleavage. This has not always been recognized. Christopher Walton failed to recognize it, and other commentators have treated the difference as if it were only a regrettable incident best forgotten. It was left to Mr. Hobhouse, when dealing with an aspect of Law to which his relation with Wesley was only incidental, to point out its fundamental nature.[3]

As invariably occurs in controversies of this kind, the protagonists found themselves driven to accentuate their differences rather than attempt to compose them, with the result that the 1756 Letter affords us one of the clearest and most comprehensive of all Wesley's statements of his doctrinal beliefs, while Law's various comments on the letter and other relevant passages, written with Wesley in mind, express the opposite view in sharp contrast.

There are many today, however, who, while accepting broadly one of the two systems, would gladly incorporate elements of the other.

Many, for example, who insist as strongly as did Wesley on the centrality of saving faith in the atoning efficacy of our Lord's death, readily agree that forensic ideas, based on human legal theory and practice, have coloured the thought of God's justice. They assert with Law that in His gracious dealings with mankind God is more concerned with future righteousness than with past guilt, and are loath to set God's mercy and His justice in opposition. 'If we confess our sins, He is faithful and *righteous* to forgive us our sins.'[4] They would with equal emphasis reject Wesley's materialistic conception of hell.

[3] vide *supra*, p. 132.   [4] 1 John 1[9].

SUMMARY AND CONCLUSION 189

Others to whose temperament Law's doctrine of the indwelling Christ is congenial and for whose thought it is formative, would combine with this an emphasis on the value of the historical Incarnation, more reminiscent of Wesley than of Law.

While the disagreement between Law and Wesley has thus thrown into clearer relief the two opposing standpoints, and thereby enabled us to appreciate the distinctive contribution made by each to the religious life and thought of eighteenth-century England, the issues raised by our inquiries are by no means confined to that period.

A striking example of this is the 'faith and works' controversy. While this inevitably arose between Law and Wesley as a result of their contrasted systems of doctrine, it has also reappeared at various times in the history of the Church, beginning in the New Testament itself.

In modern times, too, the extreme liberal and humanistic schools of theology have held interpretations of the Atonement embodying features akin to those of Law, while the Barthian protest, and other German movements which insist on the 'once-for-allness' (*einmaligkeit*) of God's redeeming act in Christ, are in this respect, though not necessarily in others, in harmony with Wesley.

The operation of God's saving grace, however, does not depend on right opinions, as is manifest from our study of these two Christian contemporaries, who along such different paths were led by God's Spirit from νόμος to χάρις. Both men permanently enriched the Christian tradition alike by their life and character, not only by the separate contribution each made along the line of his individual genius, but most of all, perhaps, by the renewed zeal for Christian Perfection, for which they were jointly responsible. This ideal has fired the imagination and won the allegiance of countless Christians all over the world since their day and will continue to do so.

While this was directly due to Wesley's preaching and organizing ability, it received its initial impetus in his own experience as the result of the impact on his mind, already prepared by a study of à Kempis and Jeremy Taylor, of Law's *Christian Perfection* and *Serious Call*.

Bibliography

I. WILLIAM LAW

The Works of the Reverend William Law, M.A.
In nine volumes.
London: Printed for J. Richardson (1762).
Privately reprinted for G. Moreton, Setley, Brockenhurst, New Forest, Hampshire (1892).

II. JOHN WESLEY

The Works of the Reverend John Wesley, A.M.
In fourteen volumes.
Third edition. London (1829).
The Journal of the Reverend John Wesley, A.M.
In eight volumes.
Standard edition: edited by Nehemiah Curnock. London (1904-16).
The Standard Sermons of John Wesley.
In two volumes.
Edited by Edward H. Sugden. London (1921).
The Letters of the Reverend John Wesley, A.M.
In eight volumes.
Standard edition: edited by John Telford. London (1931).

III. OTHER WORKS CONSULTED

Allen, G. W. Article on Jacob Boehme in *Encyclopaedia of Religion and Ethics.*
Arminian Magazine (1797).
Atkins, G. G. *The Making of the Christian Mind.* London (1929).
Aulen, Gustav. *Christus Victor.* Translated by A. G. Hebert. London (1931).
Baillie, John. *Our Knowledge of God.* London (1939).
Beet, J. Agar. Article in *London Quarterly Review,* January 1920.
Berridge, Rev. Mr. *A Fragment of True Religion.* London (1760).

Bett, Henry. *The Hymns of Methodism in their Literary Relations.* London (1913).
Bett, Henry. *The Spirit of Methodism.* London (1937).
Bready, J. W. *England: before and after Wesley.* London (1938).
Bretherton, F. F. Articles on 'The First Apology for Methodism' in the *Proceedings of the Wesley Historical Society.* Vols. XIX and XX, December 1924, June 1925.
Byrom, John; *Remains of.* 4 Volumes. Chetham Society (1854).
Carter, Henry. *The Methodist.* London (1914). Revised and enlarged edition (1937).
Cell, G. Croft. *The Rediscovery of John Wesley.* New York (1935).
Clarke, W. N. *An Outline of Christian Theology.* Edinburgh (1920).
Coke & Moore. *Life of the Reverend John Wesley.* London (1792).
Curtis, O. A. *The Christian Faith.* London (1905).
Dobrée, Bonamy. *John Wesley.* London (1933).
Edwards, Maldwyn. *John Wesley and the Eighteenth Century: A study of his social and political influence.* London (1933).
Ewing, Alex. Introduction to 'The Atonement', by the Rev. William Law. *Present Day Papers,* London (1869).
Flew, R. Newton. *The Idea of Perfection in Christian Theology.* Oxford (1934).
Gibbon, Edward. Remarks on William Law in the twentieth edition of the *Serious Call.* Romsey (1816).
Gillman, F. J. *The Evolution of the Christian Hymn.* London (1927).
Gordon, Alex. Article on Christopher Walton in *Dictionary of National Biography.* Vol. XX. London (1909).
Green, J. (Bishop of Lincoln). *The Principles and Practices of the Methodists Considered.* London (1760).
Green, J. R. *A Short History of the English People.* London (1895).
Green, Richard. *The Works of John and Charles Wesley: A Bibliography.* London (1896).
Green, R. *Anti-Methodist Publications; A Bibliography.* London (1902).

Gregory, A. S. *Praises with Understanding.* London (1936).
Harrison, A. W. *Arminianism.* London (1937).
Hellier, Benjamin, Life of. Edited by his Son and Daughter.
Hobhouse, Stephen. *William Law and Eighteenth-century Quakerism.* London (1927).
Hobhouse, Stephen. *William Law, Selected Mystical Writings.* London (1938).
Hobhouse, Stephen. Review of *Die Stufenfolge des Mystischen Erlebnisses bei William Law* (1686-1761), by Conrad Minkner (Munich 1939) in *Expository Times*, March 1941.
Inge, W. R. *Studies of English Mystics.* London (1906).
Inge, W. R. *Christian Mysticism.* (Third edition.) London (1912).
Jackson, Thomas. *Lives of the Early Methodist Preachers.* Six Volumes. London (1865).
Jackson, Thomas. *Memoirs of the Rev. Charles Wesley.* London (1875).
Jones, Rufus M. *Spiritual Reformers in the Sixteenth and Seventeenth Centuries.* London (1914).
Jones, Rufus M. *New Studies in Mystical Religion.* London (1927).
à Kempis, Thomas. *De Imitatione Christi.*
Knox, Alexander; Remains of. Edited by J. J. Hornsby. Volume I. London (1834).
Knox, Alexander. *Works.* (4 Volumes.) London (1836).
Laver, James. *Wesley.* London (1932).
Lecky, W. *A History of England in the Eighteenth Century.* Seven Volumes. London (1892). Volume III.
Leger, Augustin. *La Jeunesse de Wesley.* Paris (1910).
Loofs, Friedrich. Article '*Der Methodismus*' in *Realencyclopaedia.*
Lunn, A. H. M. *John Wesley.* New York (1929).
Mackenzie, D. Article on 'Synergism'. In *Encyclopaedia of Religion and Ethics.*
Maltby, W. R. *Christ and His Cross.* London (1935).
Maurice, F. D. Introduction to Law's *Remarks on the Fable of the Bees.* Cambridge (1844).
Methodist Hymn-book. London (1933).
Minutes of the Methodist Conference, 1939.

Moore, Henry. *The Life of the Rev. John Wesley in which are included the Life of his Brother, the Rev. Charles Wesley, and Memoirs of their Family.* (2 Volumes.) London (1824 and 1825).
Moulton, W. J. Article in *London Quarterly Review.* July 1925.
Mozley, J. K. *The Doctrine of the Atonement.* London (1933).
Overton, J. H. *Life and Opinions of the Rev. William Law, M.A.* London (1881).
Overton, J. H. *The Evangelical Revival in the Eighteenth Century.* London (1886).
Overton, J. H. *John Wesley.* London (1891).
Palmer, W. Scott. *Liberal and Mystical Writings of William Law.* London (1908).
Piette, Maximin. *John Wesley in the Evolution of Protestantism.* English Translation. London (1938).
Platt, F. Article 'Christian Perfection' in *Encyclopaedia of Religion and Ethics.*
Pope, W. B. *Compendium of Christian Theology.* London (1875).
Rattenbury, J. E. *The Conversiom of the Wesleys.* London (1938).
Simon, J. S. *Revival of Religion in England in the Eighteenth Century.* London (1907).
Simon, J. S. *John Wesley and the Religious Societies.* London (1921).
Simon, J. S. *John Wesley and the Methodist Societies.* London (1923).
Simon, J. S. *John Wesley and the Advance of Methodism.* London (1925).
Simon, J. S. *John Wesley: The Master Builder.* London (1929).
Simon, J. S. *John Wesley: The Last Phase.* London (1934).
Southey, Robert. *The Life of Wesley and the Rise and Progress of Methodism.* London (1820).
Stephen, L. Article on William Law in *Dictionary of National Biography.* London (1892). Volume XI. London (1909) (reissue).
Taylor, Jeremy. *Rules and Exercises of Holy Living.* London (1857 edition).
Taylor, Jeremy. *Rules and Exercises of Holy Dying.* London (1857 edition).

Telford, John. *Wesley's Veterans.* Seven Volumes. London.
Telford, John. *Life of John Wesley.* London (1899).
Telford, John. *The New Methodist Hymn-book Illustrated.* London (1934).
Townsend, W. J.
Workman, H. B., and } *A New History of Methodism.* 2 Volumes. London (1909).
Eayrs, G.
Trevelyan, G. M. *History of England.* London (1926).
Tyerman, L. *The Life and Times of John Wesley.* Three Volumes. London (1871).
Underhill, Evelyn. *Mysticism.* London (1911).
Underhill, Evelyn. *Worship.* London (1936).
Vulliamy, E. C. *John Wesley.* London (1931).
Walton, Christopher. *Notes and Materials for an Adequate Biography of William Law.* London (1854).
Watson, P. S. Article on 'Justification' in *Expository Times.* August 1940.
Watson, Richard. *Institutes of Theology.* Edinburgh (1836).
Wesley, Charles; Journal of. Edited Jackson. Two Volumes. London (1849).
Wesley's Hymns and New Supplement. London (1876).
Wesley, John and Charles. *Hymns and Sacred Poems.* 1739.
Wesleyan Methodist Magazine. Two Volumes. 1848.
Whitefield, George. *Works.* Six Volumes. London (1771).
Whyte, Alexander. *Characters and Characteristics of William Law.* London (1893).
Whyte, Alexander. *Jacob Behmen: An Appreciation.* Edinburgh and London (1894).
Wiseman, F. Luke. *Charles Wesley, Evangelist and Poet.* London (1933).
Workman, H. B. *Methodism.* Cambridge (1912).
Young, G. Introduction to Law's *Serious Call.* Glasgow (1827).

Index

ABSTINENCE, 99, 179
'Academicus', 84
Adam, 49, 110, 115f., 130, 133f., 143, 148f., 153
 and Eve, 115f., 117, 143
 the second, 115f., 148f.
Aldersgate Street, 18
Allen, G. W., 110, 113
America (*see also* Wesley in Georgia), 169
Angels, 84, 114f., 130, 137f., 142
Anglicanism; 73, 119
Antinomianism, 84
Arminian Magazine, 21n.
Arminianism, 58
Assurance, 108, 150f.
Atkins, C. G., 103f.
Atonement, the, Law's view of, 33, 128–39
 Law's criticism of Wesley's view, 145f.
 mystical and evangelical views, 153, 157, 189
 need of, 43
 Wesley's criticism of Law's view, 24, 143ff., 146ff.
 Wesley's doctrine of, 84, 105, 117–28
Augustine, St., 68, 117, 132
Awakening, need of moral, 66, 130

BAILLIE, DR. J., 68
Barclay, Robert, 107
Barry, James, 86
Barthian theology, 189
Beet, Dr. J. Agar, 65n.
Berridge, Mr., 57f.
Bethlehem, 137
Bett, Dr. Henry, vii, viiin., 65n., 73, 182
Bishop, Mary, 60, 118
Black, William, 59, 177

Boehme, Jacob, angels, theory of fallen, 114
 biographical details, 110
 Law, influence on William, 31n., 32, 34, 53, 84, 92, 188
 learning, lack of, 92, 110
 Methodism, and early, 59, 167, 170
 philosophy in his religion, 48f., 110ff., 113ff.
 scripture, method of interpreting, 112
 style, literary, 107, 111
 Walton, in view of Christopher, 167f., 170, 172
 Wesley, influence on Charles, 182
 Wesley's criticism of, 48n., 49f., 56, 61, 104, 107, 109, 112ff., 167f.
Böhler, Peter, faith, view of saving, 17, 21
 Law, interview with William, 23ff., 27f.
 Law's criticism of, 25ff.
 Walton, in view of Christopher, 163
 Wesley, influence on, 17ff.
Bolton, Ann, 14
Booth, William, 174
Brackenbury, R. C., 68
Bramwell, William, 172
Bray, John, 41f., 152
Bretherton, F. F., 9
Briggs, Philothea, 59
Bristol, 122
Brooke, Henry, 61, 138
Browne, Dr. Peter, 156
Byrom, John, 15, 51, 53f., 57-60, 106, 152, 155n.

CALVINISM, 58, 75f., 84, 117, 121f.
Cards, playing, 86
Catholic piety, 12, 73, 132, 135, 187
Cell, Dr. G. C., 13, 65, 187
Children, Christian training of, 99

Christian perfection. *See under* Perfection, Christian.
Clarke, Dr. Adam, 177
Clarke, W. N., 144
'Classicus', 179
Cockfighting, 97
Coke, Dr. Thomas, 61
Coldness, spiritual, 50, 150, 152f., 157
Conversion, antecedents of, 66
  Catholic and Evangelical, 13
  Law's view of, 76, 151f.
  Perfection, and Christian, 68, 76
  Wesley's (*see also* Wesley), 11ff., 17ff., 67, 84, 123
Creation, 113ff.
Cross of Christ, the (*see also* Atonement), faith in Christ and, 23, 136
  individual sinner and, 127f.
  necessity of, 134ff.
  New Birth and, 135
  Perfection, and Christian, 85
Curnock, Nehemiah, 123. *See also* Wesley's *Journal*.
Curtis, Dr. O. A., 65n., 176n.

Dancing, 86
Darkness, spiritual, 107
Deal, 17, 19
Death, sin and, 119
Debtors and creditors, 145
Deism, Christianity and, 118, 141
  Walton's view of, 170
  Wesley's view of, 43, 117, 148, 153
Devils, 142
Dionysius, 109
Dobrée, Bonamy, 41
Dodd, William, 26
Dress, 98, 179
Drink, 179
Dublin, 61

Early rising, 95
Eayrs, G., 8
Education, 99
Edwards, Dr. Maldwyn, 92

Election, doctrine of, 58, 75
Eternity, truths of, 156f.
Ethics (*see also* Perfection, Christian), and conversion, 66, 86
  and faith, 28, 76
  and mysticism, 69
'Eusebius', 43
Evil, origin of, 110, 129f.
Experience, Christian (*see also* Conversion and Sanctification), 81

Faith, saving
  Christ, in, 18, 21, 23, 28, 118, 149, 154, 157, 165
  Justification and, 125
  Law's view of, 22f., 28, 34, 149, 165
  Salvation and, 121
  Works and, 125, 189
Fall of Man, the, Boehme's view of, 49, 84
  Law's view of, 38, 70, 92, 115, 129f., 133ff., 146
  Wesley's view of, 116, 119, 147
Fasting, 96, 179
'Feliciana', 179
'Flatus', 179
'Flavia', 179
Flew, Dr. R. Newton, ix, 65n., 69, 73, 81, 88, 92, 181n.
Fog's Journal, 8f.
Forgiveness, 125, 133, 145-6
Furly, Dorothy, 59
  Samuel, 46

Genesis, 114, 119, 129, 143
Geometry, 93
Gerhardt, Paulus, 67, 82
Gibbon, Edward, 6
  Hester, 39
  of Putney, Mr., 5, 39
Grace, free, 58, 120-2
Green, Dr. (Bishop of Lincoln), 58
  Richard, 46n., 50n., 61
Gregory, A. S., 174f.
Guilt, 133

HAPPINESS AND RELIGION, 91, 119
Hell, 50, 133, 146, 156f., 188
Hellier, Benjamin, 180
Henshaw, Fanny, 31n.
Herodotus, 162
Herrnhut, 122
Hildesley, Bishop, 54
Hill, Mr., 104, 126
Hoadly, Bishop W., 4, 32f.
Hobhouse, Stephen, 3ff., 6, 21, 30, 31n., 32, 34-7, 43, 60, 103, 114, 116, 129n., 132, 155, 161f., 188
Holiness (*see also* Perfection, Christian), 74f., 106
Holy Club, the, 8
Spirit, 44, 77, 81, 84, 105, 124, 149f.
Humility, 89, 95, 99, 112, 150
Huntingdon, Countess of, 51, 53, 127
Lord, 118
Hutchinson, Mrs., 39
Hutton, James, 17

IMPUTED RIGHTEOUSNESS, 107
Incarnation, the, 136, 157, 189
Indwelling Christ, 50, 153, 182, 189
Ingham, Benjamin, 43
Isaiah, 147

JACKSON, THOMAS, 10, 15, 77f.
James, St., 50
Jews, the, 141, 153
John, St., and Johannine Christianity, 36, 38, 48, 50, 76, 79, 107f., 111, 167, 188
the Baptist, vii, 72, 154
Johnson, Samuel, 6
Jones, J., 79
Rufus M., 92, 103, 110
Judgement Day, 138
Justice of God, 50, 141-4, 188
Justification by faith, atonement and, 127f., 133, 144f.
faith as condition of justification, 125

Methodism, distinctive mark of, 57, 176, 187
mysticism and, 107, 112
sanctification and, 76, 122, 124 133, 152, 157, 176
Wesley, in Conversion of, 14, 29
Wesley's criticism of Law's view of, 50, 107, 112, 126f., 141, 144, 148
Wesley's teaching of, 60, 76, 79, 122, 124-8, 144ff., 187

KINGSCLIFFE, 3, 39, 41, 91, 98, 128
Kingswood School, 177
Knox, Alex., 187
John, 174

L., MR. J., 155
Mr. T., 139
Lambert, Canon C. H., 9
Langcake, Mr., 51, 53, 138, 166
Lavington, Bishop, 104, 169
Law, the, 32, 71f.
to grace, from, 32, 71, 189
Law, William: general: Atonement, view of, 117, 126, 128-39, 143-5
Boehme, influence of Jacob, 32, 34, 109, 143, 168, 188
Böhler, and Peter, 25, 27
character of, 40, 91, 152
Churchmanship of, 4, 6, 36, 44, 57, 129
controversialist, as, 28f.
death, 59
early life, 3f.
evangelical understanding, deficiency of, 28, 124, 149, 166
Fictitious characters in Law's writings:
Academicus, 84
Classicus, 179
Eusebius, 43
Feliciana, 179
Flatus, 179
Flavia, 179
Matilda, 179

Law, William:
  fictitious characters in Law's writings:
    Miranda, 60, 179
    Ouranius, 155
    Penitens, 82
    Susurrus, 180
    Theogenes, 43
    Theophilus, 43, 82
  influence, present, 37
  irony in writings, 22f.
  last years, 56, 59
  Methodism, influence on, 37, 44f., 117, 152, 161ff., 169ff., 172, 175-83, 187
  middle life, 39
  Mystics and, 32, 69, 71, 128, 136, 155
  perfection, and Christian, 10, 65, 69, 83, 171, 189
  philanthropist, as, 98
  Quakerism, and, 31n., 70, 147
  sacramental views, 36, 148, 153f., 155
  Scripture, and, 154f.
  war, denunciation of, 83
  Wesley compared with, 41, 91f., 154, 157, 169, 172
  Wesley, critical judgement against, 52, 55
  Wesley, influence upon, 7, 11, 52, 65, 68f., 182
  Writings of:
    Address to the Clergy, An Humble, Earnest, and Affectionate, 57, 61, 81, 92, 137
    Animadversions upon Dr. Trapp's Late Reply, Some, 61
    Answer to a Scruple, 145
    Answer to Dr. Trapp's Discourse, 31, 46, 61, 69
    Appeal to all that Doubt, 31, 35, 61, 69, 129f., 134f.
    Case of Reason, 61
    Collection of Letters, 51, 53, 55-7, 61, 135
    Confutation of Dr. Warburton's 'Divine Legation', 57, 61, 168
    Demonstration of ... Errors of late Book called 'A Plain Account of ... Lord's Supper', 23f., 28, 31, 34, 165
    Dialogue on Justification, 57f., 61
    Letters to the Bishop of Bangor, Three, 4, 31
    Perfection, Practical Treatise on Christian ..., 3, 5, 7, 11, 20, 22, 31, 37, 46, 61, 65, 69f., 74, 76, 78, 81f., 88, 90, 165, 170f., 177, 179f., 189
    Regeneration, Grounds and Reasons of Christian, 31, 35, 42f., 124, 136, 151
    Remarks on 'Fable of the Bees', 4
    Serious Call to a Devout and Holy Life, A, 3, 6, 20, 22, 31f., 37, 46, 60f., 65, 69f., 75, 78, 82, 86-91, 94-6, 98-9, 137, 155, 165, 170f., 176-80, 189
    Spirit of Love, 36, 43, 48, 61, 71, 78, 113, 130, 132, 134f., 137f., 140, 142, 144f.
    Spirit of Prayer, 36, 38, 43, 48, 61, 82, 113f., 131, 136, 140ff., 146, 148, 151, 166f.
    Unlawfulness of Stage Entertainment, 6
    Way to Divine Knowledge, 36, 61, 84
Lawley, Mrs., 11
Learning, 55, 92, 112
Leger, M. Augustin, 10f., 19
Lincoln College, Oxford, 5, 8, 98
Lindsay, John, 53
London Chronicle, 7, 55, 166
Lord's Prayer, 112, 145f.
Love (see also Perfection, Christian;)
  Enemies, Loving, 87
  God in man, love of, 81, 150
  God loves, as, 88, 131
  Neighbour, loving our, 87, 95
Lucifer, 110, 130
Luke, St., 87, 89, 115
Lusatia, 110
Luther, Martin, 117, 126, 132

INDEX

Mahometans, 153
Man, nature of, 118f., 131, 148
Manchester, 54
Mandeville, Dr. Bernard, 4
Marriott, Thomas, 9
Martin, Mr., 57
'Matilda', 179
Matthew, St., 98, 145
Maurice, F. D., viii
McClintock, John, 176
Means of grace, 50, 84, 106f., 153ff., 157
Mercy of God, 133, 188
Messiah, 141
Methodism (*see also* Wesley, Law),
  architecture of, 181
  Calvinism and, 75f.
  discipline of, 178, 180
  doctrinal standards of, 67, 176
  early, aims of, 68, 78
  early, growth of, 40, 45, 52, 171
  England, and Church of, 119, 170, 181
  fellowship of, 84, 105
  Hymnbook, 173-6
    1739 Edition, 68, 84, 105, 169
    hymns in 1933 Edition:
    Gerhardt, by Paulus, 'Jesu, Thy boundless love' (430), 67
    Spangenburg, by A. G., 'What shall we offer?' (784), 75
    Tersteegen, by Gerhard, 'Thou hidden love of God' (433), 67
    Watts, by Isaac, 'We give immortal praise' (40), 109
    Wesley, by Charles
    'Ah, Lord, with trembling' (480), 79
    'And can it be?' (371), 85, 121
    'Good Thou art' (59), 121
    'Jesus, my Saviour' (478), 80
    'Love divine, all loves excelling' (431), 82, 182n.
    'O for a heart to praise' (550), 182n.
    'Open, Lord, my inward ear' (465), 120
    'Since the Son hath made me free' (468), 77
    'The God of love' (372), 127
    'To the haven of Thy breast' (459), 85
    'What is our calling's glorious hope?' (557), 75, 182n.
    'What shall I do?' (77), 122
    'Where shall my wondering soul begin?' (361), 122
    'Would Jesus have the sinner die?' (173), 120
    'And when we rise' (omitted from 1933 book), 182
    'O that we now' (omitted from 1933 book), 182
    (Numbers in brackets refer to hymn number of 1933 Hymnbook.)
  nature of, 187
  Oxford, at, 9
  preachers of, 177f., 180
  thrift and, 99
Ministers, qualifications of Christian, 55, 92f.
Minkner, Conrad, 129n.
Minutes of Conference, 1744, 76
  1770, 81
  1939, 174, 176, 180f.
'Miranda', 60, 179
Money, 98, 180
Moore, Henry, viin., 72
Moral, awakening, 66, 130
Moulton, W. J., 65n.
Mysticism (*see also* Boehme), atonement and, 153
  justification by faith and, 112
  Law, in teaching of William, 32, 34, 69, 71, 82, 135f., 157
  Methodism and, 104, 108, 167, 171, 173, 181, 183
  nature of, 103, 104
  sacraments and, 148
  Scripture and, 107ff.
  Wesley's critical view of, 14, 18, 56, 103f., 107f.

200   INDEX

Mysticism:
  Wesley's moderate view of, 47, 60f., 73, 108f.

NATURE, PROPERTIES OF, 114, 116, 129
New Birth, 38f., 50, 87f., 124, 135, 148f., 153, 157
New York, Methodist Centenary Celebration in, 176
Newton, John, 6, 68

OMNIPOTENCE OF GOD, 49, 140f., 147
'Ouranius', 155
Overton, J. H., viii, 21, 27f., 30, 45, 50, 75, 80n., 161f.

PAIN, 119, 130
Paul, St., and his Epistles, 17f., 50, 66, 68, 88, 105, 108, 111, 117, 148, 150, 152f., 183
Pawson, John, 177, 181
'Penitens', 82
Perfection, Christian, amusements and, 96
  atonement and, 84f.
  Church and Tradition of the, 73, 187
  communion with God, as, 81
  conversion and, 68, 76f.
  degrees of, 80
  differences between views of Wesley and Law, 82-5
  dress and, 98
  education and, 99
  ethical ideal, limitation of, 72, 76
  fasting and, 96
  gift of God, the, 75, 77
  God and man, to, 87f.
  humility and, 89
  individual and social, 82, 106
  instantaneous, 80
  inwardness of, 77
  Law, in teaching of William, 10, 65, 69, 83, 171, 189
  learning and, 92
  loss, possibility of, 79
  man, in nature of, 74
  Methodism and, 68, 175-80
  money, and use of, 98
  mysticism and, 69, 84
  prayer, and private, 94
  self-denial and, 88
  self-discipline and, 94
  time, and redemption of, 95
  universal, purpose of, 74, 117
  Wesley, ideal of, 10, 65, 67, 171, 173, 175-80, 189
  worldliness and, 90
Peter, St., 44, 50, 148
Philips, Mr., 59
Philosophy and religion, 48f., 93, 111, 129, 140f., 149
Piette, Father Maximin, 11f., 16, 66n.
Plato, 99
Platt, Dr. F., 65n.
Pointer, Mr., 57
Pope, the, 53, 56
Prayer (*see also* Law; Spirit of Prayer), family, 179
  fervent, 82, 150
  God, and union with, 150, 152
  individualism in, 82f.
  Lord's, 112, 145f.
  private, 82, 94, 123
  schemes of, 86
Predestination, 122
Public worship, 50, 153, 155
Punishment, 131, 133, 143, 156
Purgatory, 138, 157
Pythagoras, 99

QUAKERISM, 71

RATTENBURY, DR., J. E., 12ff., 16f., 65n., 84n., 139, 181n.
Recreation, 181
Regeneration, 152
Repentance, 78
Riches, danger of, 89

INDEX

Ritchie, Eliza, 59f.
Roman Catholic Church, 108
Romans, Epistle to, 17ff., 66

SACRAMENTS, THE, Baptism, 35, 148
   Lord's Supper, 33-6, 148f.
   validity of, 32
Sacred and secular, 91, 93, 181
Salvation (*see also* Atonement), 70, 74, 77, 117, 120f., 132, 144
Sanctification (*see also* Perfection, Christian), 65, 68, 75, 76, 79, 122-4, 133, 171, 176, 180
Satan, 137, 146
Schurman, Anna Maria Van, 147
Scripture, languages of, 55, 92f.
   supremacy of, 93
Self-denial, 88f., 180
Self-discipline, 94
Sermon on the Mount, 96, 175
Sex, 115f.
Shackleton, Roger, 43
Shakespeare, 97, 181
Simon, Dr. J. S., 9, 177
Sin, 75, 79, 85, 117-19, 132
Sleep, 95
Sobriety, 99
Socrates, 99
Solitary religion, 83ff., 105ff.
Spangenburg, A. M., 75
Stage, the, 92, 97
Stillness, 50, 60, 153-5
Sugden, Dr. F. H. (*see also* Wesley's Sermons), 12, 56
Sunday, 154f., 179
'Susurrus', 180
Swift, Dean, 61

TAULER, JOHN, 50, 104, 110
Taylor, Ann, 60
Taylor, Jeremy, 7, 65, 67, 89, 94, 170, 173, 178, 183, 189
Telford, John (*see also* Wesley's Letters), 29, 177
Tersteegen, Gerhard, 67
'Theogenes', 43

Theologia Germanica, 10, 20, 23ff., 28
'Theophilus', 43, 82
Time, redeeming the, 75
Townsend, W. J., Workman, H. B., and Eayrs, G., 8n.
Tragedy, 97
Trapp, Dr. J., vii, 36, 44ff., 69f., 173
Trinity, the Holy, 35, 130, 182
Tucker, Josiah, 44ff.
Tyerman, Luke, 12ff., 21, 26, 55

UNDERHILL, EVELYN, viii
Union with God, 70, 116, 135
Universal grace, 121f., 137
Universalism, 157
Usher, Archbishop, 73

WALKER, W., 152
Walton, Christopher: Boehme, on Jacob, 167, 170, 172
   conversion, on, 164
   correspondence of 1738, and, 21, 25, 163f., 168
   correspondence of 1756, 58, 165-9
   historian, as, 162
   Law's writings, his use of, 30, 31n., 36-9, 43, 47, 51, 53, 58, 60, 138
   Law, admiration for William, 162, 172
   Law, biographical details of William, 3, 4n., 60
   Methodism, and, 163, 169ff.
   perfection, on., 171
   purpose of, 161
   style of, 161f.
   theories, criticism of his, 172f., 188
   Wesley, his criticism of, 166f.
Walsh, T., 79
War, 83, 119
Warburton, Bishop, 44f., 53, 57, 61, 173
Ward, Mr., 53, 55
Watts, Isaac, 109
Wauer, Dr. G. A., vii

Wesley, Charles (*see also* Methodism; Hymnbook) conversion of, 18, 162
   Georgia in, 11, 15
   hymns of, 174, 181
   Journal, 15, 18, 41f., 72, 172n.
   Law, on William, vii, 72, 183
   Law, visits William, 15, 41f., 152
   Memoirs, 10n., 15
   Wesley, and John, 42, 56, 79
Wesley, John: general: Boehme, and Jacob, 103, 111ff., 116, 128
   Böhler, influence of Peter, 17ff.
   controversialist, as, 29, 47, 112ff., 144
   conversion of 1738, Evangelical, 11f., 14, 17ff., 29, 65, 72, 123, 162, 164, 168, 174, 187
   early life, 4ff., 56
   England, and Church of, 73, 119, 129, 181
   experience of 1725, 11ff., 17
   Georgia, mission to, 10f., 17, 20, 91, 104, 123
   hymns, translator of, 175, 181
   Law, compared with William, 40f., 91f., 128, 131, 154-7, 169
   Law, divergencies from William, 16, 18-29, 76, 103, 124, 127, 137, 139, 140-57, 188
   Law, indebtedness to William, 65f., 73, 86f., 175ff.
   Law, modifies views on William, 59f.
   Law, view of style of William, 47
   Law, visits William, 10
   Law, will not visit William, 19
   Letters to Law of 1738, 18-29, 103, 106, 117, 124, 163f.
   Letter to Law of 1756, 30, 47-54, 85, 103, 113, 117, 124, 139, 140-57, 163, 165ff., 188
   Methodism, founder of, 174
   mysticism, critical view of, 14, 18, 56, 103ff., 108f., 123, 157
   mysticism, more favourable view of, 47, 60f., 73, 126
   Ordination, 8
   Oxford, at, 5, 10, 19, 44, 67, 95, 98, 120
   practical sense, 45, 166
   Scripture, view of, 50, 55f., 93, 112, 116, 118, 128, 141, 144, 154f., 157
   theologian, as, 117, 122f., 156, 187
   writings of
      Address to Clergy, 54, 56, 92
      Boehme, Thoughts on Jacob, 110
      Doctrine of Original Sin, 118
      Earnest Appeal to Men of Reason and Religion, 96
      Farther Appeal to Men of Reason and Religion, 119
      Forms of Prayer, Collection of, 95
      Journal (references to Curnock, Standard Edition):
         Vol. I, 5, 7f., 10f., 14, 17-20, 108, 123, 147f., 155
         Vol. II, 42, 107, 109, 122
         Vol. III, 24, 43, 107
         Vol. IV, 7, 54
         Vol. V, 61, 97, 106, 126
         Vol. VI, 97, 108
         Vol. VIII, 19-22, 27, 106
      Letters (references to Telford, Standard Edition):
         Vol. I, 14, 20f., 24f., 27, 29, 89, 91, 93, 96, 104, 165
         Vol. II, 14, 66
         Vol. III, 26, 30, 46, 48-50, 59, 85, 107f., 113-15, 129, 140f., 144, 147, 153-6, 166
         Vol. IV, 7, 55f., 68, 93, 107, 167
         Vol. V, 59, 69, 127
         Vol. VI, 59f., 108, 118
         Vol. VII, 60f., 177
         Vol. VIII, 68, 86, 97, 175
      (Letters of 1738 and 1756 *also* appear under Wesley, general.)
      Logic, Compendium of, 94
      Minutes of Some Late Conversations, 119

Wesley, John, Writings of:
   Notes on the New Testament, 67, 174
   Perfection, Plain Account of, 66, 73, 80f.
   Preservative against Unsettled Notions, 50
   Primitive Physic, 94
   Principles of a Methodist, 43f., 125-8
   Remarks on Mr. Hill, etc., 104, 126
   Rules for United Societies, 94
   Rules of a Helper, 94f.
   Sermons (references to Sugden, Standard Sermons), 169, 174f.
   1. *Salvation by Faith*, 77f., 120f.
   5. *Justification by Faith*, 124f., 127
   12. *The Means of Grace*, 109, 155
   13. *The Circumcision of the Heart*, 10, 12, 67, 88f., 91, 175
   14. *The Marks of the New Birth*, 87f.
   22. *Sermon on the Mount*, VII, 96
   23. *Sermon on the Mount*, VIII, 98
   35. *Christian Perfection*, 175

Wesley, John, Writings of:
   39. *The New Birth*, 119
   40. *The Wilderness State*, 107
   42. *Self-Denial*, 88f.
   44. *The Use of Money*, 99
   49. *The Lord our Righteousness*, 107, 109
   Preface, 93
   Sermons not included in *Standard Sermons:*
   Free Grace, 122
   On Redeeming the Time, 95
   The More Excellent Way, 94
Wesley, Samuel (elder), 4
   Samuel (younger), 14, 104
Wesley, Susannah, 4, 13, 173, 183
Wesleyan Methodist Magazine, 8f., 19
Wesley Historical Society, Proceedings of, 9
Whitefield, George, 40f., 53, 103, 122
Whyte, Alexander, ix, 161
Witness of the Spirit, 109
Workman, Dr. H. B., 8, 108f., 117
'World, The', 90-2
Wrath of God, 43, 50, 53, 131-3. 142-5

ZINZENDORF, COUNT N. L. VON, 44